Advance praise for
Best Minds: How Allen Ginsberg Made Revolutionary Poetry from Madness

"Stevan Weine met Allen Ginsberg when Weine was in medical school. His relationship with Ginsberg and his comprehensive research into Ginsberg's poetry, experiences with mental illness, and his mother's psychiatric treatment culminate in *Best Minds: How Allen Ginsberg Made Revolutionary Poetry from Madness*. Weine, now a professor of psychiatry, received unprecedented access to Ginsberg's personal archives as well as his and his mother's psychiatric records. He utilized these remarkable sources to reveal new dimensions of Ginsberg's story. Weine's keen analysis of Ginsberg's journey makes *Best Minds* an essential book for any student of poetry, human sexuality, and the American counterculture."

—**Jack Drescher, M.D.**, Clinical Professor of Psychiatry, Columbia University; Adjunct Professor, New York University; Training & Supervising Analyst, W. A. White Institute

"This sympathetic and insightful account of Allen Ginsberg's relationship to madness, psychiatrically determined mental illness, and creativity is buttressed by the author's exclusive access to Ginsberg's psychiatric records and those of his mother, Naomi Ginsberg—records that even Ginsberg himself never saw. A psychiatrist specializing in trauma who has also long nourished a personal interest in poetry, Stevan Weine makes a profound contribution to the emerging field of 'mad studies' by demonstrating how a young poet with a dire prognosis from the psychiatric establishment and a fragile sense of self emerged as a mid-twentieth-century cultural icon by turning the raw and genuinely anguishing materials of his 'madness' into new directions in poetry, social relations, and values."

—**Maria Damon**, University of Minnesota; author, *The Dark End of the Street: Margins in American Vanguard Poetry*

"*Best Minds* will stand as a landmark study of creativity that can occur when an artist titrates a descent into madness while staying aware that this descent is also a strategy. Stevan Weine shows Ginsberg's writing to be more than a road-trip narrative of sex, drugs, and lawlessness. Rather, he chronicles Ginsberg's life as a spiritual journey, from seeking revelation through visions and hallucinations, to redeeming lost lives by bearing witness to suffering, to restoring personhood for those whose lives had been erased by trauma, social exclusion, or mental illness, starting with his mother and her lobotomy. Through his poetry Ginsberg still can touch each of us."

—**James Griffith**, Professor of Psychiatry and Behavioral Sciences, George Washington University; author, *Religion That Heals, Religion That Harms*

"In Stevan Weine's illuminating study, madness is no mere metaphor. Using Allen Ginsberg's medical records and those of his mother, Naomi Ginsberg, *Best Minds* explores the secrets of Ginsberg's experiences with madness, providing a refreshing new look at his most famous poem, 'Howl,' and expanding what we know of the poet's life. Ginsberg, who consented for Naomi's lobotomy, would speak of the lack of tenderness in the mindset of midcentury America and then write about new hopes and liberations. *Best Minds* offers an in-depth look at a bygone era of radical medical solutions to human problems and one gifted individual's suffering, guilt, survival, poetry, and optimism."

—**Regina Weinreich**, Department of Humanities & Sciences, The School of Visual Arts; author, *The Spontaneous Poetics of Jack Kerouac: A Study of the Fiction*

"As psychiatrists have been attempting to understand the relationship between psychiatric illnesses and creativity, it is wonderful to see this volume. In this superb book, Stevan Weine takes on the challenge of understanding Ginsberg, his background, his mother's illness, and his poetry. Clinical psychiatry cannot occur in a vacuum. Understanding the patient's experiences in the context of their development, family, and social circumstances is key. Combining information from multiple sources, Weine offers as complete a picture as possible of the pain of someone who was the foremost poet of the Beat Generation. We are grateful to Weine for producing a stunning history of Ginsberg and helping us understand his creative genius."

—**Dinesh Bhugra**, Emeritus Professor of Mental Health and Cultural Diversity at the Institute of Psychiatry, Psychology and Neuroscience at King's College London; author, *Textbook of Cultural Psychiatry*

Best Minds

BEST MINDS

How Allen Ginsberg Made
Revolutionary Poetry from Madness

Stevan M. Weine

FORDHAM UNIVERSITY PRESS

NEW YORK   2023

Fordham University Press has no responsibility for the persistence or accuracy of URLs for external or third-party Internet websites referred to in this publication and does not guarantee that any content on such websites is, or will remain, accurate or appropriate.

Fordham University Press also publishes its books in a variety of electronic formats. Some content that appears in print may not be available in electronic books.

Visit us online at www.fordhampress.com.

Library of Congress Cataloging-in-Publication Data available online at https://catalog.loc.gov.

Printed in the United States of America

25 24 23   5 4 3 2 1

First edition

CONTENTS

CONTENTS

PROLOGUE

ONE DAY IN November 1949, at the elite New York State Psychiatric Institute (PI) perched high above Riverside Drive in upper Manhattan, a twenty-three-year-old bespectacled patient was presented to the chief of service, Dr. Nolan Lewis, at the weekly case conference.[1] The patient's therapist gave the staff gathered in the auditorium a brief summary of the case history and treatment. The patient had been raised in a Jewish family in Paterson, New Jersey by a mother afflicted with schizophrenia and a father who taught high school English and wrote poetry. The patient excelled at school and received an early admission to Columbia University, where he studied literature with Lionel Trilling and other top professors.

After inexplicably writing antisemitic obscenities ("Fuck the Jews") on his dorm room wall, this brilliant young man was suspended for a year but eventually graduated. While finishing two incomplete papers and living off campus, he wrote poetry, had visions of God, and fell in with drug users and a criminal gang. After a scandalous arrest that made the *New York Times*, a deal with the prosecutor was struck, and he was hospitalized at PI for eight months. He was diagnosed with a serious mental disorder and received treatment in the form of psychotherapy to ward off further collapse into psychosis, drug use, homosexuality, or criminality. At PI, the nurses were instructed to curb any homosexual contact with other patients, encourage dancing at parties, and reassure him that he wasn't psychotic.

On that November day, the patient was escorted into the PI auditorium by a nurse and sat down across from Dr. Lewis, who conducted an interview in front of the audience. The patient acted as if he had something to prove—that he wasn't mad like his mother, who had recently been released from Pilgrim State Hospital following a several-year stay and a prefrontal lobotomy. He was talkative and brash but cooperative and aware of the audience around him, curious, receptive, and prepared for a judgment on his prognosis. He was grandiose, like many people in the throes of psychosis, but also demonstrated literary talents and ambitions not commonly seen among the patients presented at the clinical case conference.

After the interview, the patient, whose name was Allen Ginsberg, was invited to share his poems and paintings with the psychiatry department audience. This event may have been at a psychiatric hospital way uptown in Washington Heights, but it was still Columbia University and New York City, and Ginsberg was all in.

During his hospital stay, Ginsberg had been working on a group of poems about a "Shrouded Stranger," a deranged tramp wandering the railroad tracks and waterfront, calling for someone, in some versions a child, to lie down with him in the night. When the shrouded stranger speaks, his voice has a singsong tone both menacing and sympathetic. These poems offered characters more compelling and language more emotionally charged than any poem he had yet written.

To his therapist at PI, the poem was a personal breakthrough for Ginsberg. The shrouded stranger seemed rooted in the patient's experience of his psychotic mother, whom he had been describing in psychotherapy sessions—scary and predatory but also loving and intensely appealing.

Another poem read that day at PI, "Paterson," could not have been more different in how it portrayed a man who would "rather go mad."[2] The protagonist rejects bureaus, clerks, cloakrooms, psychiatry, employees, and all such attempts to structure living. Instead, he chooses madness, heroin, marijuana, peyote, travel, even misery. He likens himself to a wild modern American Christ, in "hideous ecstasy" and "screaming and dancing against the orchestra in the destructible ballroom of the world."

This figure was a mythic amalgam of many friends Ginsberg had made during those years in New York City—Lucien Carr, William Burroughs, Jack Kerouac, Neal Cassady, and Herbert Huncke—who embraced what they together called a "new vision." These were the friends who the PI psychiatrists thought were encouraging Ginsberg's deviant behavior. For eight months they had been urging Ginsberg to keep away from them and follow a more conventional path if he wanted to get better. Yet in "Paterson," Ginsberg was presenting madness as a deliberate choice and exhilarating ride that offered social value.

The patient showed the case conference attendees several of the paintings he made in art therapy at PI. These were engaging but not nearly as well composed as the poems. His therapist noted: "The paintings are large, rather highly colorful, very primitive drawings of phallic symbols, vaginal symbols, faces. Interspersed throughout all these are various other figures such as therapist, father, mother, etc. The painting has a repetitive theme in each of his paintings, each painting is usually a circle surrounded by satellite figures and phallic symbols."

Afterward, the patient was politely asked to leave the room while the doctors discussed his case. Dr. Lewis shared his grim assessment. The "patient was a severe schizoid, who would probably go definitely schizophrenic someday, but was near genius level in creating." At the time, psychiatrists recognized that schizophrenia occurred at higher rates in some families, perhaps through genes or interpersonal interactions.[3] Given his mother's serious mental illness and Ginsberg's expression of psychotic symptoms, Dr. Lewis had reason to be concerned.

Looking from today's vantage point, the way Dr. Lewis hedged his prognosis raises concerns about the inadequate rigor in psychiatric diagnoses, which has long been a major challenge for psychiatry. In a famous study from 1973 called the Rosenhan experiment, eight people without any mental illness were instructed to say they were hearing voices. They were admitted to psychiatric institutions, where they were given diagnoses of mental illness and directed to take antipsychotic medication.[4] When Ginsberg came to PI, could he have been incorrectly diagnosed?

Dr. Lewis's ominous prognosis, which came from one of the top psychiatrists at one of the most prestigious institutes in the United States, was never shared with Ginsberg. To the contrary, Ginsberg left the hospital believing he had been declared sane and no longer at risk of ending up like his mother, who had spent much of the past twenty years in and out of state psychiatric hospitals in New Jersey and New York. For Ginsberg, this was a tremendous relief.

He walked away "very pleased" with the case conference. He enjoyed being in front of an audience and "seemed bolstered up by their positive reaction to . . . his poetry and his paintings." He knew he was no painter, but he thought his poems were coming along. While at PI, Ginsberg wrote poems depicting madness as either liberatory or damaging. It would take many more years of living and working with the tensions between those two perspectives on madness—and between the promise of his PI poems and the doom predicted in Dr. Lewis's formulation—for Ginsberg to blow these concepts wide open in his poetry.

Naomi Ginsberg, being visited by her son Eugene, at Pilgrim State Hospital, shortly before her death, late May/early June 1956. *Courtesy Lyle Brooks.*

In 1955, five years following his discharge from PI, Ginsberg wrote "Howl," a poem that became a generational touchstone for its challenge to the cultural status quo, not only in the United States but internationally. The poem catapulted him out of relative anonymity and into the headlines. "Howl" is a witness to its own explosion: "I saw the best minds of my generation destroyed by madness."[5] In "Howl," Ginsberg finally managed to turn the many versions of madness he encountered in his own life—that of his mother, his friends, his psychiatric hospitalization at PI, and of a postwar world turned upside down—into a literary call to arms defending the human spirit against social oppression. "Howl" became an overnight sensation, the focus of a highly publicized obscenity trial, and many years later a feature film starring James Franco. It remains one of the most widely read poems in the United States.

"Kaddish for Naomi Ginsberg" (1962), widely considered Ginsberg's greatest poem, also addresses madness, albeit very differently from "Howl." It contains Ginsberg's first and only retelling of the ravages of his mother's serious mental illness. It was so painful for Ginsberg that he rarely read it in public.[6] It is one of the earliest and most powerful family member's first-person accounts of schizophrenia, conveying the humanity of Naomi and her struggle to find meaning and dignity despite serious mental illness and devastating treatments.

"Kaddish" documented Naomi and Allen Ginsberg's lives, but as a poem it does so with remarkable innovations of rhythm, language, structure, and image, especially regarding the use of the "long line," which Ginsberg described as capturing "the unspoken visual-verbal flow inside the mind."[7] According to the literary scholar Tony Triglio, "Kaddish" revises the Jewish traditional prayer and offers a new language for prophecy, which builds upon and redeems Naomi's heroic struggle with madness.[8] It is also a tour de force of madness as a social diagnosis, as it would later be explained by antipsychiatry theoreticians such as R. D. Laing, who was influenced by "Kaddish" and "Howl."[9]

But despite this poem's fame and notoriety, the madness referred to in "Howl," "Kaddish for Naomi Ginsberg," and multiple other poems remains an enigma even today. Biographers, literary critics, and readers do not fully grasp it when they assume madness is largely a cultural construct.

Psychiatrists hardly ever speak of madness or its meanings and instead diagnose and treat mental illness, such as schizophrenia, which they regard as a brain-based disorder akin to other medical diseases. They tend not to see their diagnoses or treatments in cultural or historical context or to consider the phenomenological dimensions of their patients' experiences.

This book aims to bridge these gaps in the understandings of madness and mental illness in relation to Allen Ginsberg's poetry and life. It does so by introducing and examining from a multidisciplinary perspective documents never seen before that give new accounts of Allen and Naomi Ginsberg's involvement with mental illness and psychiatry during a bygone era of American psychiatry.

More than fifty years since these poems' publication and worldwide reception, several key questions remain unanswered. What is the madness Ginsberg depicts in his poems, and how can it be at times either so fantastically liberating ("Howl") or so terribly damaging ("Kaddish")? How did Ginsberg grab hold of the mental illness and madness in and around him and turn them into powerful poems that set off cultural explosions?

To grasp Ginsberg's achievements as a poet and countercultural leader and what they still mean for us today, these questions need answers. Mental illness and madness have not yet been adequately explored in the existing biographical and scholarly writings on Ginsberg. This includes his experiences growing up with a seriously mentally ill mother, having visions at age twenty-two, and being psychiatrically hospitalized at age twenty-three, about which little is known. These gaps are striking because Ginsberg, known for literally disrobing at poetry readings, so often made us feel we knew everything there is to know about him. He gave the impression that he kept no secrets and that his poems accurately depicted his life.

In 1986, as a Columbia University medical student preparing to enter psychiatry, I was especially curious about literary views of madness. I read John Berryman, Sylvia Plath, William Blake, Ezra Pound, Robert Lowell, Antonin Artaud, Michel Foucault, and many others. I reread William Burroughs and Allen Ginsberg. I had questions, so I worked up the courage to write to Ginsberg, one of my heroes, and asked him how he reconciled the different views of madness in his art and life. Much to my surprise and delight, Ginsberg called me and asked to meet the very next day. He let me interview him and offered access to his archives and psychiatric records, as well as to his mother's psychiatric records, which nobody outside the hospital had seen. In multiple meetings over several years, Allen, as he asked to be called, mentored and encouraged me to pursue my investigation, making this book possible. In accordance with his request and consistent with the rapport that made this book possible, I will largely refer to him as Allen.

Best Minds shows how Allen's poetics involved a lifelong imaginative and hopeful reworking of many different experiences of mental illness and madness. He approached both with great empathy, innovations in language, and an urgency to connect with larger meanings and experiences about being human. In Allen's hands, as a poet and countercultural leader, though madness is always linked with hardship and suffering, there remains hope that these experiences can be put to use and lead to redemptive aesthetic, spiritual, and social changes. He was committed to leading others toward new ways of being human and to easing pain through his revolutionary poetry and social advocacy. Reckoning with mental illness and madness was a core component of this project. Madness is not only an individual but also a social condition, and thus it calls for action at multiple levels. Allen's poems and other interventions concerning madness have been an inspiration to antipsychiatry theorists, to mental health practitioners, and to other artists who are asking similar questions today, when madness seems to be breaking out all around. He was only human, and along with these achievements of Allen come some important and consequential flaws, which I will also discuss.

This book introduces new facets of Allen Ginsberg to those who feel like they already know him but want to learn more, as well as to those who are only familiar with his most famous poems. It also contains a personal narrative about how I as a young student came to know Allen, the access he gave me to his psychiatric records and those of his mother, and what he taught me. From these a new picture of Allen emerges along with fresh readings of some of his most famous works. It is a voyage into the worlds of mental illness, madness, psychiatric treatment, and poetry led by Allen and Naomi. It does not aim to be a comprehensive study, neither covering his whole life nor all of his most famous poems.

Allen's poetry expresses a commitment to personal, sexual, social, and political liberation in response to real-world threats to freedoms in the second half of the twentieth century. What Allen attempted in his writings and activism still inspires today, and this book shows what has come— culturally, intellectually, therapeutically, and politically—from Allen's poetic, pragmatic, and hopeful approach to madness—and how much can still be learned.

As a case study of one of the most famous artists in the mid–twentieth century to focus on madness, this book explores the complex relationships between mental illness, psychiatry, trauma, poetry, and prophecy. It also provides historical insights into the paternalism, treatment failures, ethical lapses, and limitations of American psychiatry of the 1940s and 1950s.

I bring to this book my experience and expertise as a mental health professional, psychiatric researcher, and cultural scholar. I introduce theory and empirical knowledge from different fields, including psychiatry, history, traumatology, and cultural and literary studies. Psychiatrists working with patients sometimes offer interpretations as provisional explanations for behavior, motivations, or experiences for which there is incomplete evidence. Although Allen was never my patient, I will sometimes offer interpretations, based on my direct conversations and experiences with Allen and my analysis of his journals, correspondence, interviews, and poems, and will alert the reader when doing so.

Like several other notable artists and thinkers before him, especially William Blake and Arthur Rimbaud, Allen derived inspiration, ideas, and techniques from his encounters with mental illness and psychiatric treatment. Beginning in his childhood, Allen was exposed to his mother's serious mental illness and failed psychiatric treatment, and as a young adult he faced his own mental health problems and inpatient psychiatric treatment and psychotherapy.

Drawing from these life experiences, Allen's poetry enlivened, explored, and elaborated a madness that for him was far more than a mental illness: It was a disruptive and potentially redemptive life force. Madness encompassed many experiences, including hardship, suffering, deviancy, derangement, ecstasy, visions, inspiration, liberation, and more. Through his poetry and countercultural leadership, Allen offered himself as a qualified witness to both the liberatory and damaging powers of madness. He also became a powerful advocate for changes in consciousness, culture, and society that could bring on changes akin to the redemptive aspects of madness and nurture a cherished essence of being human, which in "Footnote to Howl" he called the "supernatural extra brilliant intelligent kindness of the soul."[10]

The story begins in Chapter 1 with Naomi Ginsberg's death at Pilgrim State Hospital and Allen missing her funeral, which drove him to later write the "Kaddish" she was denied. In Chapter 2, I reach out to Allen to learn more about his experiences with madness and end up discovering an important traumatic event he had not openly discussed. Chapter 3 tells the story of Naomi's serious mental illness and Allen's complicated involvement with her care and then his joining the Subterranean gang in New York City, who hatched a "new vision" for society. Chapter 4 reconstructs a detailed chronological account of Allen's 1948 Blake visions and his attempts to use them to write visionary poetry. Chapter 5 covers Allen's ten-month stay and treatment at the New York State Psychiatric Institute and its many-sided impact on his life and poetry. In Chapter 6, we learn about the life changes and writing work that Allen achieved over the next five years, which led to his breakthrough poem "Howl." Chapter 7 examines his "Kaddish" and the life experiences and social meanings behind this powerful elegy for Naomi and reflection upon her madness. Chapter 8 explores how once established as a poet, Allen did not let himself become defined by madness yet drew from lessons learned and applied them in innovative ways in new public activities. Chapter 9 considers Allen's later poems "White Shroud" and "Black Shroud," which revisit "Kaddish," and also looks at Allen's lifelong commitment to support persons with mental illness. The Epilogue reflects on why Allen's involvement with mental illness, madness, and psychiatry still matters and also discusses some of Allen's flaws, which became a public controversy when he was in his sixties.

A life and art revolving around madness cannot be approached by simply offering up explanations; instead we must enter the mystery of poetry arising from life experiences of mental illness, psychiatric treatment, trauma, family conflict, spirituality, and social adversity. The intention of this book is to take you there and discover a place where poetry and artistic breakthroughs emerge from vulnerability, risk taking, struggle and resilience.

For the love of Jesus I do not know how I got this sickness. It's up to you to find out.

Your loving mother, Naomi

To Allen Ginsberg from his mother, Naomi, written in Building 12, Pilgrim State Hospital, New York, 1947

Chapter 1

Death and Madness, 1997–1998

A WEEK BEFORE his bones and flesh were burned into a small mound of ash, Allen Ginsberg gave detailed instructions to Bob Rosenthal, his loyal personal secretary of more than twenty years, to divide his ashes into three and send them to his father's family plot in Newark and the Buddhist centers of his two gurus.[1]

Without a doomed body to worry over, Allen was released from pain in his bones, money worries, publisher deadlines, the exhaustion of public life, demanding students, and his long-term partner Peter Orlovsky's Benzedrine-fueled manic tantrums. After his organs peacefully quit, as a practicing Buddhist, the time of his rebirth was to come.

Nearly one year later, on May 14, 1998, Allen's adorers let him go with a great celebration at the Cathedral of St. John the Divine, just a few blocks from his alma mater, Columbia University. Friends and admirers came to listen as the punk rocker and poet Patti Smith recited his poem "On Cremation of Chögyam Trungpa, Vidyadhara." Backed by her band and Philip Glass, she solemnly read: "I noticed the Guru was dead . . . noticed mourning students sat crosslegged before their books, chanting devotional mantras."[2] The peace activist Dave Dellinger said that "a star has fallen."

The Mourners' Kaddish chanted that misty day in New York City's Morningside Heights neighborhood was not over a freshly dug grave, as has been done for Jews since days of old, but in a church, of all places. Thousands upon thousands chanted Kaddish in the largest church in New York City, in a rousing farewell so unlike his mother's pathetic burial.

* * *

Naomi was buried at age sixty on June 11, 1956, at the Beth Moses Cemetery in West Babylon, Long Island. Only seven people and a sexton laid her to rest. Allen's father, Louis Ginsberg, Naomi's ex-husband; and Allen's brother Eugene, her oldest son, were there. Also present were Eugene's wife, Connie; two cousins, Abe and Anna; and Uncle Max and Fannie. Later Eugene told Allen it was probably the smallest funeral on record. To her loved ones, Naomi had already been gone a long time.

Allen was then residing in the Bay Area, having landed in California two years prior after travels in Mexico to explore Aztec ruins and experiment with the native hallucinogenic yage under his close friend William Burroughs's tutelage. Allen did not return to the East Coast for his mother's funeral. Eugene wanted Allen to know everything that happened on that long, sad day so later in the evening he sat at a hotel room desk and wrote Allen a letter.

Naomi's body had been transferred the day before from the morgue at Pilgrim State Hospital to the funeral parlor in Hempstead, Long Island. They said she had a cerebral aneurysm and went fast. Schizophrenia, on the other hand, had done its gruesome work intermittently and episodically over several decades. Moreover, the injurious psychiatric treatments and years of confinement in dismal mental hospitals had no doubt made her worse. Nobody from the psychiatric hospital came to pay their final respects, even though she had been a patient there for much of the past decade.

The body lay in an open casket. Her face was recognizable and looked sad. They had had a short service at the funeral home. In the middle of the service the sexton had to ask her name, and even then, he mangled it.

The sun was shining brightly, and the sky was clear and blue. The cemetery itself was not as bad as Eugene thought it would be. It was far less crowded with tombstones than the old Jewish cemeteries one drives past on the way through Queens out to Long Island.

Naomi's gravesite at Beth Moses was one hundred yards from Elanor's grave, her only sister. Naomi had not known that Elanor had died a few months prior. The family thought it would upset her too much, so they didn't tell her. Withholding information was one of the only gestures of care left for a family exhausted by her decades-long illness.

At the graveside, the sexton looked away as he told the mourners he regretted not being able to recite the Jewish prayer for the dead. To chant this Mourners' Kaddish there had to be at least ten Jewish adults to make a minyan. Her loved ones could not complete their mourning for Naomi.

As the casket was being lowered, Louis shook his head and said, "Naomi is let down for the last time."[3] Her loved ones needed no further reminders that neither they, her doctors, nor God had been able to save her from a devastating mental illness.

"So ended a somewhat pathetic life,"[4] concluded Eugene's brief letter. It would have been hard for anyone present at the funeral to predict that years later Naomi's life and Allen's grief would become icons of madness and mourning. Never discount the miracle and mystery of poetry.

Two days before the funeral, Allen received news of his mother's death via a Western Union telegram from Eugene in New York. It was addressed to "Allen Ginsberg, care Orlovsky." His companion and lover, Peter Orlovsky, not yet twenty-three, the son of Russian immigrants and a poet himself, read it. "Naomi Ginsberg died suddenly Saturday afternoon. Would appreciate your communicating this to Allen Ginsberg. He may call me at Hotel Regent . . . Eugene Brooks."[5] Orlovsky placed the telegram on Allen's writing desk and went out looking for him. Later in the evening, Allen returned to their cottage and read the telegram and Orlovsky's handwritten note.

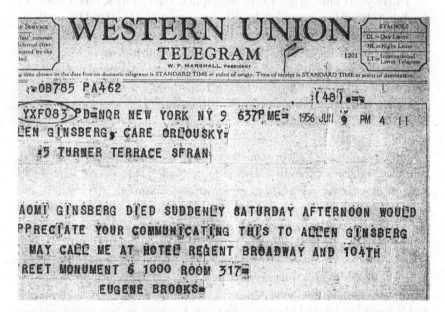

"a telegram from Gene, Naomi dead" ("Kaddish"). © *Allen Ginsberg Estate; Courtesy Columbia University Libraries.*

I got this at 9:30 PM, and here at 10:4 PM. out to find you.
be book soon. Shes. in the sunshine now.

Jane
Peter.

Peter Orlovsky: "She's in the sunshine now." © *Allen Ginsberg Estate; Courtesy Columbia University Libraries.*

Allen pushed open the screen door and stood alone in the small yard under the hazy night sky. At that sorrowful moment, Allen remembered all those visits to the psychiatric hospitals when he was young. It was much harder to recall from years long gone her smile and the warmth of her colorful still-life paintings, before the mental illness and the doctors' treatments took them away. After all the horrors she had endured, there was no doubt in his mind she was better off now. The low-hanging clouds made it impossible to see any stars.

Thirty years later, Allen's first biographer, Barry Miles, asked him why he didn't attend her funeral. A Jewish son is expected to attend his mother's funeral and say Kaddish for her. Allen could have offered an explanation. He could have said he didn't have the money. But instead he said a most unusual thing, according to what Miles later wrote: "Allen did not go to the funeral, for reasons he can no longer remember."[6] Bill Morgan, another Ginsberg biographer, described how at the time Allen was completing his maritime service training at Fort Mason and working on board ship during the day.[7]

Neither Louis nor Eugene made an issue of Allen's not being at the funeral. Louis thought it was because of Naomi that Allen had visions, befriended eccentrics and drug addicts, was expelled from Columbia, got arrested, and was admitted to the New York State Psychiatric Institute (PI) at age twenty-three. Louis would never say so, but maybe he thought it was better Allen did not come back from California. Being there would remind him of Naomi's hospitalizations, psychiatrists, paranoia, shock treatments, and visions. It may pull Allen back in and risk exacerbation of his mental health problems just when he had established some separation from the mental illness and traumas in his family and found his voice as a poet. Louis knew better than anyone that Allen had been too devoted to Naomi for his own good.

* * *

Chanting Kaddish at Allen's memorial in 1998 had a significance beyond Jewish ritual and prayer because of his "Kaddish for Naomi Ginsberg" (1962), considered Allen's masterpiece, an elegy for his mother, an immigrant child raised in New York and New Jersey, who suffered a life of mental illness and died alone in a psychiatric hospital. "Toward education marriage nervous breakdown, operation, teaching school, and learning to be mad, in a dream— what is this life?"[8]

In "Kaddish," Allen discovered a rhythm of rhythms built around his sounds of grief over Naomi's loss, incorporating the Hebrew Mourners' Kaddish, Thelonious Monk's syncopated jazz rhythm, Shelley's "Adonais," Ray Charles's "I Got a Woman," and many other influences across the ages. To some readers, these innovations may seem to have emerged whole out of a person himself gripped by an inspired madness, an interpretation Allen did not discourage. Allen was telling his readers that one way to access and share the truths and emotions of modern life was through the spontaneous summoning and recording of naturally disjointed experiences—such as he had done in "Kaddish" and many other poems.

Allen's poetic innovations also derived from his ongoing exchanges with his fellow writers Jack Kerouac, William Burroughs, John Clellon Holmes, and the more senior William Carlos Williams; his reading of his literary forbearers William Blake and Walt Whitman; and his personal stores of intelligence, devotion, hardship, compassion, journeying, discipline, and hard study, all of which he had invested into his poetry writing for years. "Kaddish" had a deliberate structure, and the poet wanted others to see what he did and how he did it and to make it seem accessible, so it might inspire and guide them in their own spiritual and aesthetic quests.

"Kaddish" bore witness to a world so full of crises, conflicts, binds, and traumas that it drove the innocent young immigrant woman to madness and then passed it to her son. "O glorious muse that bore me from the womb, gave suck first mystic life & taught me talk and music, from whose pained head I first took Vision." Allen was referring to his own 1948 visions, which within a year landed him in a psychiatric hospital.

"Kaddish" said things about madness, psychiatry, and death that had never before been said to the greater public. A mental illness and treatments like Naomi's, "Tortured and beaten in the skull," could be a defeat even worse than physical death. If you lose consciousness or are gone beyond joy and reflection and lose your connections with others, then you lose what it means to be human.

Yet as much as "Kaddish" documented the awful, destructive potential of serious mental illness, it also found and documented Naomi's passion, love, spirit, and insight. This is reflected in what was claimed to be Naomi's last letter to Allen, written at Pilgrim State Hospital just before her death: "The yellow of the sunshine also showed a key on the side of the window."[9] Through the example of Naomi, the poet insisted that even those caught up in the most extreme madness are capable of making meaning and expressing hope, which challenges conventional psychiatric and lay assumptions, even today.

In "Kaddish," the God Allen praised blessed the casualties of the strange new times— marked by homosexuality, drugs, war, paranoia, migration, and madhouses. "Blessed be He in homosexuality! Blessed be He in Paranoia!" "Kaddish" took what were adversities, traumas, and failures of modern life and found in them spiritual traces and keys to existence. "Kaddish" gave to its many readers all over the world new takes on madness, death, and modernity. But no matter how moving, the powerful poem could not bring Naomi back, but instead inscribed the memory of her tragic loss.

In the 1940s and 1950s, an era when psychiatrists had little to offer the severely mentally ill other than confinement and damaging treatments, far too many difficult responsibilities fell upon loved ones. Allen was often alone with her and responsible for her care when just a child. She was frequently hallucinating, delusional, nudist, and suicidal. She filled his young mind with her suspicions about Louis and his family, and as his parents' marriage was collapsing, Naomi drew him to side with her. Yet Allen loved her and thought he was doing what any dutiful son would do for his mother, but her behavior was often frightening and exasperating, and he was unable to make her better, despite everything he tried.

One day in 1942, when she was breaking down, Naomi persuaded Allen, just fifteen years old, to take her to a countryside rest home, a several-hour-long bus ride away. When a few days later Naomi ended up at New Jersey's Greystone State Hospital against her will, Allen felt he had cruelly abandoned her. For the remainder of his life, wherever he roamed, Naomi was never far from his mind. Anything could trigger thoughts of her. She kept coming to him in dreams, which upon awakening, he habitually recorded in his journals.

As a young poet, Allen made madness a subject in many of his poems. In the spring of 1948, within a year of Naomi's commitment to Pilgrim State Hospital on Long Island and when he was twenty-two years old, Allen had visions of God and wrote more than a dozen poems about the madness of visions in the style of William Blake and other classic mystical poets. His own psychiatric hospitalization at PI, soon thereafter, led Allen to write about a madness that portended not divine inspiration but catastrophic mental collapse inspired by Antonin Artaud, one of his early literary heroes and the author of "Van Gogh: The Man Suicided by Society." However, neither the poems of ecstatic nor degrading madness reached the great literary or saintly heights Allen ambitiously aspired to climb. Having tried to examine madness from both directions, the liberatory and the destructive, but not yet getting any poems published, Allen still didn't know how to rise up.

Then in 1955 came "Howl," which took the real-life stories of those he knew and turned them into a blazing testimony of the madness of a generation trying to break from the social oppression of postwar America. With the long breath lines, bluesy rhythms, and informal hip speech of "Howl," Allen leaped onto the scene as the modern heir to William Carlos Williams, Walt Whitman, and, of course, William Blake. "Howl" drew from Naomi's life but did not mention her by name, substituting Carl Solomon, a young Bronx Dadaist intellectual Allen met his very first day on the PI fifth-floor ward in 1949, and a brotherhood of other friends and acquaintances riding the wave of madness.

At its first reading, "Howl" created an instant sensation among the gatherings of poets, leftists, bohemians, and intellectuals at San Francisco's Six Gallery, all seeking meaning and purposeful exit from Eisenhower's vision of America. Michael McClure, a Bay Area poet friend who also read that night, later wrote about the cultural and political break that "Howl" instantly instigated: "Ginsberg read on to the end of the poem, which left us standing in wonder, or cheering and wondering, but knowing at the deepest level that a barrier had been broken, that a human voice and body had been hurled against the harsh wall of America and its supporting armies and navies and academies and institutions and ownership systems and power-support bases."[10]

Naomi died at Pilgrim State Hospital several months before "Howl" was published, while Allen was still just beginning to absorb the new vibes the first public reading of "Howl" had set resonating. Allen found himself explaining to skeptical critics and journalists that the poem was not a simplistic emotional rant but a meticulously constructed work of art.[11] Suddenly, with her death, however, the painful realities of Naomi's mental illness came crashing down once again on him.

Allen tried responding to her passing as a poet, at first writing some fragments about her life in his journal. In prior years, he had written very little about her in his journals, letters, and poems. After her death, the images and memories kept coming, at first in little drips, then eventually in huge torrents of grief. Several days after her passing, he wrote in his journal, "My childhood is gone with my mother. My memory becomes less clear. My body will go. There is no me left. Naomi is a memory. Naomi is a memory. My 30 years is a memory to me."[12]

Allen believed in his heart that he and Naomi were bound by madness. But what kept them connected also, heartbreakingly, drove them apart. His mother was a mental patient who had been confined to a state mental hospital in New York for the last ten years of her life. Allen, by age twenty-nine, was a poet who also had been in a psychiatric hospital but believed he had been certified sane (despite what Dr. Lewis said in the case conference) and had gone on to turn a literary take on madness into a global cultural sensation. Naomi's path through madness was one of deteriorating illness, whereas Allen's star was rising as he transcribed the divine madness of his generation. Nevertheless, he could not forget her, her suffering, and how she fought back against illness and hospital treatment. Allen believed himself to be her appointed artistic witness: He had to tell her story. If he didn't, who would?

We will never know exactly why Allen didn't join his father and brother at Naomi's burial for the reading of the Kaddish. He must have had a good reason for neglecting his filial duties, despite his devotion to her. For whatever reasons, he wasn't witness to the rabbi lowering the casket and pronouncing the end of his mother's life. Remaining out west couldn't have been an easy decision, but it may have given him a margin of space and peace with which to see what a poet who once wanted to be a saint might someday do with all the memories and emotions linked with her madness and death.

Allen was not the only one who had a difficult life with Naomi. She divorced Louis several years prior to her death and for a time became involved with a maritime doctor who put her to work in his office at the Union Hall on Tenth Avenue in Manhattan. Ten days after the funeral, Louis wrote to Allen and confessed his continued attachment to Naomi. "There was no day during which I was in a crowd or happy that thoughts of Naomi, torn within herself and cooped up in a desolate room, did not invade my mind."[13]

As Naomi's pine casket was lowered into a hole in the ground, Louis was overwhelmed by memory and emotion: "The pathos and tragedy of her well-meaning life, the constant struggles within her, the flashes of our happy early moments together—all blinded me." Louis expressed the emotions associated with both Naomi's awful deterioration and their happier times together. A thrilling family outing to the World's Fair in Queens. Amazing summers upstate at a communist family camp. And all those breakdowns and hospitalizations. With this expression and his loving support, Louis gave Allen a beacon to follow that led him eventually to write his own "Kaddish." As a high school teacher, published poet, and avid correspondent, Louis was in a position to transmit valuable life lessons to Allen, if only he would listen.

Louis Ginsberg, 1963. © *Allen Ginsberg Estate.*

Allen had not seen his mother for three years. He and Eugene visited her at Pilgrim State Hospital, where she was tearful but quiet. She complained about the wires in her head, her unremitting complaint. The doctors had no answers. His previous visit to the hospital, in January 1953, had gone horribly. She looked like a walking corpse. In the ward's day room, she told him to get out before he was struck down. Allen fled in tears, later that night recording notes in his journal about the visit, which eventually became part of his "Kaddish."

Not long before Naomi's death, Eugene sent Allen all the letters he received from their mother while she was held against her will at Pilgrim State. She wrote in one of her letters: "God's informers came to my bed, and God, himself, he saw it in the sky—it was after Jan 1, 1956. The sunshine showed it too, a key on the side of the window for me to get out. The yellow of the sunshine, also showed me the key on the side of the window. I'm begging you to take me out of here."[14] This too would find its way into "Kaddish," lending a note of hope to an otherwise bleak landscape.

Just two weeks before Naomi's death, Allen wrote to Eugene: "The main problem for Naomi is that nobody wants or can help her really. Perhaps we can find a place to settle her. I had not thought of it before reading her letters but they seem mild enough. It's not necessary that she be sane to live outside, just peace[ful], & the new pacifying drugs seem to do that from what I read in the papers."[15]

Allen's proposal was to have his mother live on Long Island with his partner Peter Orlovsky's mother, Kate, and a caretaker. His innovative idea anticipated the deinstitutionalization of the mentally ill, which was facilitated by the psychopharmacologic breakthrough that produced chlorpromazine (marketed as Thorazine), which became available in 1953. Naomi was first prescribed chlorpromazine on April 21, 1955, but died shortly before Allen's hopeful plan could ever be realized. Allen failed to get her released from the hospital, which was her only wish. However, he could still write an epic poem about his mother, but it couldn't only be about her misery and death. Hers had to be a story of empathy, remembrance, and hope that could speak to many people whose lives were shadowed by social suffering and mental health problems. Allen held on to Naomi's image of the sunshine-key in the window.

In early July, a few weeks after the funeral, Allen shipped out from San Francisco on a freight ship delivering supplies in the Arctic Ocean. He needed some time away and an infusion of cash. When they made port in

Seattle, Allen received a letter from his mother, dated June 11, 1956, mailed by the hospital staff after she passed.

Naomi wished Allen a happy birthday and thanked him for sending her the poems that would be in his new book. She was glad his poetry was finally getting published but still worried about her baby boy. You need to get married and to find a real job, she wrote. She had read the copy of "Howl" and picked up on its drug references. "I hope you are not taking drugs as suggested by your poetry."[16] Her message was clear: How on earth could you put drugs in your body? Didn't you see how my brain was damaged by all the treatments they gave me? Naomi missed her family and the life she lost a long time ago. "I wish I were out of here and home at the time you were young; then I would be young. I'm in the prime of life now."[17] Reading this belatedly delivered letter, Allen knew she was already gone, and he was already dreaming about how she would later be given a new life in the great elegy he planned to write about her. But where to start?

He wrote to Louis from on board the ship on July 29, 1956, asking him to send him a Jewish prayer book with the Mourners' Kaddish, which, as a nonobservant Jew, Allen was not very familiar with. Louis sent the prayer book with this note: "Those chants therein have a rhythm and sonorousness of immemorial years marching with reverberations through the corridors of History . . . and laden with the tears of things."[18]

Back in San Francisco just days after Naomi's death, Allen spent one afternoon walking around San Francisco with Jack Kerouac and Peter Orlovsky. They passed a synagogue near Telegraph Hill and decided to step inside. Allen tried to rally the rabbi and get the Kaddish said for her, but the worshippers said that once again there were not ten Jewish men present to form a minyan. She could not go to God just yet. According to Jewish belief, her soul would have to wait longer still.

The "Kaddish" Allen eventually wrote and finally published in 1961 bore witness to the family tragedy brought about by Naomi's devastating mental illness and ineffective and harmful treatments. It told her history "of the hospital" and "remembrance of electrical shocks." One hundred and seventy-six long-line verses in five parts on thirteen dense pages.

The bulk of "Kaddish" was written in a drug-fueled forty-hour compositional blitz in November 1958 in New York City. The night before he began to write, Allen stayed up late in a Chelsea apartment with a friend, listening to Ray Charles albums, injecting morphine and methamphetamine, and letting himself tell the story of his mother's life. His friend brought out an old prayer book, and together the two read the Kaddish for Naomi. Then after he returned in the morning to his apartment at 174 East Second Street, the poem "burst from my hand in a day."

Part I begins with Allen walking the streets of lower Manhattan and reminiscing about his mother's life and loss. Part II, the longest section, tells the story of her experiences with mental illness and going in and out of psychiatric hospitals through his eyes, ending with an excerpt from one of Naomi's last letters. "Hymn" gives praise to God and to all the manifestations of the Holy One in the many madnesses of our lives. Part III is a short crowning section focusing on the sunlight and visions Naomi had soon before her death. Part IV had been written a year earlier in his journal while Allen was living in Paris. In these lines he bids his mother farewell and recounts the life she saw:

> with your eyes going to painting class at night in the Bronx
> with your eyes of the killer Grandma you see on the horizon from
> the Fire-Escape
> with your eyes running naked out of the apartment screaming into
> the hall

From Paris's Left Bank, Allen wrote to Kerouac: "I sat weeping in Café Select, once haunted by Gide and Picasso and the well-dressed Jacob, last week writing first lines of great formal elegy for my mother."[19]

In October 1960, after several years of revising and editing, "Kaddish" in its entirety was finally ready for publication. Allen had now written a poem that said everything he had to say about Naomi's life, madness, and death. "Kaddish" centered on a woman crushed by serious mental illness but not deprived of her humanity. Decades of suffering were chronicled, hurts forgiven, and a degraded life redeemed through poetry. Her madness was transformed through its retelling as the story of a twentieth-century immigrant woman driven mad by an even madder world.

"Kaddish" spoke of experiences that would otherwise stay silent, not only at burials but in life, experiences including homosexuality, mental illness, incest, and death. The poem charted an emotional terrain that extended far beyond what was then permitted in ordinary speech, Jewish tradition, or American poetry.

Since its publication, Allen's "Kaddish" has inspired several generations on how to bear family illness and death and how to mourn, preaching open heartedness toward downtrodden loved ones. We will return to "Kaddish" in Chapter 7.

When Allen was seventy, he collaborated with the record producer Hal Wilner on an MTV Unplugged concert more typical of rock-and-roll artists, rehearsed in public performances at New York's Knitting Factory. Sadly, it was cancelled when Allen became ill with liver cancer. Allen was never satisfied with being just a poet; he had always wanted to be a rock star, like the Beatles, the Grateful Dead, and the Clash who looked up to him. Bob Dylan and Bono each promised Allen that they would visit his loft and play music together, but because Allen's passing was so quick, those sessions never took place.

In the decade before his death, Allen wanted to learn more about his mother and what was wrong with her. He was curious about the possible gap between her actual life history and the stories he had told about it. After all, there was quite a space between Irwin Allen Ginsberg, born 1926 in Newark, New Jersey, and the legendary figure named Allen Ginsberg, crowned the May King of Prague in 1965 and leader of a global literary movement.

Allen could not find his way back to his younger days and in his later years lacked the time and energy. So he welcomed those willing to help him get the job done. He didn't even have to look for them; they came looking for him. He sometimes got fed up with academic experts who brought too much intellectual and professional baggage, preferring young, enthusiastic, open-minded persons.

Chapter 2

An Unspeakable Act, 1986–1987

ONE AFTERNOON IN a reading room on Columbia University's Morningside Heights campus in May 1986, I discovered an event of great emotional and moral weight, one not revealed in Allen's "Kaddish for Naomi Ginsberg." I am shocked because I think that in "Kaddish" Allen had committed to telling her entire tragic history, no matter how traumatic, painful, or embarrassing. At the time, I assumed that Allen's poetry had to directly represent actual life experiences and be factually accurate. This assumption seemed consistent with the code he worked by, Jack Kerouac's "Belief & Technique for Modern Prose: List of Essentials" from 1958, which pledged to deliver "the unspeakable visions of the individual."[1]

The event I discovered is documented on several pieces of paper kept in a folder of correspondences from 1947 in his personal archives at the Rare Book and Manuscript Library on the sixth floor of Columbia's Butler Library. It concerned his mother's lobotomy. When these documents turn up, I think this event from his personal life may be a secret. I have already read everything I could find on Allen Ginsberg and located no mention of it in his poems, essays, interviews, or in the critical and biographical writings. That an event so significant has remained largely unknown to his readers all these years, escaping the gaze of critics, scholars, and journalists, I find absolutely unbelievable.

Unspeakable is a word associated with the emotional impact of traumatic events, those involving exposure to death, disfigurement, life threat, or major loss. The psychiatrist and trauma expert Judith Herman wrote, "The *ordinary response to atrocities* is to banish them from consciousness. Certain violations of the social compact are too terrible to utter aloud: this is the meaning of the word unspeakable."[2] Was the event that became unspeakable for Allen a traumatic event or atrocity in this sense? Listening to Allen tell me about it, showing distress and confusion, suggests it was.

Moreover, we know that for family members, being proximate to life-altering and threatening medical events such as surgeries or ICU stays are often traumatic. Family members can experience distressing memories, emotions of guilt and shame, and withdrawal from interpersonal relationships and social activities. These experiences can be even more traumatic when the family member already has an ambivalent attachment to their loved one, which Allen certainly did, given her decades of mental illness and associated absences, disturbing behavior, marital conflict, and divorce. Add to that Naomi's poor outcome from the lobotomy, Allen's guilt for having given his consent for the procedure, and Allen's long-standing grief over missing his mother. As is typical of those exposed to traumas, Allen often avoided reminders of the lobotomy, sometimes including seeing Naomi herself, and had avoided talking about it for many decades.

This surprising discovery occurs because a few months earlier, in April 1986, Allen gives me access to the papers held in his personal archives. I am a third-year medical student at the Columbia University College of Physicians and Surgeons in New York City. I arrived in Manhattan from Ann Arbor, Michigan, straight from college into medical school.

Allen has been my hero ever since the eighth grade, when I first read "Howl," "America," and "Kaddish" at the Southfield Public Library and realized that poetry could be just as thrilling as Bob Dylan or the Beatles. As a fourteen-year-old reader, I loved the emotional intensity and outrageous language with which the poet drew the ecstasies and darkness of his world, which in time came to feel very close to my own.

I am a student of literature and history and a dabbler in poetry who, after medical school, is planning to become a psychiatrist. I seek not only to treat psychiatric patients but to better understand the relationships, if any, between madness and poetry, between art and life. While reading Allen again, I see that in 1949 he was on an inpatient ward at the New York State Psychiatric Institute (PI), where I am now a medical student learning psychiatry. I want to learn more, so I read whatever I can find in published books and articles, but there aren't many details, and it is mostly from Allen's point of view.

How did the psychiatrists diagnose and treat him? Was it helpful? Was there a relationship between this personal episode and the madness he wrote about in his poems? Maybe I should try to ask Allen himself. I decide to write him a letter where I pose some big questions about his experiences with madness, asking his permission to study and write about him. "What was the madness that required hospitalization? Should I call it 'madness'? What characterized it? What meanings did it have to you, with regards to your art (how should it be separated from Blake's presence?), political beliefs, stance in your community of Beats, position in post-war America, family? What is your perspective on the responses from medicine, psychiatry (traditional and less traditional), and how your personal experience has been used, or possibly manipulated by all of these collectives?"[3] I send the letter to his publisher, hoping but not expecting it will actually end up in Allen's hands. Several days later, I am thrilled beyond belief to hear Allen's deep voice on my answering machine when I return to my walk-up on Haven Avenue in Washington Heights late one spring evening. "Hello, Steve Weine, this is Allen Ginsberg calling you back. Yes, I was at PI for eight months of psychiatric treatment. Call tomorrow and ask my secretary to have you speak with me."

I skip class to call him back at exactly 11 a.m. the next day. I speak first to Bob Rosenthal, who passes the phone to Allen. The very first thing Allen asks is if I am writing a book about him. I swallow and say, "Umm, yes."

He starts answering the questions from my letter and without any hesitation encourages me to pursue my project. After ten minutes on the phone, Bob reminds him it is time to go. "The car is waiting for you downstairs." They are headed to Brooklyn College, where Allen was recently appointed a distinguished professor of English and creative writing. Before hanging up Allen says: "Meet me tomorrow at the Museum of Modern Art at six o'clock."

"Isn't MOMA closed on Tuesday?" I ask. As a student member I go often and know the visiting hours.

"There's a poetry reading with some Indian poets at seven. I'll get us in."

Of course he will. He is Allen Ginsberg.

I wait for the man on Fifty-Third Street in front of the museum entrance. He arrives promptly, we shake hands, and the guards let us in. He wears a blue blazer, shirt, and tie. We sit at a table in the cafeteria near the wall of windows overlooking the sculpture garden and speak for forty minutes as the workers set up microphones and chairs for the poetry reading. I try to calm my nerves. "Call me Allen," he says, and he speaks to me with the kindness of an uncle and the seriousness of a professor. "So, you're studying psychiatry at PI?"

"I'm a medical student who will become a psychiatrist. I am doing a research project on creativity and madness that led me to you. I have been trying to understand more about your experiences at PI and what that meant for you."

"By and large they were helpful to me. Although I have some issues with psychiatry uptown at Columbia. I just think that their practice should be more open."

Allen asks me what I am being taught about psychiatry at PI. I tell him I have been working with people who are homeless and chronically mentally ill. When he sees homeless mentally ill on the street, he thinks they are better off than being in "big loony institution bins. My mother died in Pilgrim State." His demeanor changes and his voice quickens. "It was very different for my mother. I'm still having dreams about that. I had a dream of being reunited with my mother whom I found living on the streets. I wrote a poem about that called 'White Shroud,' which is in my new book."

Allen volunteers that if I want to learn more about those early years, I can look through his personal archives at Columbia. He asks, "Have you seen my psychiatric records?" and within a week he gives me his written consent to review his medical records from PI. Allen has never seen those records. Nor have any of the literary critics or biographers who have written about his visions, madness, and psychiatric treatment. Allen is curious about what we will find in those records. Throughout the evening's reading, which is nothing less than wonderful, my mind is racing with thoughts about undertaking a literary adventure with my hero. Most of the time, I am an attentive listener. That night it is hard to focus and keep from dreaming.

"I am a third-year Columbia medical student. I come here with a special request. A former patient from long ago, Allen Ginsberg, gave me permission to review his records, and I am here hoping to confirm they are in fact still at the Psychiatric Institute." I show them the letter giving permission.

The young woman behind the counter loses a bit of her charm when she frowns and turns around to face a middle-aged man in a bow tie sitting behind a desk piled high with psychiatric records. He steps up to the counter with a diplomatic smile and asks me to explain again. To my complete surprise, the explanation satisfies the director, who instructs the clerk to fetch the record.

Not long after, the clerk returns with a gray folder more than an inch thick, places it in the director's hands, who, without pausing, passes it over to me. "You can look if you'd like. Have a seat at that desk over there."

Even if there is somewhere I have to be, I am not going to refuse this invitation. Allen Ginsberg's psychiatric record! What was his diagnosis? Were they visions or hallucinations? What kind of treatment did he get? Who treated him? Was it one of my professors? Did the psychiatrists recognize he was a genius? Did they imagine he would go on to become who he is today?

I flip through the chart and see Allen's admission photo (see cover). I, who am learning how to conduct diagnostic interviews, can't decide if in the mug shot he was genuinely mad or just looking like a young intellectual thinks a mad person looks. I read the lengthy medical history, the social work summary, and skim through the daily psychotherapy progress notes. Unlike today's antiseptic notes, they are long and thick with juicy details. It is all there. Some of the questions I have are easy to answer—yes, they really thought he was sick. Others are not—did they really help him? Other questions I can see I don't know how to ask properly, let alone answer, without expertise in psychiatry and psychotherapy. I am, after all, just a medical student.

Allen and I meet a couple of times that spring and summer. Between meetings I comb through his poetry and his personal archives and read all the books he tells me to read, hoping to unlock invaluable stores of knowledge and inspiration. One thing I hope to learn from him is how you can make such a difference in this life when you know you yourself are so imperfect. How can you help others if you yourself need so much help? My psychotherapist, Burton Lerner, is helping, but Allen could help on a whole other level, I hope. In one of our meetings on a stoop in the East Village, he declares, "I'm going to make you into my kind of psychiatrist."[4] More on that later.

The book I am then imagining I will write will explore how mental illness and madness turns into creative breakthrough. It will include Naomi's mental illness, which Allen endured from birth on, and his own difficult struggles, which emerged when he was in his early twenties. I am especially interested in his experiences with visions in 1948 and his subsequent hospitalization at the New York State Psychiatric Institute, where I am now being taught psychiatry. I know enough not to fall for easy understandings that either pathologize creativity or make light of mental illness.

Nobody has yet told an accurate and complete story of Allen's involvement with mental illness and madness in relation to his poetry. What good fortune for me, as a longtime Ginsberg reader, aspiring author, and psychiatrist in the making, to be in a position to tell the story. Of course, as a medical student, I am also thrilled I am going to learn about mental illness and madness not only from my Columbia psychiatry professors but also from Allen Ginsberg, former PI patient, brilliant poet, and countercultural icon. What kind of book will I write? Neither a Foucauldian critique of psychiatry[5] nor a standard psychoanalytic psychobiography. Allen deserves better, and I picture this project as more of a collaboration with my brilliant subject.

However, the project, which at first seems like a dream come true, gets more complicated for me when not long after, looking through Allen's papers, I find out about a past event that has not been openly discussed.

A few months before the thirtieth anniversary edition of "Howl" is published in 1989, and after we have explicitly discussed it, Allen tells me he will mention this event in the passage he wrote to reintroduce the poem's protagonist, Carl Solomon. At his place, he shows me the page proofs where he wrote in a footnote: "I had signed the papers giving permission for her lobotomy a few years before."[6]

Few readers will likely notice, but I do. Undoubtedly, I am more sensitive to the event because it involves psychiatry, which has just become my chosen profession. How could the psychiatrists who advocated for lobotomies have been so wrong? Being identified with the psychiatric profession makes me feel uncomfortable when sitting with Allen, as if I was in part responsible for a horrific event that took place thirteen years before my birth.

Anyone can find further mention of this event in Barry Miles's biography of Allen Ginsberg, the first of now three biographies.[7] The very day Miles's book comes out in 1989, I rush to the Yale Co-op, grab the book off the shelf, and go straight to the index to see if it is mentioned. One note on page 95 briefly mentions the lobotomy.[8] I am relieved. If I am to write about it, I will not be the traitor who discloses Allen's lobotomy permission from days gone by.

Most of the time, I am not shy. However, the lobotomy is an event so difficult for me to speak of that at first I am afraid to say anything about it to Allen. I am afraid of what he will say. I talk with my book-loving friends from the medical student reading group at Columbia. To stay sane, while immersed in microbiology and pathophysiology, we read Robert Coles, William Carlos Williams, Walker Percy, and Raymond Carver. That week I give them "Kaddish," and at our lunchtime meeting in the Bard Hall cafeteria, which Allen himself visited when hospitalized at PI, we discuss the dilemma over my approaching meeting with Allen: "I thought Ginsberg's revolutionary poetry was built on the premise that nothing of emotional or moral weight was ever to be left out. All stories have to be put in the open and all experiences revealed. No poem better embodies this premise than 'Kaddish,' Allen's elegy for his mother. Why then did he leave it out?"

"Some things are better left unspoken," says my friend Bob.

"That is where art comes in. Art is after truth, not necessarily what really happened," adds Dawn.

"OK, but this is an opportunity to talk with him about what happened. Should I do it?" My classmates know very well I will often not hold something back that needs to be said even at the risk of causing discomfort. However, I was reluctant to do it this time with Allen. "I am afraid to say anything to Allen about it."

I bring my concerns to my mentor, the PI psychiatrist Dr. David Forrest, who as a medical student had studied with the poet e. e. cummings.[9] Meeting for coffee in the PI cafeteria, overlooking the Hudson and the Palisades, I say, "What good would it do to mention it? He doesn't need to be bothered, especially from me. On the other hand, you shouldn't hide from memories and feelings that are buried inside. You shouldn't run from the past. Isn't that what psychotherapy teaches?"

"Who knows? You can ask him if he remembers talking about the lobotomy in therapy. You don't need to have an explanation. Just ask. Invite him to talk about it."

So I add the lobotomy to the long list of potential questions for Allen written in my composition notebook.

We are sitting in Allen's East Village apartment one late afternoon in September 1986, after he returns from his summer travels to Yugoslavia, Hungary, and Poland. I open my notebook, but Allen stops me before I can get off a single question: "Do you want to tell me what you saw first or would it be more interesting for you and your project if I didn't know what you found in those files at PI to give my fresh answers at the moment without any forethought?"

After some nervous stammering, I say, "I want to first hear what you thought."

"Yes. I was very conscious that my mother had been in the hospital, and here I was in the same spot. In the same kind of trouble. So that was a bit scary. Half my life was over, and I was getting into a state similar to hers. That's a phrase in 'Kaddish.' And there is also in 'Kaddish' a recollection of a resolve. People disapproved of what I was doing and warned me that I had better watch out whether my sanity was a question. I better watch out, or it might get me in trouble. So I was quite aware of that."

Allen speaks at length about the circumstances preceding his being at PI. He speaks of the experience of having visions, of living with a junky friend, Herbert Huncke, and of the spectacular car crash that led to his arrest and eventual hospitalization. His father and teachers criticized him harshly for hanging out with criminals. But these were his friends. In his and their defense, Allen points out that Huncke eventually became a published author. "My judgment was right, I think." He adds, "More extreme, however, and more questionable was what was my relation to the visionary experiences I had with Blake, what was that and what had I concluded from it? What did I rationalize out of it, and was what I had rationalized out of it something that was unworkable, and impractical, and too metaphysical, and something that was getting me in trouble, because it was too absolutistic?"

Allen shares his memories of eight months at PI. He speaks of the mind games he played with his novice psychotherapists. Allen recalls once insisting to one of his therapists: "The walls were alive; that exists in some form of energy. That is deposited. You can call its presence everything its presence in that presence involves a certain amount of energy. But I was just banging my head against the wall with him. I didn't want to get in trouble by having them consider me a complete nut. My aesthetic insistence was really not worth the practical trouble, because I think there was a question of whether I'd get out on weekends."

Over several hours I listen and take it all in but I want to ask him about the lobotomy. If I don't say it now, I may never get another chance. Already long into our conversation, I finally tell Allen, "I ran across a letter from Pilgrim State, dated November 1947."[10]

"To?"

"To yourself."

"Where did you find it? In PI?"

"No, in your personal archives at Columbia."

"What did it say?"

"Please be advised that your mother, Mrs. Naomi Ginsberg, was seen in consultation with the assistant director and it was decided that her mental condition is serious enough to warrant a prefrontal lobotomy."

"Please be advised? November 1947? That was 1948?"

"November 1947."

"Now that's interesting. I would have guessed it to be in the 1950s."

I thought this might happen, so I bring my handwritten notes to the interview. I pull them out, and we both look over the papers to confirm that

Form 90-Adm.

State of New York
Department of Mental Hygiene

HARRY J. WORTHING, M. D.
SENIOR DIRECTOR

PILGRIM STATE HOSPITAL

West Brentwood, Long Island, N. Y.
November 14, 1947

Re: Naomi Ginsberg

Mr. Allan Ginsberg
200 West 92nd Street
New York 25, N. Y.

Dear Sir:

Please be advised that your mother,
Mrs. Naomi Ginsberg, was seen in consultation
with the Assistant Director and it was decided
that her mental condition is serious enough to
warrant a prefrontal lobotomy. If you are
interested in more details in regard to this
type of operation and its possible complications,
you can discuss this problem with the doctor in
charge of the case of your mother on the next
visiting day.

In the meantime, we are enclosing a
permit for the operation which you can sign and
return to us if you so desire.

Very truly yours,

HARRY J. WORTHING, M. D.
Senior Director

GEC:TF

"Please be advised." © *Allen Ginsberg Estate; Courtesy Columbia University Libraries.*

I have it right. He then pauses in silence, looks down, and says, "Hmmm. That's a very extreme thing."

"What are you thinking?"

"I wonder to what extent there is a relation to my whole change of mind during that time, psychotic breakthrough, so to speak. Because I had to do the signing for that."

"How did it make you feel?" (That's either a hack psychiatric question or a reconfigured Dylan line. Perhaps both.)

"Well, I just had to cut my feelings out to do it. It had to be done. They said that, and I inquired further, somehow or another the decision for that fell on my head."[11]

Nearly forty years earlier, Allen gave his written consent for the doctors at Pilgrim State Hospital to perform a prefrontal lobotomy on his mother. I had found a letter dated November 14, 1947, addressed to Allen Ginsberg, in Paterson, New Jersey, from Harry Worthing MD, senior director of Pilgrim State Hospital in West Brentwood, Long Island. Allen, just back from several months' travels in Texas, Louisiana, and Dakar, was supposed to sign and return the letter by mail, which would forever change his mother's life, and also his own. He was twenty-one years old.

"My mother was in a state of high pressure, high tension, high blood pressure, and a stroke was imminent. If she didn't have a lobotomy, she would likely bash her head against the wall and likely have a stroke and die. She would explode literally. She was in such a state of anxiety, tension, and violent agitation that in order to save her life, they needed to give her a lobotomy to cut the affect. Is that possible?"[12]

Our psychiatry professors at PI don't teach us anything about lobotomies. It is regarded as the dark past of psychiatry, and the faculty is trying to impress upon us medical students that today psychiatry is just as scientific and professional as any other medical specialty. In medicine, memories of misadventures are short; hubristic efforts to cure, whatever the cost, are relegated to the long-gone days of ignorance. Modern psychiatry has long since left the lobotomy behind. If not for Allen and my discovering this letter, I would have, too.

To learn more, I visit the PI library and read their annual reports from the late 1940s and early 1950s describing the experiments being done with lobotomy. They tout them as achievements of a modern scientific psychiatry. Walter Freeman, the psychiatrist who promoted lobotomies and did more than 2,500 in twenty-three states, said the idea was to "apply a simple operation to as many patients as possible in order to get them out of the hospital."[13] What these papers didn't state was that women were much more likely to be lobotomized, even though more men were institutionalized.[14]

I read the original scientific articles by Dr. Worthing and the other leading lobotomists, which related their high hopes for psychosurgery in that bygone era. Historical reviews published far more recently show that not only were

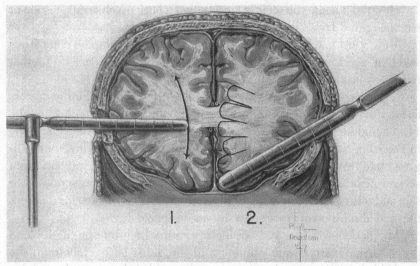

Figure 15. (1) After the sweeping incisions have been made with the precision leucotome, (2) they are deepened with a somewhat wider blunt knife called a radial stab incisor.

"Sweeping incisions." Walter Freeman and James Winston Watts, *Psychosurgery in the Treatment of Mental Disorders and Intractable Pain* (London: Charles C. Thomas, 1950), 42.

the promises of lobotomy not fulfilled but also that lobotomies were pursued in haste and without adequate regard for basic principles of science and ethics.[15] By the 1960s, the consensus opinion was shifting against lobotomy. There were reports of serious adverse effects, negative media portrayals, and the new option of chlorpromazine (Thorazine). The more I learn about lobotomies, the more I understand why many in psychiatry would rather forget this part of its history. This wish to forget can also extend to some family members of the mentally ill who, from no fault of their own, signed up their loved ones for an irreversible procedure many would later regret.

A prefrontal lobotomy is a surgical procedure that was used by psychiatrists to treat schizophrenia and other types of mental illness. It involves making burr holes in both temples, then inserting a sharp, bladed instrument called a leucotome to make sweeping incisions in the frontal lobe, irreversibly severing the white-matter connections between the prefrontal cortex and other brain areas.[16] At the time, some psychiatrists in state hospitals were using lobotomies widely. This was especially the case in New York State, which in the 1940s had one-fifth of the nation's institutionalized mentally ill persons.[17] Clinical experience and preliminary research suggested to these doctors that lobotomy might help with intractable mental illness, and the procedure became increasingly common, even though the benefits and risks had not been fully evaluated scientifically. The psychiatrists at Pilgrim State and many other institutions believed lobotomy was the hoped-for treatment that would revolutionize psychiatric care for the severely mentally ill. Before 1955, an estimated thirty thousand lobotomies were performed in the United States.[18] Naomi got caught in this wave of desperate measures to help empty the overflowing state mental hospitals.

Over the next several decades, the use of prefrontal lobotomy began to be regarded as harmful and ineffective. It became clearer that lobotomies caused a lack of emotional capacity and produced passivity and apathy. These personality changes were not effects of the original mental illness.[19] It came to be widely held that it was a misuse or even abuse for those psychiatrists to have lobotomized so many people with mental illness.

Even in 1949, there were dissenters within mainstream psychiatry. Dr. Nolan Lewis, who had interviewed Allen at PI, asked in *Newsweek* whether lobotomy was merely a way to "make things more convenient for the people who have to nurse."[20] He objected to the "number of zombies" made by lobotomy and cautioned psychiatry to stop "before we dement too large a segment of the population." Yet many of the psychiatrists of the day ignored such calls and got carried away by their own explanations, their research agendas, and their belief that they had found a cure for the most devastating of all mental illnesses.

One evening in 1986, when Allen and I discuss the lobotomy, I share my personal opinions: "I think psychiatry should apologize for the tragic history of lobotomy. It's the right thing to do. The American Psychiatric Association should issue an official apology."

"I suppose so," Allen says, "but the psychiatrists, like me, were only doing what they thought was right. In those days, nobody had any better answers."[21]

At the time of Naomi's lobotomy, psychosurgery was not only an accepted treatment for mental illness; it was even lauded. The first Nobel Prize ever awarded to a psychiatrist was given to the Portuguese psychiatrist Egas Moniz in 1949 for developing the prefrontal lobotomy (aka leucotomy). To understand the enthusiasm for lobotomy, we have to remember that back then psychiatry had little hope to offer to the seriously mentally ill. Effective antipsychotic medications had not yet been developed. State hospitals all over the country were overflowing with persons afflicted with intractable symptoms and with no hope of ever going home. Psychiatrists, families, and society were desperate for anything that could help make the mentally ill more manageable.

Naomi's family felt that way. By 1947, she had been severely mentally ill for more than thirty years. She had been hospitalized four times, for years each, and had received electroshock, insulin therapy, and metrazol therapy, with little to no apparent benefit and many awful side effects. At the time he signed consent, Allen was doing what almost any family member would do in these circumstances. Something had to be done.

The man who had written for Allen's consent, Dr. Worthing, was one of the most prolific lobotomists in the United States. At the PI library I find some of his articles, including a paper entitled "350 Cases of Prefrontal Lobotomy" published in October 1949. Naomi was one of the first one hundred operations performed between May 13, 1947, and June 4, 1948.

Dr. Worthing reported that between May 1947 and May 1951, he performed six hundred lobotomies. His colleagues at Pilgrim State reportedly performed another six hundred during the same period. Dr. Worthing wrote: "Among the unmeasured and perhaps immeasurable gains from lobotomy, one may number the improved appearance and subjective state of the patients, the family attitude toward the improved state, and, finally, the effect on certain details of hospital management and morale of personnel, which follows the elimination of chronic severe behavior disorder from continued-treatment wards."[22]

For several years, lobotomy was believed to be psychiatry's breakthrough. The media coverage of lobotomy was "uncritical and sensational,"[23] further raising the hype. Dr. Worthing believed lobotomy would help make patients easier to be cared for by their clinicians and, by implication, their families as well. But making them easier to manage was not a cure and not without cost. However, these matters were seldom considered and, in any case, did not dampen enthusiasm for the lobotomy among the psychiatrists at Pilgrim State Hospital or the families of the mentally ill. Before long, they hoped, everyone would see that lobotomy was the neurosurgical answer to America's mental health crisis. By the mid-1950s, the adverse effects and lack of effectiveness of lobotomies were too obvious to ignore, and with chlorpromazine now available, psychiatrists stopped offering them.[24] But this was little consolation for all those patients who had endured the irreversible operation and for their family members who saw their loved one irretrievably lose a core part of their personality.

Allen said the request from Dr. Worthing came to him because after his parents divorced, he became the family member primarily responsible for Naomi's care. Allen wasn't sure about what the doctors at Pilgrim State said about her physical problems and what that had to do with her mental problems. Were they the same thing? As a medical student with little knowledge of psychiatry, I didn't understand this either. With Allen, I do not pretend to know. He says there really was no choice. They told him that for her sake, he had to sign. I believe him.

Some forty years later, as Allen speaks about the lobotomy, he sounds confused. He believes Dr. Worthing's statement that she needed the operation to survive. But he questions Worthing's professionalism. "Some time back I looked into Dr. Worthing's background and found out that Worthing was a nut who performed a lobotomy on his own wife."[25] I do not know what to say. To this day I am unable to confirm this outrageous claim, but what strikes me about it is Allen's belief that Worthing had taken his commitment to the lobotomy to such an extreme degree. It is almost like Allen identifies with Worthing, as paradoxical as it may seem. This brings to mind Dr. Walter Freeman, one of the leading lobotomists, who on October 13, 1948, was on the cover of *Time* and at the time regarded as a savior of the mentally ill and their families.

Allen knows so well from his own experience that there's something about serious mental illness that pushes the people who care for such persons in all kinds of desperate and difficult ways. That's true for psychiatrists, spouses, children, and poets. At the time he signed for the lobotomy, neither he nor her doctors knew what else could be done for her. Naomi had been asking her doctors and family to please kill her. Why not see if lobotomy could release her from her suffering?

For as long as he can remember, Allen tells me, he thought the lobotomy was done much later, sometime after 1951, during Naomi's lengthy final hospital stay at Pilgrim State, which lasted until her death in 1956. But the lobotomy happened at least four years earlier, meaning it actually preceded his "psychotic breakthrough,"[26] as he called it. I needed to investigate the possible relationships between these events if I wanted to understand how his life experiences, madness, and poetry may be related.

This begins with acknowledging that giving consent for his mother's lobotomy was itself a very difficult and traumatic experience for Allen, as it would be for almost anyone in his position as a family caregiver and son. It can be considered a medical trauma, which refers to traumas that occur in medical settings, in this case Allen deciding that Naomi should receive irreversible brain surgery.

As dreadful as the lobotomy was for Naomi and Allen, it is a mistake to focus only on this one event. After all, the lobotomy did not happen in isolation, having been preceded by many years of Naomi's deteriorating mental illness, repeated lengthy hospitalizations, other harmful and ineffective psychiatric treatments, and the consequent family tensions and marital breakup. Trauma to family caregivers, such as Allen, can also come from caring for someone with severe and life-threatening illness and disturbing behavior, like schizophrenia, especially as a child. On top of that, Naomi's repeated and prolonged confinement in psychiatric hospitals was a major loss for the young Allen, who grew up without his mother for years at a time.

For example, her psychosis relapsed when he was four years old. Naomi became irritable toward Louis, arguing about communism and berating him for writing poetry. Her hallucinations returned; she kept repeating "dog chasing me" and "fear, leer, tear" and was sent to the hospital.[27]

Another experience comes from fifteen-year-old Allen's journal, where he wrote his mother "Is still a little —."[28] Blanks hid the words he could not bear to write to describe her mental illness. He couldn't get himself to write what he thought was wrong with her, even in his private diary. As a youth, he did not allow himself the words to describe either her condition or what it was like to live with her. Nor apparently did Louis or Gene. Perhaps he thought some things are better not spoken.

The loss associated with a family member who has severe mental illness can be considered an ambiguous loss. "Ambiguous," because the person is physically present but not cognitively or emotionally present due to the psychotic illness. Or, in another sense, because the person is alive but confined in a hospital. Ambiguous losses are difficult to manage and often leave people with more prolonged and complicated grief responses.[29]

As for the lobotomy, we can only imagine the difficulties young Allen would have, putting his mother through a risky, very possibly deadly or debilitating operation, and the numerous conflicting feelings behind that decision and motivating it. For years the son had been responsible for caring for his mother, a mother he loved but was deeply ambivalent about. A lobotomy was known to be a risky operation, despite Dr. Worthing's calm platitudes. But even this was charged with ambivalence. Could it possibly kill her? Would she die if he refused to sign? Allen alone had to decide and to sign. He didn't talk with his brother or his father. It was all left up to him. He never told her what was about to happen and that he was the one who had consented.

These types of traumas can leave some people with symptoms of posttraumatic stress disorder, and they can leave others feeling bereft, hopeless, alone, and/or guilty. At the same time, traumatic experiences like these challenge one to find ways to cope, to draw upon existing strengths or to develop new ones, which can sometimes involve spiritual and creative approaches, among many others.[30]

Could Allen's lengthy silence associated with the lobotomy have generated a longing to give a voice and a story to Naomi to make up for the irreversible harm done to her? Perhaps, but even the poems that mention lobotomy still present Naomi's lobotomy as not fully utterable. "Howl," his signal poem of protest, said little explicitly about Naomi's mental illness and nothing about her lobotomy. But it did have the protagonist Carl Solomon showing up, "on the granite steps of the madhouse with the shaven heads and harlequin speech of suicide, demanding instantaneous lobotomy."[31] According to Dr. Walter Freeman, it was not uncommon for patients and their families to actually send letters requesting lobotomies, which, based on glowing media portrayals, they saw as a miraculous life-changing surgery.[32]

"Kaddish," on the other hand, seemed to say everything there was to say about Naomi's mental illness and treatment. In contrast with "Howl," which many fans know line by line, it is a poem not even hardcore devotees can recite. It is too sorrowful to keep in your heart or mind, too irregular to keep the rhythm, and at moments too painful to bring out of your throat without being reduced to tears. "Kaddish" is also full of painful mysteries; it mentions "a scar on her head, the lobotomy,"[33] but does not further describe how or why Naomi got the lobotomy scar.

Upon learning about the lobotomy, I have a different response to one line in particular in "Kaddish." After a thorough and exhaustive telling of Naomi's life story, he asks her:

O mother/what have I left out

Even after reading this telltale line, it probably seldom occurs to most readers that Allen left anything out of this exhaustive poem. It never occurred to me until I learn about him giving consent. But is he saying right here that he did? Is he pleading with his mother to keep him honest? Naomi never did answer, not in a letter, poem, or in life. She never knew Allen signed consent, and she was gone before the poem was written. Her spirit might have said: You left out the fact it was you, my dear son, who signed the consent that put me through that awful operation. They cut me and put wires in my brain. You let them ruin me. My son, why didn't you protect me?

* * *

When I learn about the event left out of "Kaddish," I wonder if it could also shed some light on Allen's reluctance to read "Kaddish" in public. Despite his pride in "Kaddish," Allen read the poem in front of audiences only a small number of times. In 1966 he explained: "I was afraid that reading it over and over, except where there was a spiritual reason, would put the scene into the realm of performance, an act, rather than a spontaneous poetic event, happening, in time."[34] There is something intensely personal about this poem. We might say "Kaddish" is closer to the son than to the poet. Allen does not want to share this poem with just anybody on any occasion. The moment has to be right. But when is the moment ever right to talk about something so painful and difficult?

Although Allen is not an observant Jew, in Jewish law, mourners are not supposed to read the Kaddish for more than eleven months after the death of their loved ones. You need to let yourself move on. There may also be personal reasons for keeping his distance from "Kaddish"; reciting the poem to an audience could bring him too close to the emotional distress associated with her illness and the lobotomy.

The lobotomy, he seemed to fear, may have killed her. Cerebral hemorrhage, after all, was one of the most common causes of mortality following psychosurgery.[35] There is no knowing for sure, but we can speculate whether the lobotomy could in part explain the mystery of why Allen did not attend his mother's funeral. He may have felt too guilty about the lobotomy and what he feared he had done to her to attend her burial. He later recalled: "There's still, unresolved, a sort of guilt at having not been able to take care of her properly when she was alive and having, in fact, been the one to have had to sign the papers for a lobotomy, after the doctors at Pilgrim State Hospital warned me that she would have a stroke and perhaps perish unless something were done to cut the emotional torrent."[36] He further said:

> The emotions that I felt, of grief and affection for my mother were, in a sense, forbidden social emotions, even though she was . . . *because* she was . . . in a bug-house, and therefore outside the pale—and in those days they used to cut pieces of their brains out, remember—the prefrontal lobotomy or tenectomy for the eyeball—so people were being treated as objects and experimented with, and that was something that I was supposed to not talk about, and not relate to other people about, and that it was a deep dark family skeleton secret, but actually, I loved my mother, and the social manners didn't seem to fit in with the family tragedy.[37]

The lobotomy may have done triple work for Allen and his mother: driving him away from her funeral, where he would miss the chance to recite the Mourners' Kaddish; leading him toward taking on her visions, then resurrecting her and reworking the meanings of madness through poetry; and burdening him with ambivalent feelings about the human costs associated with his poetic breakthroughs.

That was my thinking as a medical student. How much better if we could be there with Allen, to see how he put to work these experiences with mental illness and psychiatry so as to write poems that changed his world and ours. This becomes my new mission. But because I keep bringing up things Allen doesn't like talking about, and because one of those is a disastrous operation done by some psychiatrists, the profession I am now associated with, I fear Allen will not want anything more to do with me. He will surely tell me to end my investigation and go away. But instead Allen tells me, "I like you. I like your project. I like talking with you." He unexpectedly asks: "Have you tried to get her records?"

"Not yet."

"Go ahead and try."

My mission now had Allen's permission. When Naomi's records finally come in the mail, which would not happen for many years, the doctor's and nurse's notes contain more pieces of her untold history.

Chapter 3

Refrain of the Hospitals and the New Vision, 1943–1948

IN HIS POEM "Kaddish for Naomi Ginsberg," published five years after her death, Allen wrote, "Over and over—refrain—of the Hospitals—still haven't written your history—leave it abstract—a few images."[1] Part II of "Kaddish" gives an account of Naomi's illness and hospitalizations as a social diagnosis (driven by social processes), which will be discussed more fully in Chapter 7. This chapter gives an account of her illness and hospitalizations based on other sources, including Naomi's medical record from Pilgrim State Hospital, and her letters in the Allen Ginsberg archives, both of which I read with Allen's permission. They give a devastating picture of Naomi's symptoms and suffering leading up to her 1947 admission to Pilgrim State Hospital, where she eventually underwent a lobotomy.

On April 24, 1947, a feeble fifty-one-year-old Naomi entered the examining room at Bellevue Hospital in lower Manhattan, teetering on her feet and almost falling over. When she sat, her head sank onto her chest, and her voice dropped to a whisper. She had hypochondriacal complaints and reported visual and auditory hallucinations. As she continued talking, however, her voice picked up and became more energetic. To the examining psychiatrist, her mental content had a touch of ecstasy.

She told the doctor she had had three or four attacks of fear in her life but added, "I hang on to a happy thought and wouldn't let it go. I fought for the joy of life."[2] She made an opaque statement about being embroiled in political situations and asked, "Is there such a thing as outside spirits haunting you?" She had seen God, who was tall, strong, and handsome. God told her to "Have patience and keep saying 'I don't care.'"

Her gestures consisted of a characteristic head movement. Sometimes she jerked her head about on an imaginary axis drawn perpendicular to the floor. At other times she threw her head onto her chest and let it hang there. She hung her head because "I can't keep trying to hold on to a happy thought."

When asked about her husband, she said, "That's where my trouble started, everyone knows my life. It's a case in history. My husband killed his brother and child. My husband is a well-known poet. I left him four years ago. I got tired. We separated. . . . His mother organized a gang to get something in America for the Jews. They went wild with killing. I was always a progressive internationally minded."

She described the vision in which she saw God and heard his voice: "All of a sudden a vision came to me when I first became sick. It said: 'Have patience, it comes to the needy'—I was so happy I tried to get him again."

She was at the end of her rope. "I can't endure the suffering. . . . I feel as though I'm dead, but I am not dead." Naomi was exhibiting and describing many of the classic symptoms of schizophrenia, such as delusions, paranoia, disorganized thinking, hallucinations, and agitation. She also had the rich language of schizophrenia, including idiosyncratic semantic associations and word approximation.[3]

News of her admission got to Allen, who later that day wearily wrote in his journal, "Naomi, Bellevue, radio back. Etc. etc. Depression, relieved, but settling in; sexual stasis again."[4] From Bellevue she was transferred to Pilgrim State Hospital in Brentwood, Long Island.

After it opened in 1931, Pilgrim State Hospital quickly became the largest psychiatric hospital in the world, and by the early 1950s it held more than 13,000 patients.[5] Under the directorship of Dr. Norman Brill, Pilgrim State Hospital also became a major center for lobotomies. Not long after her transfer, Allen visited her at Pilgrim State Hospital but wrote nothing of this visit in his journal.

Naomi was born April 1, 1896, the second of four children to Judith and Mendel Livergant, both educated, in the village of Nevel in the Jewish Pale between St. Petersburg and Odessa.[6] Before she turned ten, Naomi's life became a story of migration, part of the historic movement of Jews from Russia and Eastern Europe to the United States in the late nineteenth and early twentieth centuries.

In 1904, to escape being drafted into the Russian army, first Mendel and his brother immigrated to the United States. Until they got settled enough to send for them to come as well, their wives and eleven children stayed in a two-room cabin in Vitebsk, birthplace of the painter Marc Chagall. One year later, the two families boarded a ship and were reunited in New York. Mendel's family settled on the Lower East Side's Orchard Street, where he opened a candy shop.

The Pilgrim State record included four typewritten pages of the "Abstract of Case History" of Naomi, which had been compiled in New York's posh and private Bloomingdale Hospital in 1931.[7] On the top of the first page in bold letters it states:

CONFIDENTIAL AND PRIVILEGED—FOR PROFESSIONAL PURPOSES ONLY—NOT TO BE USED AGAINST THE PATIENT'S INTERESTS. THIS RECORD IS NOT TO BE SHOWN TO THE PATIENT.

Neither Naomi nor Allen nor any other family member ever saw this record. In 1973, Allen and his brother Eugene had tried to get the records by writing to Director Henry Brill, but their request was denied. I find the following in the section entitled "Personal History":

Her periods began at age 16. She remembers she was distressed at menses late onset and wondered if a sexual experience at 9 was in any way responsible. This episode was an attempted assault by a male boarder. There was contact but no penetration of the penis. . . . Patient was masturbated by a female cousin two years her senior when she was 5 or 6.

Today, US mental health professionals would regard these experiences as sexually inappropriate behaviors occurring in childhood. Sexual stimulation by an older child or an adult is believed to be deeply disturbing to a child's psychological development and sense of physical and psychological integrity and can lead to serious behavioral or psychiatric problems.[8]

As far as we know, Naomi did not speak of these experiences either with her family or her doctors at Pilgrim State. None of her Pilgrim State medical records mention it. By today's criteria, Naomi was subject to child sexual abuse. Moreover, these events likely shaped her emotional life and her own sexual behaviors, including those toward her sons. Survivors of childhood sexual abuse are known to have higher rates of psychiatric disorders and of hallucinations.[9] Some studies show that survivors of childhood sexual abuse have higher rates of schizophrenia, though these studies are not definitive.[10] Some, but certainly not all, victims of childhood sexual abuse are also more likely to have difficulties in interpersonal relations, especially involving intimacy, or to engage in sexualized behavior with their own children.[11]

In the 1950s, however, serious mental illness was believed to be largely genetically inherited, and little attention was paid to childhood traumatic experiences. Today, more weight is put on childhood trauma, and while genetic factors are known to be important for schizophrenia, they nonetheless explain less than half of the variance, and there is much about gene-environment interactions that is still not understood.[12] Although the psychiatrists of the 1940s and 1950s put little emphasis on traumatic experiences, we should acknowledge their likely contribution to Naomi's mental illness.

The family eventually moved to Newark, New Jersey, where Naomi attended grammar school and then Barringer High School. Growing up, nothing about young Naomi seemed out of the ordinary. Then at age eighteen, Naomi had her first "nervous breakdown." According to her sister Elanor, their parents thought Naomi's troubles came from living under financial pressures, typical of recent migrants to America. However, Elanor thought it had more to do with her infatuation with a man who didn't reciprocate her attraction. None of the family knew for sure whether these romantic delusions were a cause or a symptom of an emerging mental illness.

Not long thereafter, Naomi met Louis Ginsberg, a teacher and published poet. When she was twenty, they began their courtship. His father came from Galicia, a former province of the Austro-Hungarian Empire, and his mother from Ukraine. Louis was born in Newark and raised in a strong extended family with socialist political views. Naomi never got along with Louis's mother, Rebecca, who apparently didn't think Naomi was good enough for Louis. It didn't help that Naomi was raised a communist. At the time, socialist and communist groups in the United States were in deep conflict, leading to many bitter and dramatic debates in the social halls, newspapers, and cafes where the new immigrants made their lives, and debated over the state of the world.[13]

Naomi attended the Newark Normal School to become a teacher, but all was not well. According to the medical record from one of her first psychiatric admissions, she suffered prolonged distress over the infatuation for the first man: "All through Normal School, she pined for him, became despondent, lost her appetite and weight and slept poorly." Nonetheless, Naomi graduated at age twenty-one and began work as a teacher in a primary school. Maybe everything was going to be alright.

In 1918, when Naomi was twenty-two, her mother, Judith, died in the global influenza epidemic, which claimed tens of millions of lives.[14] This flu

Naomi and Louis Ginsberg, c. 1920. *Courtesy Lyle Brooks.*

struck quickly and cruelly. A person picked up the contagion on the street or from casual contact and within hours became consumed by the most terrible pneumonia, lost their breath, and died. For Naomi, losing her mother was devastating. Within a year she had another breakdown. This time, according to what Allen was later told, "Light was painful to her. Every noise was a blow."

Despite his parents' objections, Louis and Naomi married in 1919 at a ceremony in Woodbine and then took an apartment in Newark. In 1920, Louis wrote a poem, "Roots," which became his major poetic work. He received a prestigious award from the *New Masses*, an American Marxist magazine, and had poems published in the *New York Times Magazine*. Naomi accompanied Louis to meetings of the Poetry Society of America in Greenwich Village. His reputation as a poet grew.

Naomi became pregnant, and their first son, Eugene, was born in 1921. For the next several years, when she was taking care of Eugene, the medical records indicate that Naomi did not have any overt mental health problems. Motherhood was good for her, it seemed. After Eugene turned three, her condition worsened again. The medical records from New York Hospital, where she was admitted, reported: "She became distressed and excited over a threatened divorce in her husband's family. She said she had trouble in her head and heard voices. She kept repeating, 'Fear, leer, and tears' over and over."

Once again, she became pregnant in the hope of correcting this trouble. A second son, Irwin Allen Ginsberg, was born on June 3, 1926, at Beth Israel Hospital in New York. Unfortunately, their mother's pregnancy as prevention strategy didn't work as planned: "After her delivery she began to complain of something turning over in her head. She was very much afraid of another pregnancy and used contraception daily."

For Allen's first three years, Naomi was well enough to stay away from the psychiatrists. However, soon enough it became apparent Allen's birth had not saved her. In 1929, she became physically ill and had gallbladder surgery. While Naomi was recuperating, Allen and Eugene moved in with her sister Elanor and her family. Soon thereafter, Louis moved the family to Paterson, New Jersey, where he received a teaching position at Central High School. Amid all these life changes, Naomi's psychiatric symptoms returned:

> In August 1930 [age thirty-four], she developed considerable irritabil-
> ity which was directed toward her husband and children. She began
> to brood and worry about petty matters. She had heated arguments
> with her husband about communism. She resented her husband's
> complacency and his poetry. She experienced a recurrence of hallu-
> cinations and repeated various stereotypes such as "fear, leer, tear"
> and "dog chasing me." She feared insanity, lost weight, and ate and
> slept poorly.

Naomi was admitted to the psychiatric ward at Westchester Division, New York Hospital (aka Bloomingdales), on May 7, 1931, at age thirty-five. The records report: "She expressed numerous hypochondriacal ideas and inti-mated that she had auditory and visual hallucinations. Things seemed unreal to her. . . . She occupied herself with long division or mathematical problems to divert herself from unpleasant bodily sensations."

Naomi was released from the hospital against medical advice on September 19, 1931, as Louis Ginsberg could no longer afford to pay the bills. Her diagnosis was "Psychoneurosis, Psychasthenic Type." This diagnosis, which is no longer in use, refers to a mental disturbance including phobias, obsessions, compulsions, or excessive anxiety. Naomi returned home but didn't recover her prior level of functioning and never returned to teaching. "Adjustment was considered as poor."

Back home, Naomi was able to maintain her activities in the local Communist Party branch. She took Allen and Eugene to meetings and large public speaking events. The family spent two pleasant summers at camp Nisht-Gedaiget ("Not to worry"), a camp for families of the Communist Party in upstate New York. For Allen, it was great to be in the countryside and to see his mother getting somewhat better. These became his most idyllic childhood memories. Louis, disheartened by Naomi's illness and financial problems, turned to his poetry for strength and relied upon the emotional support of his family and friends.

Several years later, at age thirty-nine, Naomi had another relapse. She did not want to go back to the hospital, was treated with sedatives at home, and got somewhat better within two months. The next year, Naomi relapsed and became much worse. This time she had auditory hallucinations and paranoid delusions that Louis and his mother were trying to poison her.

With no funds to pay for private treatment, Louis brought Naomi to the New Jersey State Hospital at Greystone Park, which had nearly five thousand patients and relied on electroshock and insulin therapy. Its most famous patient was Woody Guthrie, committed there in 1956, and in 1961 it was visited by Bob Dylan, who called the hospital "Gravestone."[15] Naomi's diagnosis was again "Psychoneurosis, Psychasthenic Type." This time she would need a long hospital stay, the doctors told Louis. However, Louis could not tell Naomi without further arousing her suspicions. Being that Greystone was a public hospital, at least he didn't have to pay and go further into debt.

Allen recalled those years: "As I grew up, I had to take care of her on and off because my father was teaching in college, and so, when I was 9, 10, 12, 13, I visited her by myself in mental hospitals, which were grimy, huge drab prisons in those days, where she'd had shock treatment—insulin and metrazol and lobotomy and electro-shock."[16]

Nearly every weekend, Louis took the boys on a several-hour bus ride to visit her at Greystone. Sometimes Naomi came home on passes. But she was still not well. On June 24, 1937, Allen wrote in his journal: "My mother locked herself in the bathroom early in the morning and my father had to break the glass to get in. She also went back to the Sanitarium."[17] Louis later explained to the boys that she was depressed, suicidal, and had cut both her

State Insane Asylum, Morris Plains, N. J.

Greystone Hospital, 1923.

wrists. She was sent back to the hospital in an ambulance. What could they say or do?

After more than three years of treatment, Naomi was "paroled" on April 16, 1940, and then discharged the following year, on April 16, 1941. This time her stay at home would last less than one year. Allen was fourteen. All he wanted was a normal mom. The boys received much-needed loving support from Louis's side of the family.

In the winter of 1942, at age forty-six, Naomi's condition became worse yet again. According to the next admission note: "Patient continued to complain of pain in her head and believes that her mother-in-law was instrumental in her hospitalization. . . . Stated that a New York doctor was sending his henchman to kill her. He had thrown fumes at her that contaminated her husband and if he touched her, it would poison her. She searched the house for Dictaphones. She complained of insomnia and was afraid to be alone."

Naomi was admitted to Greystone for the second time. The doctors reported:

She was fearful, over productive, overactive and almost screaming in a high pitch voice. She showed occasional flight of ideas with pressure of speech and a tendency to rambling and circumstantiality. She noticed she was being watched and whispered about by people on the street. Mrs. Roosevelt told someone to tell her the labor movement was fighting Hitlerism and this confirmed her feeling that she was being persecuted. She has always tried to help the poor people and has "felt" for them. Hitler has been preparing for her persecution for a long time and has been spreading germs.

Persecutory delusions, a common symptom of schizophrenia, often take on a political dimension, borrowing from the headlines of the day. Given the severity of her symptoms during this hospitalization, Naomi received forty insulin and metrazol shock treatments. Using insulin and metrazol in combination to induce seizures and coma was, at the time, a new treatment being used by psychiatrists to try to lessen the symptoms of schizophrenia. The original scientific reports touted significant rates of remission and symptomatic improvement.[18] But this treatment also led to weight gain, spontaneous seizures, and memory loss. Naomi developed all these complications. But apparently there was enough improvement in her delusional symptoms for her to be discharged, after a nineteen-month stay, on October 6, 1943. Upon leaving the hospital, Naomi promptly divorced Louis, whom she still regarded as her enemy, and went to live on her own in New York City.

Allen always had more questions than answers about his mother's condition. Back in the 1940s, families were told little by psychiatrists about what was wrong with their loved ones. They were burdened by stigma, ashamed of their mentally ill loved one and even blamed themselves. Much later in life, many years following Allen's own experiences with visions and psychiatric hospitalization, he decided he wanted to know more. By then his mother and father were long gone. When he was young, Allen had nowhere to turn for help with understanding Naomi's illness.

Mental illness manifests itself uniquely in each person, yet there are recognizable patterns. The signature feature of Naomi's illness was the presence of psychotic symptoms persisting over many years. This indicates Naomi had a type of severe chronic psychotic mental illness. Beginning at age eighteen, she had multiple episodes of paranoia, delusions, hallucinations, and disorganized speech, which are all hallmarks of a severe chronic psychosis. During these episodes and between episodes, she was unable to work, to care for herself, or to care for her family. For these reasons, she was given a diagnosis of "Dementia Praecox" (premature dementia), which was the original designation of schizophrenia described by Emil Kraepelin in 1883.[19] Were she to be assessed by a psychiatrist today, the most likely diagnosis would be "schizophrenia, paranoid type, chronic, severe."[20]

Allen did not know whether Naomi's condition was physical or mental. There is no evidence to suggest she had some kind of neurological or neuropsychiatric disorder that caused the psychosis. This is not to say that there wasn't a neurobiological basis for her mental illness. Scientific evidence increasingly indicates that schizophrenia is attributable in large part to biological changes in brain functioning.[21] This, however, does not account for the fits and movements Allen wondered about in Naomi's later years. Regarding those symptoms, it is likely the neurological problems she began to have later in the course of her illness were largely side effects of the treatments she had received, including the electroshock, insulin, and metrazol therapies and especially the lobotomy.[22] As in other areas of medicine, like oncology, sometimes the treatments are just as bad or even worse than the disease itself. This was certainly true for psychiatry in the 1940s and 1950s, before antipsychotic medications were discovered.

For Allen, who for much of his life was racked by guilt over handing his mother over to doctors who did more harm than good, there was an extra reason for being confused about the issue of physical causality. If he thought Naomi had a physical problem to start with, then it could possibly assuage his guilt over the harm to her caused by the lobotomy.

Naomi also had marked disturbances of mood with periods of depression and agitation. I am unsure how to account for her mood disturbance diagnostically. It could be part of another diagnosis now called schizoaffective disorder, or it could be depression comorbid with schizophrenia. This has become a useful distinction because there are different treatment regimens for each disorder, but back in the 1930s and 1940s, this was not the case. There were no effective medications. There was psychotherapy, electroshock therapy, insulin therapy, metrazol therapy, and lobotomy. None were as fine-tuned for particular types of mental illness as are psychopharmacological treatments today. Some medications can be effective in diminishing hallucinations, delusions, and depression. Nonetheless, it is of concern that Naomi's first presentation of mental illness sounds more like depression. Had she been adequately treated for depression, perhaps she would have not developed such a debilitating psychotic illness. This is a great and discomforting "what if?"

Naomi's mental illness had a devastating effect upon her family. There were clearly other tensions in the marriage, provoked by the bad blood between

Naomi and her mother-in-law. Today, these tensions would not be regarded as the cause of her mental illness, although the tensions may have contributed to her many relapses. Whatever tensions were present were made far worse by her paranoid delusions. In the face of all these difficulties, the marriage of Louis and Naomi was unsustainable.

Naomi's capacity to parent her children was profoundly affected by her mental illness. She was hospitalized for many years of Allen's childhood: six months when he was between ages four to five, three years from ages ten to thirteen, one and a half years from ages fifteen to seventeen. Or perhaps we should look at it another way: Despite her severe illness, Naomi was with Allen up until age four, from ages five to ten, and from thirteen to fifteen. At least they had enough time together for Allen to be strongly bonded with his mother, even if it was an ambivalent attachment, commonly seen with the children of parents who are psychotic.

Being exposed to Naomi both between and during relapses of her psychosis was difficult for young Allen to endure and to understand. In his childhood, the extreme was commonplace. In the journals he started to keep as a child, he documented the strange disjuncture of ordinary and extraordinary experiences that cast shadows on his childhood and at times left him insecure, fearful, and confused about what was happening to her and where to place his allegiance. Like many traumatized and grieving children, Allen's way of coping was to grow up too fast.

On Sunday, January 19, 1937, at age ten, he wrote: "Went to the movies and saw Parnell and Hotel Haywire. My mother thinks she is going to die and is not so good. Haven't received the key yet. Expect to go to the movies tomorrow. My brother is to graduate from high school soon, and will go to Montclair State Teachers College."[23] On May 22, 1942, at age fifteen, he wrote that upon release from the hospital, "She came home to find Lou $3,000 in debt. Is very fat, lost her girlish laughter and figure. I don't blame her for her condition." Note his sympathy toward her, as against commonly held views that blamed the mentally ill.

As her illness progressed, the times she was at home became more difficult. Naomi and Louis often fought terribly. Upon her coming home for a visit, Allen (ten at the time) wrote: "When she came home from the hospital there were violent quarrels." Naomi and Louis fought about politics, poetry, family, Naomi's nudism, and especially money.

For Allen, talking about his mother was always difficult. Naomi tried to turn him against Louis and her mother-in-law. He was drawn to Naomi's side, favoring her lush paintings and keen artistic sensibility, and was sympathetic toward her politics. He always wanted to believe her, even some of her far-out ideas. He learned to be tolerant of her strange habits, although he was put off by her walking around the house unclothed.

More than anything, he liked having her home and missed her when she was away. He hated what the hospitals did to her. They made her fat. Took away her smile and her desire to paint Impressionist still lifes and landscapes. Did any of those doctors know what they were doing? Allen thought he should protect her from the doctors and hospital where his father kept sending her.

When he was fifteen and she needed help, Allen let his mother persuade him to take her to a rest home. They took a bus into Manhattan, waited several hours, then took another three-hour bus ride to Lakewood, New Jersey. Naomi wanted Allen to leave her there and return home by bus. She said no matter what, he could not tell Louis where she had gone. By the time Allen got back home, the rest home had already called Louis. Naomi was completely out of control and had been thrown out. Much to his distress, Louis had to go in the middle of the night to fetch her. While Louis and Naomi were waiting in a drugstore to catch the bus back, Naomi became severely agitated and, according to the medical record, "screamed and implored people to protect her from being killed."[24] She was taken to Hopedell and was transferred to New Jersey State Hospital on February 19, 1942.

Allen remembered the rock-bottom day and included it in "Kaddish." There he told a vivid story of the bus ride and the drama at the drugstore that Louis had recounted to him. Did he ever realize that he'd written in the poem that the Lakewood incident occurred when he was twelve, but he was actually fifteen? Writing that he was younger reflects and emphasizes the emotions of vulnerability upon being far from home, alone, and helpless with his delusional mother. The feelings were true.

Perhaps he remembered this incident so vividly because it was the last day in his life Allen really listened to Naomi. After the Lakewood incident, there would be no more letting Naomi call the shots. For many years he had tried his best to take her side. There were times when he thought that because she trusted him more than anyone, he could persuade her through logic that the hallucinations and delusions were not real. There's nothing in the walls. Have a look. No wires leading to your head. No noises. The Gestapo is not really there. Family members of someone with paranoid psychosis are put into impossible binds.

After the Lakewood incident, Allen had no choice but to change positions and strategy. He was now on the side of his father and the doctors. He knew he could not save her. He could not talk her down from her madness. He was frustrated with himself for ever believing he could. Instead of trying to save her from the doctors, maybe the doctors could do something to help make her better? Maybe their treatments would work this time. Weren't they coming up with some new treatments these days? He had done what he could do; now it was up to others.

The rest of the family had their own lives to live. Louis had his poetry books to keep him going. Eugene was at college, preparing for a career in law, eventually graduating from New York University School of Law. By 1943, Allen was getting ready to go to college also intending to become a lawyer. He would never forget Naomi. As a labor lawyer, he could fight for Naomi's communist ideals and causes. It was the least he could do for his mother, who might spend most of the rest of her life in a psychiatric hospital. There seemed no other way to make something of the ideas possessing Naomi. That is, until his new college friends and he hatched what they called the "new vision."

By the time Naomi was discharged from Greystone in October 1943, Allen had already left home to start life as a seventeen-year-old freshman at Columbia University in New York City. Allen was a brilliant but troubled college student. He majored in English and studied with some of Columbia's most legendary professors, including Lionel Trilling, Jacques Barzun, Raymond Weaver, and Mark Van Doren. He read the classics required of all Columbia College undergraduates and took his academic studies very seriously. But he left his professors with the distinct impression he had some serious emotional baggage, which sometimes got in his way. Nobody knew exactly what, but it was obvious that some personal troubles were bothering an otherwise brilliant student.

Allen's education was never limited to Columbia College. In fact, what was truly exceptional about Allen's college career was all the learning he did outside of the classroom with his friends and mentors around the city and through nonstop reading and journaling. In his freshman year, he met Lucien Carr from St. Louis, who was far more worldly, educated, and bohemian than Allen. Carr introduced Allen to the nineteenth-century French poet Arthur Rimbaud and his "Season of Hell," where the soul can only be transformed through a descent into the self: "A poet makes himself a visionary through a long, boundless, and systematized disorganization of all the senses. All forms of love, of suffering, of madness; he searches himself, he exhausts within himself all poisons, and preserves their quintessences."[25]

Allen had never met anyone as worldly, sharp, and edgy as Carr, who engaged Allen in nonstop dialogue and debate on poetry, art, and politics.

Carr also introduced Allen to his older friend from St. Louis, William Burroughs, who had studied at Harvard and lived in Greenwich Village and who also had an extraordinary mind. He met Jack Kerouac on campus and, through him, Herbert Huncke and later Neal Cassady and began lifelong friendships and literary collaborations with them all. They were fellow adventurers dedicated to exploring the deviant social worlds of art, drugs, criminality, insanity, and homosexuality.

The journals Allen kept since he was nine years old were a space for recording facts about himself, daily happenings, family matters, World War II events, and reflections on politics and on his evolving sense of self. In December 1943, after completing his first semester at Columbia, Allen initiated a new journal entitled "The Book of Martifice." This journal announced itself as strikingly different from all the prior ones by making new claims about the role of the artist. As an epigram, he quoted from Allen Renard: "Out of the cracked and bleeding heart/Triumphantly I fashion— art!"[26] On the journal pages he reflected on the term "martifice," which was Kerouac's wordplay, combining martyrdom with artifice. Allen wrote: "When he touches an object it too dies and becomes a living soul, a symbol. He is beyond life, beyond good and evil; rather he is good; he is the high priest of God. He must therefore be worshipped."[27]

Spurred on by the artistic interests of his new friends, especially Lucien Carr, Allen turned away from labor law and toward literature. Over the next several years, he committed himself more deeply to journaling and writing. Composition notebooks offered him an arena for the documentation of daily experience, self-exploration, analysis of literary thought, and sketches for all the novels and poems he wanted to write.

In 1944, Allen started recording his dreams in his journals. He began by remembering dreams from childhood. He then began to record each dream in great detail the morning after, a habit he continued for the rest of his life, producing journals filled with page after page of the fantastic and perverse mixed with the mundane and ridiculous.

In an entry from 1944, he further explicated the idea and purpose of art. "Art = conscious selective creative self expression, which is therefore potentially communicative."[28] Allen took this to heart, and in time it became his life's work. Being communicative was always essential to Allen. Early on he recognized it meant staying away from what he would later call "flat prose."

He transcribed dialogues with Lucien Carr on art and morality. "As life wounds us, so art must wound us." Art may be redemptive, but it is not necessarily safe and comfortable. The aspiring artist may have been steeling

Hal Chase, Jack Kerouac, Allen Ginsberg, and William Burroughs, 1944. © *Allen Ginsberg Estate*.

himself for approaching the life adversities he had already faced and would later face or hurl himself into.

He wrote detailed character analyses of the others in his circle, beginning with Lucien Carr. "It may be now surmised that Lucien Carr considered that he was an artist. And, to tell the truth, it was not overly presumptuous of him to entertain this consideration, for he was endowed with a high degree of sensitivity and critical perspicuity of which he was, to be sure, aware." Allen used humor and sometimes played with a satiric voice.

Allen wrote fantasy suicide notes he intended to put in the Carr novel or some other. One read:

I am a lost child, a wandering child, in search of the womb of love. I have been intellectually perverted by insanity and adultery in my home. I have dreamed obscenities that would shock you as they once shocked me. I have thought of wildly imaginative insanity, of perversion, of humor, of loveliness and beauty. I have desired many things—the important ones, I have been denied. They are stability (economic and familial) and love (emotional).[29]

He was learning to imagine himself as a figure who could own and embrace the turbulence both around and within him.

He was drawn to express the dramas of his circle of friends more so than his family dramas. On August 14, 1944, scandal struck Columbia College when Lucien Carr stabbed to death a young man named David Kammerer who had been sexually obsessed with him. Allen wrote in detail about the events surrounding the murder, including for a class writing assignment. He thought these sketches would become a novel. For Allen, the event of the murder, and his growing dissatisfaction with his Columbia education, further solidified his outsider status and the literary ambitions he shared with William Burroughs, Jack Kerouac, and Lucien Carr. Nobody else on campus was talking and thinking like them. If they could only put it on paper.

It was, therefore, not a total surprise to those who knew him when, in his sophomore year, Allen was thrown out of Columbia for writing "Butler has no balls" and "Fuck the Jews" in the soot on his dorm window. Nicholas Murray Butler was the president of Columbia University from 1902 to 1945 and a prominent Republican politician who sought and lost the Republican presidential primary in 1920. To his buddies Jack Kerouac, Lucien Carr, and William Burroughs, it was a hilarious, harmless snub at a blowhard.

To the Columbia administration it was no laughing matter. What was inexplicable to Lionel Trilling and his wife, Diana, who were both Jewish, was Allen's antisemitism. Where on earth did his Jewish self-hatred come from? It was not only inexplicable but for the Trillings, inexcusable. Allen was told to stay away from Columbia for one year, to get some psychotherapy, and then to reapply. Unwilling to give up on his Columbia education, Allen complied.

After being asked to leave Columbia, Allen went to sea with the Merchant Marine. In his journal he wrote he was finished with poetry. Even the best he could write wasn't good enough, and this depressed him. Still he read and studied more poetry. He found Yeats's *A Vision* difficult reading but wanted to master it and thought maybe it would help him develop his own new vision. If he didn't find a way to get some creative writing done, he might end up as a professor or a critic. That may satisfy Louis, but what he really wanted to be was a novelist or any kind of creative writer.

Infrequently in his journals, Allen wrote about his mother and her mental struggles. In September 1944, when she was living in New York City and involved with a physician, Dr. Luria, Allen wrote:

> Remember to write about Nay on Dr. Luria's couch, stricken with the desire to become the Messiah, vainly trying to grasp the inspiration

that floated in his head. She sat on the couch self-consciously, closed her eyes, refused to be interrupted, and began to speak words of beauty, wishing she were really in a trance of genius. She spoke on for several minutes, pronouncing fierce truisms about educating the world from street corners, and ended lamely, unable to think of anything more to say other than we should build a new world as our hearts tell us.[30]

Naomi was not the seer that she—nor at times he—wanted her to be. Allen was noting what anyone who spends time with persons who are psychotic will observe. Psychotic individuals may produce poetic language and gorgeous images, as well as the most banal and impoverished communications. There is often a compromise in insight, making it difficult for them to know the difference. This compromise in insight often extends to something as basic as the difference between what is within the individual and what is out in the world. This leaves those living with psychotic people with a lot of struggles themselves. Do you believe what they say? Should you encourage or discourage them? Are there ways to complete what is missing in their ravings? Or should you just leave them be? In the pages of his journal, Allen showed signs of struggle with these questions and began to reflect upon his ambivalence about Naomi and her madness.

On November 10, 1944, Naomi reappeared in his journals in passages documenting arguments between Louis and Naomi written in the manner of a screenplay.

> Naomi: You're rotten to the core. Get out of my life.
> Louis: Don't go.
> Naomi: Go to hell! (slams door)[31]

Naomi goes off to get a room in a boarding house to live by herself and tells Allen she doesn't want him to follow her because he will just tell Louis. Allen comes anyway, and she shows him where she lives. "I have a cute room here. I'm happy where I am now but not at home." Back home, Allen told his father. As feared, he went in search of Naomi. She told him: "I don't ever want anything to do with you. I told you that before. Why do you bother me? (rising) Either you go or I go! (raises her voice)."

This passage is a reimagining of the trip to Lakewood when Allen put Naomi in a rest home and pledged not to tell Louis. In his journals, Allen took a climactic episode of family life and rendered it as a screenplay. In the rewriting, Naomi is able to live independently instead of being held against her will in a psychiatric hospital. Allen is shuttling back and forth between

Naomi and Louis. This is a role he played in real life, and it is a transitional space between sanity and insanity that he eventually came to use to great effect in his writings but here was just starting to explore. Although Allen was not mad like Naomi, he was learning he could legitimately speak about, from, and to all kinds of madness.

His journals were also a place for making lists and outlines: sexual terminology, the drugs he wanted to try, outlines of novels he wanted to write. The cluttered stuff of Allen's imagination, dreams, desires, ambitions, and even his most banal jottings were laid out in his diary. He was a sensitive observer of himself and his world, with a documentary eye that would be the envy of any cultural anthropologist.

As with many ambitious, romantic adolescents and young adults, Allen's journal was occasionally a place for making grand statements about literary ambitions. In March and April 1945, Allen first articulated his "New Vision" mentioned earlier. This was an idea that initially grew out of dialogues with Lucien Carr about the role of the artist in society and that was further discussed and shared with his other close friends. Together they regarded themselves as the progenitors of a new approach to existence emerging from the ruins and wounds inflicted by mainstream society. In correspondences, journals, novels, and poems, they elaborated this vision. Allen wrote in his journal: "The 'New Vision' is in a sense the product of a strictly rationalized system. In it I affirm the power of the mind's reconstructed intelligence. . . . The new vision lies in a highly conscious comprehension of universal motives and in a realistic acceptance of an unromantic universe of flat meaninglessness."[32]

Drawing from Rimbaud, Allen believed the writer should take in the world as it is, "without ordered, rational preconception,"[33] then, through writing, create an entirely new order and consciousness. It was up to Jack and Allen to write this new vision into reality. But how? Allen had started writing long poems, "The Last Voyage" and "Death in Violence," and Kerouac was at work on a novel, *The Town and the City*. In his journals Allen approached this by making more lists of how to implement the new vision, such as by exploring the city's range of decadent behaviors: "Cultural types to investigate."[34] This included all the different types of bars in New York City, defined by their different types of patrons. There were sailor bars, gay bars, student bars, art bars, lawyer bars, etc. If he visited enough of them, he would get an impression he could then write about.

Allen was also thinking more and more about the self and personality, becoming interested in psychology, neurosis, and psychoanalysis. In a debate in his journal, Allen proclaimed: "It's the crippled soul which you can't evade."[35] He probably didn't know what "crippled soul" really meant, but he knew the new vision involved looking directly at one's mind and innermost feelings but not being bound to current thinking and perceptions. He looked for ways to get help in this area and became especially interested in psychoanalysis.

In 1945, Allen entered into a dual psychoanalysis, with Jack Kerouac, conducted by the completely untrained William Burroughs, who was his friend and very-well-read follower of Wilhelm Reich, a highly heterodox psychoanalytic theorist. So what if he wasn't qualified. William knew Allen and Jack as well as anyone. They could never afford a real psychoanalysis. But they could go each day to William's place and lie on the couch or floor and open themselves up to him. Allen learned both Jack and he had mother issues. Their analysis ended in 1946, when William left for Texas. Allen missed the opportunity afforded by the sessions to be so closely listened to. But Allen's other pressing problems could not be addressed there. He remained unable to fulfill the artistic dreams he had for himself.

"This journal is at least a beginning in prose; although it has no literary value from a technical point of view. I allow myself slipshod expression and confused motivation, which should not do for a novel."[36] Literature and especially the new vision demanded extraordinary capacities for viewing the self and the world anew. How could he get there?

The only available answer was to pursue psychological study and a "proper" psychoanalysis. That was what everybody was talking about on campus and in the art bars. He could free himself of neurosis by becoming a psychoanalyzed man. Allen approached psychoanalysis with a degree of intellectual curiosity, as well as with skepticism. He wrote: "The Freudian language must be revised" and reflected on castration as a symbol for intimidation.

In one passage, he staged an imaginary conversation between "conscience" and "the muses." The muses said: "You still can't say what you mean in real terms." To be healthy and to be an artist, the soul must change. "Only when the soul discovers its weakness, and submits to interrelation, the imposed pattern, the trauma, the castration, the guilt, need it take demand." The kind of self-discovery Allen called for is not only found through talking on an analyst's couch but can be achieved through experience, action, and actually changing your life beyond language.

He was looking at himself through the eyes of William Burroughs, his friend and mentor. He loved William but wasn't getting all he wanted from him, which had to include help with making art, always his top priority. The work with William was, he reluctantly concluded, "inconclusive psychoanalysis." What he didn't seem to know—but accurately surmised—was that for many analysands, psychoanalysis is indeed inconclusive.

Allen pondered what was missing: "I need a frame of mind that serves me, suits me, is me. How can I write when, looking through Bill's analytic eyes, I see that what I write is not me?" On September 20, 1946, he wrote, "I am beginning to suspect Bill." In a letter, William's wife, Joan, confirmed Allen's skepticism, telling him that William may not be able to help Allen with his sexual problems. At other times Allen thought: "Analysis has made me healthier." He decided to apply to get a real analysis from Dr. Kardiner's clinic at Columbia University. Maybe a real analyst with proper training could do better.

Allen's reading lists from the time showed he read widely about parapsychology, telepathy, and hallucinations. One day, he met a college friend, Russell Fitzpatrick, in an uptown bar. Fitzpatrick was studying theology and reading St. John of the Cross. Fitzpatrick "can't dispense with stylistic sentimentalisms about the possibility of God, 'which one mustn't ever lose the sense of.'" Was this just another sentence being tossed out, or did it reflect some serious new intellectual or spiritual commitment? The latter, it turned out. Less than one year later, while sitting by the window in Fitzpatrick's East Harlem apartment, something happened that Allen spoke of for the rest of his life.

Allen was interested in using drugs, including marijuana, heroin, morphine, and Benzedrine, as a path toward something larger than himself, perhaps even toward achieving the new vision. However, when he did drugs, his letters became sloppy, his mind slipped, though he liked the sensations. Dead, broken, direct, and unordered, like the new vision called for. Could he write that kind of novel? First, he had to create a personality, discover it, find its spontaneous delight, develop it and know it. No more settling for half knowledge of the world, only whole knowledge.

Allen got a further taste of the visionary at a New Year's Eve party in 1947. They were drinking wine and sitting in a homemade Reichian orgone accumulator at a friend's apartment, listening and drumming to jazz tunes. While drumming with his friends Bridget and Norman, Allen felt vibrations, about which he journaled:

a lot of energy in my chest and abdomen, very sexual, and it pushed itself down to my genitals whenever we seemed to particularly agree on a beat, we were all "sent" simultaneously, and I suddenly felt, at one of those moments, an orgasmic sensation. . . . As we beat on we reached, a point of clairvoyance, I had an out-of-this-world, short, mystical, visionary sensation of telepathic communication with Bridget and sometimes, not often, with Norman.[37]

Since about age eight, Allen was aware of his attraction to boys, which became more explicitly sexual attraction in his teenage years. He was physically attracted to Jack Kerouac and Lucien Carr but kept those feelings secret, until one night in college confessing to Kerouac. Allen had one experience of mutual masturbation with Jack and several other sexual encounters with men he met at a gay bar and at the Museum of Modern Art.

After Neal Cassady, a ruggedly beautiful and highly literate young man raised in the slums of Denver, the "cocksman and Adonis of Denver," arrived in New York in late 1946, he and Allen met at the West End Bar and enjoyed a "wild weekend of sexual drama."[38] But immediately thereafter, Allen fell back into despair, wanting Neal in ways he could never reciprocate. Allen wrote a suicide letter to William Burroughs in which he proclaimed himself to be at a dead end, ruminating, "I never escape the feeling of being closed in, the continual relentless anxiety, the frustration, the sordidness of self, the uselessness."[39]

In January 1947, in an enormous letdown, Allen was rejected by Dr. Kardiner for psychoanalysis. At the time, he wrote in his journal of a dream in which Lucien changed to Aunt Edie and then to Naomi. Allen felt sexual toward her. "I am thinking about her black breasts, and choking and clucking and gasping like an infant."[40] He asked himself: "Do I think of Lucien as a mother?" This vision of a frightening and damaged mother threatening her child is the first such image Allen wrote down, and it was an image that would recur.

The Freudians didn't want Allen, so he tried to get a proper Reichian analyst, having been introduced to the Reichian approach by William Burroughs. In February 1947, Allen got Wilhelm Reich's address and wrote to him, asking for advice about his neurosis and for referrals regarding a proper psychoanalytic treatment. Allen contrasted his own personality with those of his friends, especially Neal Cassady. Cassady thought sixteen thoughts at once or followed them through sixteen associations. Sure, he was hard to follow, but he was not bothered by it one bit. Cassady was the polar opposite of Allen and seemed a better embodiment of the new vision than anyone else he had ever met. Allen, on the other hand, was far too bound to preconceived structures and ideas. He wanted to break out, to simply "experience" like Cassady and Kerouac, such as by smoking tea and listening to jazz. With tea one is permitted to enter a world of rhythms, and jazz can give a strange, out-of-this-world, orgasmic kick.

He wanted to get away from the need for awareness and even for verbalization. Allen could achieve this somewhat with Cassady and Kerouac, but even then, he still felt the need to verbalize and analyze. His second nature was grouchy, superficially quibbling, and even hostile. In his journals, Allen related this second nature to home life with Louis and Naomi: "At home, I received and submitted, with awareness of a true nature, to my mother's paranoid emotions: this identification with my mother's feelings."[41] Then listening to his father's complaints, he identified with Louis's emotions: "The result was that in one hour, I was on 'her side' and 'his' and continually felt called upon to make a decision in who to think with: this decision, when conscious, is the neurotic mask, when unconscious, without decision, I am flying from pole to pole: whoever I'm with I understand and identify myself with. . . . If I follow 'emotion,' respond automatically, I fear people, work, sports, etc., get into school troubles, become eccentric and disordered, melancholy, suicidal, ingrown and jejune and 'juvenile' emotionally—I become morbid and 'romantic.' If I think, I become mechanical and sterile, shallow, embarrassed, conflicted."

The only possible solution Allen could find for his emotional and writing troubles was to get out of his head, descend lower, and engage people more. He should believe in them and give himself over. This way he would be able really to feel and perhaps to create. As with his hero Rimbaud, descent into crisis without a controlling hand could provide the solution: "As I came down the impassible Rivers, I felt no more the bargemen's guiding hands."[42]

On April 24, 1947, Naomi was transferred to Pilgrim State Hospital and admitted to ward 24.3. She was fifty-one years old and had recurrent schizophrenic illness. She would remain at Pilgrim State for the next two years.

When asked whether she had been glad to see her family on visiting day, Naomi said, "I feel sorry that they come and see this sight." "I rushed my heart all day for a happy thought of the past. I'm deathly sick inside. I have tumors and ulcers. I rush my heart and it's not strong. Do me a favor and etherize me so my death will be easy." Two weeks later, Naomi stated, "There's no hope for me, I want to die." She approached the charge nurse with a piece of paper, asking whether she could sign permission for a mercy killing of herself. She stated she believed in euthanasia and felt she should receive the benefits of this. A month later, Naomi was transferred to Building 12 for symptomatic shock treatment.

Pilgrim State Hospital, 1941.

In July 1947, Naomi wrote a letter to Allen:

Dear Allen, I was so disappointed this Sunday—Elanor and Eugene didn't come to see me. I am taking shock treatment and it seems to help me—at least I am feeling better than I did. I sleep better and eat with more appetite. I did have things to tell Elanor. She should have come to see me—and Eugene too surprised me by not coming. Please write me Allen and tell Eugene to write me. I am feeling well enough to read letters. Tell Elanor to write. For the love of Jesus I do not know how I got this sickness. It's up to you to find out. Your loving mother, Naomi. To have visitors here is a Godsend. Believe me I keep your letter in my bosom. Naomi. Please tell Eugene to write more. Pilgrim State Hospital Ward 1206.[43]

A few days later she wrote him again:

Dearest Allen, Received your letter. No one gave me the other one you sent. I am getting shock treatment. Before I go to it I fall into a weakness. I guess it's due to my general condition. I've had such terrible spells here. I wonder will I get well here. My heart got somewhat stronger and I sleep better. I eat better. Am glad you are having a good time. I hope you get a job. Do not go without food—or else you'll get broken in health.[44]

Yet another letter came a few days after that:

Dear Children, Please take me out of here. I have no doctor or matron to really look after me. I was never friends with any family. I was always a person who could tend to herself—except those two years. I gave happiness with my looks, teaching, music playing, keeping house and art to others. I was a good woman! Hurry, Naomi.[45]

By the fall of 1947, Naomi's mood had shifted:

Dearest Allen, Elanor said you sent another letter but I don't know its contents yet. I'll have to go there and read it. Are you still enjoying yourself washing floors etc. etc. Make a joy out of everything you do— Don't let anything bother you too much. Only remember the good . . . Plenty of hard work also. With oodles of love, Naomi.[46]

At Pilgrim State, the doctor's progress note, from October 17, 1947, noted that Naomi

showed a remarkable improvement after her third or fourth treatment, became alert, cooperative, useful on the ward, no longer entertained psychosomatic delusions described in the previous note. However, she did not maintain the improvement very long and developed a rather severe state of acute excitement that made her more unmanageable than before treatment. The acute episode responded to treatment and she was able to maintain a fairly good behavior with about one shock application a week. It seems that this patient is subject to acute psychotic attacks, the sequence and pattern of which are very typical. Each attack preceded by a generalized paranoid trend against certain patients whom she accuses of anti-Semitism. This initial period characterized mainly by oversensitiveness and irritability was followed by hallucinations in the form of electricity in her head and her arms. These hallucinations are followed by delusions of a psychosomatic nature that become inconsistent with the rest of her mental trends. If symptomatic shock treatment is given at this stage, the more acute symptoms can be prevented. At present, she needs a treatment once every 7 or 10 days.

By November 11, 1947, the doctors decided a prefrontal lobotomy was needed. Lobotomy, psychiatrists believed, would reduce the patient's suffering and bring on docility, making her far easier to manage on the ward or even at home.

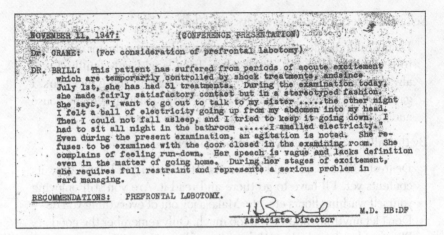

NOVEMBER 11, 1947:   (CONFERENCE PRESENTATION)

Dr. CRANE: (For consideration of prefrontal lobotomy).

DR. BRILL: This patient has suffered from periods of acute excitement
which are temporarily controlled by shock treatments, and since
July 1st, she has had 51 treatments. During the examination today,
she made fairly satisfactory contact but in a stereotyped fashion.
She says, "I want to go out to talk to my sister ......the other night
I felt a ball of electricity going up from my abdomen into my head.
Then I could not fall asleep, and I tried to keep it going down. I
had to sit all night in the bathroom ......I smelled electricity."
Even during the present examination, an agitation is noted. She re-
fuses to be examined with the door closed in the examining room. She
complains of feeling run-down. Her speech is vague and lacks definition
even in the matter of going home. During her stages of excitement,
she requires full restraint and represents a serious problem in
ward managing.

RECOMMENDATIONS: PREFRONTAL LOBOTOMY.

                                                      M.D. HB:DF
                              Associate Director

Lobotomy is recommended, 1947. © *Allen Ginsberg Estate.*

A few days later came a letter from the psychiatrist, Harry Worthing MD,
addressed to Allen Ginsberg:

> Please be advised that your mother, Mrs. Naomi Ginsberg, was seen
> in consultation with the assistant director and it was decided that her
> mental condition is serious enough to warrant a prefrontal lobotomy.
> If you are interested in more details in regard to this type of operation
> and its possible complications, you can discuss this problem with the
> doctor in charge of the case of your mother on the next visiting day. In
> the meantime, we are enclosing a permit for the operation, which you
> can sign and return to us if you so desire. Very truly yours, Harry J.
> Worthing M.D. Senior Director[47]

On November 16, 1947, Allen visited Naomi, spoke briefly to the doctors,
and signed the consent. Nine days later, he wrote this entry in his journal:
"Allen don't die." He was bottoming out, perhaps even suicidal.

On January 13, 1948, Naomi was transferred to Building 23, Ward 3, and
a prefrontal lobotomy was performed.

Allen had arrived back in New York just a few weeks earlier. He had been
away since June, Naomi's second month in the hospital. He had traveled to
join William Burroughs, Joan Vollmer, and Herbert Huncke in New Waverly,
Texas, then in July to see Neal in Denver, arriving back in Texas near the
end of August. Then in early September he shipped out to Dakar with the

Merchant Marines rather than return to school. Columbia could wait. Upon his arrival back in New York, he received the lobotomy letter from Dr. Worthing in mid-November.

Allen said he didn't like the idea of a lobotomy. It sounded extreme, and he knew it was irreversible. But the doctors told him it was absolutely necessary to save her life. They were the doctors, and they needed his decision immediately if he wanted her to live. Allen acknowledged he did not have the answers for Naomi. He thought again about the failed trip to Lakewood. Despite all his efforts over many years, he couldn't talk Naomi out of being mad. Maybe the doctors had a better answer. He hoped so. It was the only hope she or any of them had left.

The lead doctors at Pilgrim State Hospital, Drs. Worthing, Brill, and Wigderson, authored a paper entitled "350 Cases of Prefrontal Lobotomy," published in October 1949.[48] The authors told the story of how they came to perform these lobotomies. Their hospital had sent a neurosurgeon to witness the innovative lobotomy procedure being done by Drs. Freeman and Watts at the George Washington University. The authors concluded that the operation called the prefrontal lobotomy would likely be more useful if it was performed early in the course of an illness. They conducted four lobotomies in 1944 and 1945 and said they found promising results: The operation led to the amelioration or disappearance of symptoms. They didn't give specific information, so it is impossible to know for sure just what symptoms had been ameliorated. Then their neurosurgeon left the hospital. It wasn't until May 1947, when Dr. Wigderson joined the service, that the doctors at Pilgrim State could initiate a second series of operations. From the start they were thinking big. They jumped from a series of four to one hundred and then kept pushing the numbers upward.

Their article reported that the first one hundred operations were performed between May 13, 1947, and June 4, 1948. A total of 350 were done by July 8, 1949. Of the first hundred, twenty-nine were living at home and considered examples of "remission." Six were dead. Their tabulations indicated the "earlier cases" (meaning earlier in the course of illness) showed high release rates. Release from the hospital was a priority concern, given the problems of hospital overcrowding. Pilgrim State Hospital was enormous. It had a total of 15,000 patients and admitted three thousand new patients a year. If lobotomy worked, which it seemed to, then they planned to do scores of lobotomies, thereby making unimaginable improvements in their patients' lives. This appeared to be psychiatry's cure for the modern plague of schizophrenia.

Table 1

Operative numbers	Dates done	At home	Dead	Transferred to other hospitals	Imp.	Still in hospital Unimp.	Total
1–100	5-13-47 to 6-4-48	29°	6	3	...	...	62
101–200	6-5-48 to 12-28-48	28	4	1	..	..	67
201–300	12-28-48 to 5-3-49	8	3	0	..	..	89
301–350	5-6-49 to 7-8-49	0	1	0	..	..	49
Totals		65	14	4	178	89°°	267
Percent of 350 cases		18.57%	4%	1.26%	50.86%	25.43%	76.29%

°23 of the first 29 patients released have already been discharged.
°°4 of these are probably worse (schizophrenic behavior problems).

Table from H. J. Worthing, H. Brill, and H. Wigderson, "350 Cases of Prefrontal Lobotomy," *Psychiatric Quarterly* 23 (1949).

The doctors believed release was possible because the lobotomy resulted in "permanent symptomatic improvement." They reported: "There is a general tendency to report that the patient has found a much-desired calmness after a life-long tendency to over-react to minor irritations." The authors spoke of the unremitting "torment of mental illness" that psychosurgery sought to remedy. They quoted from the poet Robert Burton:

> My pain's past cure, another hell,
> I may not in this torment dwell!
> Now desperate I hate my life,
> Lend me a halter or a knife;[49]

The authors were convinced the lobotomist's knife or leucotomy successfully rid the mentally ill person of considerable psychic discomfort. How did they think it worked? Perhaps, they wrote, it is because, "there is a selective abolition of the capacity to maintain unpleasant psychotic tensions." Other writings on the lobotomy describe it as a "surgically induced childhood."

The doctors explained how they selected cases for the operation. They chose chronic patients, most with schizophrenia, who had severe behavior problems, were "shock resistant," and who had "some degree of social and economic capacity" within the past year. Following prefrontal lobotomy, 66 percent of their cases had behavioral improvements. For example: "Often, there is noted an immediate decrease of sustained hate (psychotic), with increase of reasonableness and capacity for affection." "Another reaction of great academic interest is the occasional abrupt disappearance of auditory hallucinations, with the expression of insight which resembles that expressed by a successfully treated insulin case."

The mortality was between 2 percent in newer cases and 8 percent in older cases. Although this statistic is reported neutrally, by contemporary standards, this is too high simply to overlook. The authors also downplayed the issue, already reported in the literature, of personality change following prefrontal lobotomy. It occurred in less than 1 percent of cases, they said. Much of this could be attributed to the schizophrenic illness itself, they remarked, somewhat dismissively.

In May 1949, another research psychiatrist and lobotomist, Dr. Paul Hoch, from the New York State Psychiatric Institute, presented a paper on "Theoretical Aspects of Frontal Lobotomy and Similar Brain Operations" at the American Psychiatric Association annual meeting. He expressed more concern about the issue of personality change post-lobotomy: "Clinically the most conspicuous damage is a certain inertia or apathy. The patient has no sustained effort, especially concerning intellectual performance, no drive to creative achievement."[50] Hoch theorized these changes were the consequence of the elimination of anxiety. Society is founded on anxiety. When properly sublimated, this anxiety produces a creative energy. However: "If all tension and anxiety are cut and self-evaluation becomes indifferent to the individual, the setting of goals, plans, and anticipatory activities changes into complacency." Dr. Hoch would later appear in Allen's life during his admission to the New York Psychiatric Institute.

The issue of personality change after lobotomy became more and more troubling in the ensuing decade as the practice of lobotomy was subjected to greater scrutiny. But in 1949, this was mostly an academic argument among professionals taking place in journals and at conferences. Dr. Worthing believed the personality change was caused mostly by the illness itself. Dr. Hoch believed it could be caused by the lobotomy. Neither psychiatrist thought the personality change was a reason not to do lobotomy. The benefits to the severely mentally ill appeared far greater than the liabilities. Worthing was looking for an intervention to help them empty the state mental hospitals. Hoch believed that to treat serious mental illness, a decisive biological intervention was called for, and some personality change was an acceptable price to pay. The only question was where to draw the line on how much personality change was acceptable.

Of course, no one explained any of this to the scores of loved ones who were asked to provide their consent for lobotomies, including Allen the day he visited Pilgrim State to talk with the doctors. Only afterward did he find out, when the true picture of the devastating side effects of her lobotomy surfaced and Naomi sank. Even then, the lobotomy was supported by cultural understandings that claimed that in order to heal, you have to inflict damage, as in other life-saving surgical procedures.[51]

Years later, Allen would detonate these very explanations for personality change, which underlie the lobotomy he signed off on. His poetry can be said to be based on the following claims: There is nothing more sacred to the individual than consciousness; even in madness consciousness is of the utmost value, not only to the individual but to society. If you compromise consciousness, then you diminish our humanity. Additionally, we have the capacity to change our consciousness through art, meditation, prayer, and LSD, and in doing so we can change ourselves and also society.

Changes in consciousness are certainly not the same as mental illness, though there may be some areas of overlap between such changes and the symptoms of mental illness (for example, dissociation or hearing voices). Allen was working on these issues, but he didn't come to any final resolution, nor have we today. What he did do to great effect, especially in "Howl," was take a psychiatric professional dilemma about personality loss, reframe it as a fundamental philosophical question, and compellingly put that question to society: What makes for best minds? But it would still take years for him to get there.

Allen visited his mother twice in January 1948, while she was recuperating from the lobotomy. Within one month, she stopped hearing voices. She appeared more relaxed and spoke about going home to be with her two children. She had a pain in her head for several weeks after the operation, but this eventually resolved. The doctors noted: "Her manner is vague and somewhat far away but fairly reasonable. There is moderate personality loss of a schizophrenic pattern." The latter comment is consistent with the formulation of personality change following lobotomy. Overall, it appeared there was some reason to be optimistic about Naomi's condition. This is reminiscent of the letters Dr. Walter Freeman received from some of his lobotomy patients thanking him for performing the operation, which had delivered them to a more sanguine position.[52]

In February or March 1948, Naomi wrote from Pilgrim State:

Dearest Allen, Read your loving letter. I am so happy to answer you. I was ill, physically and mentally. But I am recuperating now. I am getting some sort of treatments. Electrolysis and some sort of food. Please write Elanor, pay me a visit and bring me some money for good food if I am to build up. I feel better than when Eugene paid me a visit. I hope to see him soon. Your loving mother, Naomi.[53]

On April 20, 1948, Naomi was transferred to Building 24, Ward 6. This was a unit for patients who were being prepared for eventual discharge. Her doctors wrote:

Following prefrontal lobotomy patient continued to complain about electricity in her body, about severe headaches as well as about a number of other physical ailments. She constantly walked around with a wet towel wrapped around her head. Gradually however these symptoms cleared, she became pleasanter, did not complain any more, but started to request her release, claiming that she had been here long enough, that she had been railroaded to this hospital, that there was never anything wrong with her.

Naomi wrote to Allen:

Dear Allen, I was transferred to 24-6 yesterday; to a place where the gang are very anxious to go home, where cursing prevails, mixed in with a bit of dancing and music and a radio enlivens the room. I hope it is not for so-called experimentation under the guise of a cure. How I wish to be out walking the byways of a country watching the crop extended; making friends with nature. I used to love that as a child; the desire came back. Summer, a pool, the growing countryside. With a few wholesome people—that spells life to me at present . . .[54]

Allen journaled: "Dear Naomi: Gene tells me you will be out soon, singing and dancing in the City. . . . Musical sweet poetry."[55] However, he wrote next to nothing about his mother's lobotomy. You will find no mention of the lobotomy in his journals and correspondences from the time of its occurrence, when Allen was chasing down the new vision. There are but a few references to the lobotomy from after her death, when he was starting to write his own "Kaddish" for her, which I will discuss in Chapter 7.

Although the lobotomy was not something Allen sought out or ever wanted for his mother, having passed through it changed him forever. He never gave an explicit account of the lobotomy in journals, correspondences, or interviews. The closest he ever came was the stirring 1984 poem "Black Shroud," written thirty-five years later, which I will discuss in Chapter 9.

For Allen, giving consent for Naomi's lobotomy was experienced as a means of "descent,"[56] partly in Rimbaud's sense.

Descent is acceptance. For so long, he believed everything she said was true, but he had come to accept he could not surrender himself to her. He had to accept that she was ill, that she required treatment, and that those treatments had serious side effects.

Descent is about committing yourself to certain choices. It was high time Allen was not defined solely by the books he read but by what he did in the real world. Not to escape but to decide something of major significance, like the lobotomy.

Descent is being cast into new and unfamiliar territory. By signing consent and endorsing the doctor's authority, he pushed himself further outside Naomi's orbit, where he had spent most of his life.

Descent is risking her death and traumatizing yourself in the hope of making her better.

Descent involves finding meaning among adversity and loss. Others could be nihilists. They did not have Naomi in their minds and in their hearts. Instead of meaninglessness, he would go search for meaning via visionary madness. He would learn to become mad himself and then use his madness to write visionary poems. He would take the madness, mental illness, and visions he witnessed in Naomi and change them into something beautiful and redemptive.

For Allen, descent meant tying together the intellectualized new vision with madness' actual visions. It also meant putting complete trust in poetry to make up for life's letdowns.

Chapter 4

The Actuality of Prophecy, 1948–1949

ALLEN BEGAN TO have visions of his own. They came six months after he gave permission to Dr. Worthing to use a leucotome to sever the white-matter connections in the prefrontal cortex of his mother's brain to rid her of her uncontrollable agitation, voices, and visions. Allen was lonely, directionless, and despondent, living by himself in an East Harlem apartment subleased from his theology student friend.

Allen was studying Cezanne for a paper he needed to complete for Professor Meyer Schapiro's art history course so he could graduate. He rode the Broadway subway downtown to look at Cezanne's *L'Estaque* painting at the Museum of Modern Art. For money, he worked at the Columbia University bookstore. He read William Butler Yeats, William Blake, St. John of the Cross, William James, and other visionary literature he found on the bookshelves of his friend's apartment.

When the visions came, they took him by surprise and immediately became his new reason for living. He told his father and his friends and even strangers in bars about them. Although the visions were difficult for Allen to describe, he tried his best in letters, journal entries, and poems. They were inspiring, empowering, but also terrifying. He wanted to tap into the spiritual and aesthetic power of his visions, a mission of central concern for the rest of his life.

The visions were a mystical event to which Allen was the only direct witness. Our best way to know the visions is through his evolving descriptions,

L'Estaque, Paul Cezanne, 1885.

making it clear they are impossible to pin down into one event. The visions were not just an event that happened to Allen on a given day but a process highly dependent upon the stories he told about them as he was trying to figure out what they meant. What's more, those stories changed significantly over time, to eventually include hearing Blake's voice, ten years later.

The visions were a product of years of psychological, literary, and spiritual preparation. But it wasn't enough simply to have visions. Just as important was how Allen responded to them, especially in his writing, and then how he got others to respond as well. They were an arena in which ongoing spiritual, psychological, and aesthetic processes co-occurred and interacted. These processes were as much parts of the visions as the original experiences. Eventually, the visions raised questions about his sanity, for his father, friends, psychiatrists, and for himself.

Another notable aspect of Allen's visions is the sheer density of experience, knowledge, memory, emotion, relationships, ideas, literature, art, and history he linked with them. The longer Allen lived with and responded to the visions, the denser and more laden with meaning they became.

As a focus of so many interacting processes, Allen's visions were well suited for artistic reworking. As Lewis Hyde describes: "Ginsberg responded as an artist responds. The artist completes the act of imagination by accepting the gift and laboring to give it to the real."[1] Allen's responses to the visions, over years and decades, transformed and advanced his spiritual journey, literary project, and role as a writer. Through reworking the visions as an artist, Allen further specified and deepened his relationships with visionary madness, visionary poetry, and prophecy. At the center of it all was his experience of having been spoken to from another dimension.

When I meet with Allen forty years later, the visions remain for him a key life event and a major focal point. The visions have been trumpeted, by him and others writing about him, as the moment when Allen Ginsberg first broke through. Given that Allen's personal breakthrough also became an important literary and cultural breakthrough (as will be discussed in Chapter 8), the visions have received much attention over the years. They were the focus of one lengthy published interview from 1965 that is often quoted and several other writings.

Allen asks me to first read each of those interviews—especially the one from the *Paris Review* from 1965—before he will speak with me about the visions. I cannot blame him. I figure he is tired of repeating himself. He also does not want me to subject his visions to a reductionistic psychiatric formulation: He does not want me to dismiss them as hallucinations, mere symptoms of a mental illness, like he says his psychiatrist at the time had done. I must admit, as a medical student first studying psychiatry, I was asking myself such questions: What exactly were the visions? Were they hallucinations? Were they part of a diagnosable psychiatric illness? Was he becoming psychotic like his mother?

Even then, I knew very well that diagnostic formulations of the visions might be good enough for psychiatry, but they could never be good enough for literature or religion. Allen knew this and urged me not to limit myself to diagnostic concerns and to consider the aesthetic and spiritual dimensions of the visions. So I read the 1965 *Paris Review* interview and everything else I could find both published and in Allen's archives.

When we meet, Allen takes the time to tell me the story of his visions and to explain how he understood them. The story he tells me is very similar to the descriptions of the visions I read in his interviews. He calls them "my Blake visions" and speaks of hearing Blake's voice reciting poems, deep and ancient, "just like my own voice sounds now," he says, speaking slowly so we can both hear its deep timbre.

Sitting together in his apartment, I listen carefully to Allen's explanation of the "Blake visions," as they came to be called by his biographers and critics. Allen was unrivaled at telling stories about himself, adding layers of nuance, literariness, and politics that inform and intrigue. At the time he gave the first of the interviews about the visions, in 1965, the psychedelic era was just taking off. For Allen, talking about his personal experiences with visions was a deliberate effort to preach to the youth, public, government, and anyone who would listen about the value of alternative forms of consciousness.

The Blake visions he spoke of in 1965 helped turn him into a qualified leader of the counterculture, whereby he recommended that others discover their own visions by any available means, including taking LSD. He was still recommending LSD twenty years later, when we speak about the visions, because he sees alternate states of consciousness not as just some fad or as equivalent to madness but as an essential dimension of life, one in need of nurturing and understanding.

I take notice how most published accounts of the visions are retrospective, from many years later. This seems important. I believe what is needed to better understand the visions, begins with constructing a longitudinal account of all the first-person narrative descriptions of the visions in Allen's correspondences, journals, poems, essays, and interviews. Through making this careful reconstruction I discover something no one else has described: The visions were extensively reworked by Allen over decades; they did not actually become the "Blake visions," as they became known, until much later. Importantly, no accounts mentioned actually hearing the voice of William Blake until 1958, in a poem, and 1960, in a published article, which was many years after the visions first appeared. I think this is significant in terms of how he put his visions to work, but initially I am not sure how or why.

In taking this approach, I intend no slight against Allen. His heroism and literary achievements have long rested on his capacity to make things new through engaging with difficult experiences, transfiguring those experiences as an artist, and coming out with resonant words, images, poems, and myths. In Chapter 8, I will discuss what he was writing and saying about the visions in the early 1960s, when the Blake voice was mentioned publicly for the first time, which came after his major poetic breakthroughs "Howl" (1956) and "Kaddish" (1961). Here we will continue with his accounts from 1948 and 1949, when the visions first appeared. These early writings are an essential missing part of the story of the visions.

What I want to see is not the established writer looking back on his early years but the struggling young man and aspiring poet at work nearly two decades before the *Paris Review* interview and many years before "Howl" and "Kaddish." He was trying to live with himself after having authorized a psychiatrist to lobotomize his mother's brain, presumably to save her life—a life ravaged by psychosis and that neither she nor he thought there was much chance of salvaging, not directly anyways, given the horrible price her mental illness had already extracted.

As Allen told me, part of his response to the trauma of permitting Naomi's lobotomy came in the form of his visions. These visions could possibly have sent him down the same ruinous path into severe psychosis as Naomi, but over time, they became for him instead a personal spiritual breakthrough and the seeds of significant poetic breakthroughs.

No attempt at diagnosing, summarizing, or paraphrasing would adequately convey Allen's excitement and struggle over his visions as effectively as his own words from 1948 and 1949. I have located five prose sources from the summer and fall of 1948 where he first mentioned the visions.

Letter to Neal Cassady, May 1948. "Finally in a few moments of dispassion & self forgetfulness I experienced the first warming flashes of the transcendence which I had so long been seeking. . . . I have had moments of absolute, valid, literal knowledge: I have seen the Nightingale at last. All that in my wildest and most self consciously stylized idealizations of Love that I had celebrated & prophesized have 'descended' as from heaven."[2]

Letter to Lionel Trilling, July 1948. "I have been doing a lot of thinking about Cezanne, and through him have begun to recognize signs of truly living personality and intelligence in works of art: a literal sense that I had never before experienced."[3]

Letter to Jack Kerouac, Summer 1948. "The unreal has become for me the most real now . . . . I can't forget what I have seen . . . something dreamlike and white, Ardenesque, ghostly about us."[4]

Letter to Neal Cassady, September 1948. "I accost perfect strangers in bars to talk about Eternity."[5]

Journal entry, October 1948. "I knew they were prophetic but I didn't see the actuality of prophecy. When in Harlem I found my mind."[6]

The visions initially appeared in May 1948 and then came in force over a several-day spell in late June or early July 1948. Allen never remembered exactly which days or weeks. What mattered for Allen is that something happened in the summer of 1948 that overtook his life. Allen had made a connection with the eternal spirit, like Yeats, Blake, and St. John of the Cross before him.

He went to New Jersey and told his father. Louis promptly told him to forget about the visions and all such eccentricities. He had had enough of visions and madness from Naomi to last a thousand lifetimes. Exorcise your wild friends and especially that crazed Neal Cassady. Focus on school. At the time Louis was optimistic about getting a poem published in *Good Housekeeping.* Allen should listen to him, because he knew what it took to be a published poet. You have to slowly work your way into poetry circles, step by step. Not with a bolt of lightning.

Allen had to tell someone who would understand what had just happened and how everything had suddenly changed for him. He first wrote to Neal and Jack because they would surely understand the significance of the visions. Finally, he had broken through. Could they see it too?

The visions required bold action. He had been given a gift from above without the asking, a gift that lifted him up from the doldrums. Now he had to do something to justify that gift and to join the company of visionary literary genius. He felt an obligation to pass on the sense of divine inspiration to others, and the time to do so was now.

He could best achieve this by writing poems about the visions. So he wrote new poems unlike any he had written before, which he believed were less intellectual and more sensate. They were supposed to be poems of prophecy, like Blake's songs. The visions, he thought, had prompted the creative breakthrough he had been waiting for. Even if his father didn't understand. He was now a visionary poet and would show them all.

Truth be told, he had been trying, if only a little bit, to fit in, like his father desperately wanted. He was working as a copy boy at the Associated Press, a job he found totally dispiriting. With help from Lionel Trilling, he applied for a teaching position at Cooper Union. But he did not want to join corporate America or even a university faculty. He was interested in those who lived outside of society, like William Burroughs and Herbert Huncke. St. John of the Cross wrote that in order to fulfill a vision quest, you must empty yourself of the habits and affections of this world, so as to be more open to contact with the spiritual world.[7] Drugs and music could help, thought Allen. So could hanging out with outsiders, who cared not for how the mainstream defined happiness or success.

Allen did not dismiss the visions or seek to reestablish normal consciousness but bravely redirected his existence along a prophetic path toward an unknown future. The visions made available evocative material and stimulated entirely new creative work that embodied a new level of consciousness. Maybe this is what the "new vision" was supposed to involve.

Why did the visions come six months after the lobotomy and just before graduation? It is impossible to know for certain. But we do know his life circumstances that summer resembled what William James, in *The Varieties of Religious Experience*, described about candidates for conversion experiences. James wrote that to "get rid of anger, worry, fear, despair, or other undesirable affections . . . an opposite affection should overpoweringly break over us."[8] At the point in his life when he had visions, Allen was facing multiple crises. His severely ill mother remained at Pilgrim State Hospital following the lobotomy. He was nearly finished with college but had yet found no solid work or career. He was single, gay, closeted, and apart from his friends. He hadn't managed to fulfill the dream he had for himself as a writer. Then suddenly with the visions, everything changed.

The visions were a sensual experience of a spiritual visitation. They thrilled and frightened Allen. He basked in the delight of having made contact with the eternal. He was also terrified by the realization that so many people around him seemed to be oblivious to an eternal presence. Few people knew what he now knew about existence. The visions, which opened the doors to both heaven and hell, excited and frightened him like nothing else ever had.

The visions enabled Allen to place poetry at the center of his life. His prophetic inspiration gave him a stronger impetus for writing. The visions provided a literary subject of great sensate immediacy, personal meaning, and potentially universal appeal. He began feverishly writing poems that would reflect the visions' inspirational power. He wanted to write visionary works of poetry that would stand beside Yeats's *A Vision* or Blake's *Songs of Innocence and of Experience*. These poems gave Allen a means to channel his prophetic motivations and to bolster his identity as a poet. In time, however, Allen felt that the poems were "still clouded by the lack of concrete sensuous realism." He was not reaching the aesthetic heights of which he dreamed.

Allen did not write explicitly about the visions in relation to his mother, either in his journals or letters during the year after the visions. Yet it does not seem too far a stretch to suggest that having visions presented the poet and son a way to reimagine his relationship with his seriously mentally ill and now lobotomized mother, who for years had had her own visions of God. Decades later, *Literary Kicks* aptly wrote: "Allen was looking for the truths his mother had gotten lost within."[9]

As a child, Allen was exposed to her visions of God, paranoid delusions, voices, nudity, unpredictability, and suicidality. She was dreadfully fearful about Louis's family and tried to win Allen over to her side. One way for Allen to cope with his mother's bizarre and paranoid ideas and behavior was to believe that they conveyed some meaning, insight, or truth. She had tremendous passion for politics, religion, and philosophy and made bizarre pronunciations about FDR, communism, Jews, and war. She even had visions that she had seen God.

In 1986, Allen showed me a draft footnote he had just written for a Hebrew translation of "Kaddish": "Her suffering affected me so 'driving me out of my skull' i.e. out of my mind, vernacular phrase for 'disturb' so that I looked for a permanent answer or response or place ('eternity') for expression in poetry, or looked for a permanent vision thru and in poetry."[10]

Allen didn't say so, but it surely had occurred to him that Naomi was lost to him. Lost through the devastating illness. Lost through hospitalizations, ECT, insulin, and metrazol therapy. Lost especially through the recent lobotomy. All of these had taken her farther and farther away. And there was nothing he could do to bring her back. He had already done too much.

On an emotional level, the son's longing for his lost mother could in some way be appeased by taking into oneself a piece of her through the visions. Allen had long wanted to believe her and tried to stand with her. Believing his mother's thoughts were true meant accepting her as some kind of seer who could correctly divine unseen truths. Now he was also having visions. Eventually her visions and delusions crushed her, and he felt partly responsible for her demise. He, on the other hand, would be their master. He was

Self-Portrait, William Blake, 1802.

learning from others who had mastered their visions, like William Blake and St. John of the Cross. He could handle his visions and harness their power. Naomi and her madness would be redeemed.

For the next six months, Allen turned to literary classics on visions and tried to write his own allegories. He read Thomas Vaughan, Henry Vaughan, Plotinus, and, of course, William Blake. He wrote about his poems in his journal, noting: "I wrote a few interesting metaphysical lyrics about God and the search for God."[11] Seventeen poems from this time were later included in the collection *Gates of Wrath* (1948–1949). The ten poems written in the summer and fall of 1948 were:

"Harlem Dolors" (Summer 1948)
"On Reading William Blake's 'The Sick Rose'" (June–July 1948)
"The Eye Altering Alters All" (June–July 1948)
"A Very Dove" (July 1948)
"Vision 1948" (July 1948)
"The Voice of Rock" (August 1948)
"Refrain" (August 1948)
"A Western Ballad" (August 1948)
"The Trembling of the Veil" (August 1948)
"A Meaningless Institution" (Fall 1948)

Consider "On Reading William Blake's 'The Sick Rose,'" which belongs to this early group of vision-inspired poems from the summer and fall of 1948. It is replete with abstractions that attempt to convey the metaphysical significance of the visions. Phrases such as "black vision," "mystic charm," "magic bright," "everlasting force," "spirit shrunken," "immortality," and "doom."[12] The poem includes scattered references to visual phenomena: "black vision of my sight," "Many seek and never see," "shadow, shadow, and blind vision," "too bright," "the eye goes blind before the world goes round," "silken light of summer sun."

The poem makes some vague references to an auditory phenomenon: "Dumb roar of the white trance," "And hear a vast machinery," "voice of rock," "the literary cackle in my head," "the angels chirping cheerful." However, no actual voice is mentioned, certainly not Blake's.

The poems deemphasized sensory images and were instead dominated by abstract conceptualizations. The poems seemed to concede that the "intelligence of poets" had won out over the poetics itself. Then again, it is easy to criticize Allen for coming up short. But how difficult it must have been to describe the visions, given that his mystical experiences were anything but straightforward.

Still, this lack of sensation and overabundant vague metaphysical terminology, which dominated this and other poems from this time, made them allusive, obscure, and unengaging. Allen was affecting a prophetic and literary façade that did not let a stronger poetic voice emerge. He seemed so confident in the mystical nature of his visions that he didn't allow room for humility, doubt, or even a fear that his visions may be excessive or even a madness akin to his mother's. For readers, this can come off not as strength but as defensiveness and pride.

Allen sent some of these poems to his Columbia professors Mark Van Doren and Lionel Trilling, who had seemed supportive of his literary ambitions. Devoted to their brilliant but troubled student, they wrote back, giving encouragement but noting reservations. In September 1948, Trilling wrote:

> I'd say of these that they have a transitional and tentative quality—I have the feeling that you are trying out an idiom that you do not expect to stay with for very long. The tendency is towards lightness and sweetness. At the same time, however, I find that things become a little misty and evanescent. I found that I was a little thrown off by my sense of the frequency of the first personal pronoun.[13]

In December 1948, Mark Van Doren wrote: "Verse isn't weak. Weak verse is, but you haven't written weak verse—except in spots, where I suppose you got tired or lost faith in the poem."[14]

Trilling and Van Doren picked up on the poems' shortcomings but also recognized that the vision-inspired poems were a step ahead of the poems Allen had written earlier. These new writings were more focused, and at least he was getting work done. He may not have yet reached the extraordinarily high threshold he had set for himself, but focusing on his visions was helping move him forward. They knew Allen was aware of these shortcomings and that he and his poems were still a work in progress. He needed encouragement, and they could at least offer him some.

A few months later, William Burroughs expressed concerns about Allen's representations of the visions, in response to a letter from Allen saying his psychiatrist had dismissed the visions. In March 1949, Burroughs wrote:

> The doctors say "your mystical experiences are just hallucinations," and you think he has said something. Did he say in <u>terms of fact</u> what an hallucination is? No—because <u>he does not know.</u> No one knows. He is just throwing around verbiage. Frankly I was (and am) dubious of your mystical experiences because of their vague character.[15]

Calling the visions hallucinations pathologizes and diminishes the visions and does not begin to describe their spiritual and literary potential. Allen deserved a better response, but he was also just beginning his relationship with the visions. The visions were leading him somewhere, and he had to follow. Acting upon Burroughs's advice, Allen let himself be propelled by life events and stayed engaged with the visions until he drew more understanding and responses.

In March 1949, Naomi wrote to Allen from Pilgrim State Hospital:

Dear Allen, I feel better and gained four pounds. I prefer to be thin but I suppose I can remedy that by getting active. How I want you to know that I want to get out and cook for you and laugh and sing the rest of my life. Before I came here I was told I was made sick four times in New York. They found poison in my system in the hospital. These things made me delirious. But thank goodness I feel better! O Allen convince Eugene to take me out! Write to me good news. Love, Naomi[16]

On March 31, 1949, the doctors wrote a progress note:

The patient has improved gradually since coming to Building 12, where she resided continuously on Ward 3. She had one attack of disturbance a few weeks after admission to Building 12 where she would pull her dress up, lie around on the floor in the nude, and shout and scream. However, she got over this episode rather quickly, became more quiet and cooperative, occupied herself with some needlework and reading, became more and more interested in outside activities, her own appearance, enjoyed visiting with her family but still was harboring some paranoid delusions.

Then a few weeks later: "The patient has shown some improvement since her last note. She says, 'I feel better since the operation.' She is pleasant in her manner and well dressed, denies that she has active voices but still claims that her voices in the past were real. She claims that she no longer hears it."

On April 30, 1949, Naomi wrote:

Dear Allen, Today the sun is shining on me. They let me outside with some of the other patients. I am feeling better and they are letting me go home. I will stay with Elanor. The operation seems to have helped. The voices are still there, but not as bad. I want to be productive, to

live again. I want to cook for you and Gene like the old days. Come
and visit me. Love, Naomi[17]

Despite all she had been through, Naomi still clung to her role as a mother.

On May 1, 1949, Naomi was discharged from Pilgrim State Hospital.
She became one of the twenty-nine lobotomized patients from Dr. Worthing's case series who were living at home and considered in remission. The
operation appeared to be a success, enabling Naomi to be calm enough to
leave the hospital, live with her sister Elanor in the Bronx, and take up
housework.

Allen kept writing vision-inspired poems until something unexpected happened, when Allen was able to let a more vulnerable and worrisome side of
madness enter his works alongside the ecstatic inspiration of the visions.
Beginning in February 1949, his poems reflected the mounting frustrations
and fears involved in wholehearted dedication to the pursuit of visions.

The poems written from fall 1948 to spring 1949 were:

"A Mad Gleam" (January 1949)
"Complaint of the Skeleton to Time" (early 1949)
"Psalm I" (February 1949)
"An Eastern Ballad" (1945–1949)
"Sweet Levinsky" (Spring 1949)
"Psalm II" (March 1949)
"Fie My Fum" (Spring 1949)

These poems broke through the prophetic façade of the early vision poems
and other barriers the poet used to keep his doubts away. Now he was
admitting, like St. John of the Cross had written four hundred years prior,
that the visionary has "so tender and frail a nature" that no wall is able to
divide spiritual visions from other more troublesome forms of madness.
When Allen let himself bear this burden, his poems took on a greater urgency
and sensitivity.

In "Psalm II," written at age twenty-two, six months after the visions, the
poet imagined himself with a naked mind, vulnerable to any environmental
influence. "Bigger and bigger gates, Thou givest, Lord,/And vaster deaths,
and deaths not by my hand,/Till, in each season, as the garden dies,/I die
with each, until I die no more."[18] He wasn't proclaiming the importance of
his visions or using them to ward off fears that he was losing his mind. Instead
he was revealing the difficulties of living with visions, of possibly living on the
verge of madness. Madness was humbling, harsh, painful, maybe an illness.

Allen's words and images lent a serenity and power to the challenging realities of his visionary madness and made "Psalm II" one of the stronger vision-related poems.

The vision poems written in April 1949 are refreshingly varied in their portrayal of madness, ranging from doom to glee. "Bop Lyrics," written in 1949, gives an allegorical portrayal of visionary madness.

> I'm a pot and God's a potter,
> And my head's a piece of putty.
> Ark my darkness,
> Lark my looks,
> I'm so lucky to be nutty.[19]

As playful as a childhood rhyme, madness is portrayed as unambivalently wonderful and euphoric. God planted visions in his head and made him mad just like his mother. The poem also portrays the visionary episodes in a manner that hints of the annunciation of the Madonna, a theme he would further develop several years later, leaving a mark on how he would explain the visions to the broader public.

The visions were a gift, but they also asked a lot of Allen. When Allen was working for the visions, he was working for Naomi, to make something positive out of her illness and suffering. If this was arduous, so be it. The saints had borne their suffering, and so could he. It was nothing compared to what his mother had to face each and every day. If it turned out that he was insane, as he sometimes feared he might be, then he would face that too. In the meantime, his obligation was to keep writing about the visions.

The visions were also the tangible creative product of the psychological and aesthetic studies and spiritual preparation that had engaged Allen for several years. He approached those studies with commitment and discipline. On top of a solid liberal arts education from Columbia, he had schooled himself in literature, poetry, religion, psychoanalysis, philosophy, music, visual arts, and art theory.

In the months preceding the Blake visions, his readings were a veritable syllabus in the literature of visions. But he did not want to write a scholarly study or become a professor of religion. That was never his ambition. He wanted to write literature, perhaps a novel.[20] The problem was that he kept getting lost in abstraction and intellectualizing. He could only write his thoughts or, if he had characters, their thoughts. Deeper understanding, which could help fully realize the new vision in the very language and content of his writing, was still beyond his reach.

Like other American and European intellectuals and artists in the postwar decades, for a time he thought that psychoanalysis would show him the way. His problem, he believed, was neurosis, and if he could get properly analyzed and freed of neurotic symptoms, then he would be able to write without limits. However, it seemed that his readings and his attempt at psychoanalysis from William Burroughs had only deepened his tendency toward the abstract and that, try as he might, he couldn't break his neurosis down. He needed to find another way to break through.

His other approach to ending the endless abstractions was to descend from the intellectual to experience, that is, to get himself involved in physicality, in friendships, sexuality, love, and drugs. It could be either exciting and orgasmic or depressing and suicidal. It didn't matter. The important part of being free from abstractions was to be caught up in some circumstances, to feel them, and to confess something real about them. That was what Allen meant by "descent."

To reach this kind of freedom, he especially needed his friends. Although they were spread out all over the country, from Texas to Colorado to Long Island, their conversations continued in their letters. Allen was a dedicated correspondent, and in those letters he wrote in vivid detail of the ecstasy and challenges of the visions.

When the visions came, it was a sign that more affirmed the second strategy, that of descent. If the answer lay in new sensory experiences, these were sensory experiences that came in communication with God. Now he was moving beyond psychoanalysis. If this was psychology at all, it was the psychology of religion and conversion, à la William James, or the psychology of ecstatic experience, à la Reich, and not the Freudians' focus on unconscious conflicts related to early childhood experiences. He had less and less faith in any systems of understanding, such as psychoanalysis. Poetry was beyond systems. Now it was all upon him to be able to communicate the value and depth of the world that the visions had revealed.

To accomplish that, he turned to visionary language, to Yeats's "unity of being," Blake's "The Sick Rose," and James's "The Sick Soul." In William James, he found a veiled critique of psychiatry, for its dismissing visionaries as being mentally ill and their visions as hallucinations. He appreciated James's insight that the potential for extraordinary happenings heightens "when superior intellect and a psychopathic temperament coalesce."[21] Who knows? Maybe that was Allen's situation too. James wrote: "We have the best possible condition for the kind of effective genius that gets into the biographical dictionaries. Such men do not remain mere critics and

William James, 1906.

understanders with their intellect. Their ideas possess them, they inflict them, for better or worse, upon their companions or their age."[22]

If James was right and this was religion, then Allen knew after the visions that he was a religious man. James spoke with a scientific authority that gave him what he needed to counter his psychiatrist, who dismissed visions as hallucinations. Psychiatry had also discounted Naomi's creativity. She was a gifted painter with a fine artistic vision. Psychiatry had also irreversibly sliced her brain to save her. But he now had an ally in William James.

Allen had a channel for focusing his words and his energy and a project to work on. He was a visionary prophet whose calling was to write vision-inspired poems. Yet one year into the new writing phase, Allen was not satisfied with his progress, as the poems were still too cognitive. He wrote: "My poetry is not yet literal because I am not yet literal in my thought; and the more literal the mind & language become, the more prophetic or true it will be."[23] Just having the visions and wanting to write poems was no guarantee of success.

He turned to visionary predecessors, especially St. John of the Cross. He had already passed through the first night, the "dark night of the senses," which was having the sensual experience of seeing God. Now he had to pass through the second night, the "dark night of the soul."[24] That was a more difficult test. He needed to let go of his pride in having made contact through the visions. Let go of the visions themselves and the ecstatic sensuality he associated with them. Let go of their sweetness. Let go of society, accept abandonment from God and darkness, and commit to pure contemplation of the spiritual.

In May 1949, Allen wrote a long letter to Neal Cassady back in Denver, describing the continued burdens of the visions from one year prior, "my theoretical and visionary preoccupations—fixation, based on experience which was gifted, as it seemed, from a higher intelligence of conscious Being of the universe, or hallucinations, as the doctor dismissed it when I went to arrange for therapy beginning Sept., has left me confused and impotent in action and thought."[25] He aimed to clean up his poems for a book he wanted to publish. Earlier, he was too proud to do so unless he spoke with full prophetic authority. But now he could no longer count on more visions and was doubting those he'd already had. Despite these challenges, he needed to press on "like a man."

In June 1949, Allen wrote back to his fellow writer John Clellon Holmes in Provincetown, who was going to submit some poems to Delmore Schwartz at the *Partisan Review*, possibly including some of Allen's. On June 14, Holmes wrote back, politely asking, "I would like any and all information (nee data) on your poetry and your vision."[26] John posed four big questions about the visions, poetry, psychoanalysis, the police, and symbolism. At the time, this was an important opportunity for Allen. If he was to be a poet, let alone a visionary poet, then he had to get published. You can't change the world if nobody reads your poems. On June 16, from his father's house in Paterson, Allen wrote back, describing that "a consciousness, or awareness, or intelligence, seemed to be drifting through all things."[27]

He explained the challenge of the visionary: "He only wants to be like everybody else, in the flesh, but he is afraid of love, so he makes a system which makes him prophet, confuses everybody (they all have their own systems) and forces his misdirected will into making them think the same abstractions as he."

He redescribed the visions themselves:

> I saw nothing new in form, no angels, no smoke,—I was in the bookstore and the bookstore was the same as ever, but with the addition of a new sense of reality, or supernatural existence, indwelling in all the forms. The sense of prescience, fullness, absoluteness, and total

significance of detail were all that they are in the most otherworldly of night dreams, and all that I previously might ascribe to the mystical or religious sense of the presence of the Holy Ghost. Wherever I moved I seemed to see so deeply into things that they appeared under the aspect of eternity which had been talked about for Centuries, and see so deeply that I saw all there is to see, and was satisfied and peaceful.

At one time I also sensed, further, that the great beast of the universe was sick or sickening; slowly being consumed (See Blake's "The Sick Rose") and that human evil was part of that sickness. As if God were mad. The horror! The unspeakable horror! As if being itself were, like the sick human mind, being destroyed.

Here, Allen is putting his visions to work, not spinning off into incoherence but instead articulating a cosmology, a worldview, based on his vision experiences and grounded in the literature of other spiritual seekers. He is not doing what someone in the throes of delusion or paranoid thinking would do—offering rigid or one-sided views. He is less mad in a serious mental illness sense and more presenting a self who wants to incorporate a degree of madness, which had ties with Naomi, as part of his identity.

In July 1949, Jack Kerouac wrote back to Allen about the visions. Like William Burroughs, Kerouac knew Allen inside and out and had a knack for speaking directly to his dilemmas: "Think now I know what you mean. If only you could be straight like Yeats and come right out with it—and if I too did so."[28] Kerouac, like Burroughs, gave good advice to stop burying it in intellectual propositions and just come out with it. But what was "it"? Knowing what Kerouac meant was one thing; doing it another.

Two weeks before Naomi's discharge, Allen's visions came under additional scrutiny when in April 1949 he was arrested along with Herbert Huncke and two of his junkie friends. A few months earlier, he let Huncke, recently released from Rikers, move into his apartment. Allen hardly noticed as his place became a den of thieves and their stolen wares. Everything changed on April 19, when following a dramatic stolen car chase and crash in Queens, he was arrested along with the rest of the gang and faced the real prospect of jail time.

His lawyer, Ilo Orleans, asked for a detailed account of the events leading up to the arrest. Allen provided him with "A Confession of the Fall," a story of those days in his life, which includes the most descriptive passages about the visions he had yet written, almost a year later.

Herbert Huncke, 1953. © *Allen Ginsberg Estate.*

The first flash came when he was walking down 125th Street in the middle of the day. The people walking past him had "incredibly sleepy, bestial expressions on their faces. . . . Everybody I saw had something wrong with them. The apparition of an evil, sick, unconscious wild city rose before me in visible semblance . . . "[29] Another flash came soon after:

> I saw a vast gleam of light cover the sky, the bowl of heaven was suf-
> fused with an eerie glow, as if the world about my eyes was a vast sea
> creature and this was the interior of the leviathan. . . . I perceived
> that the guiding intelligence was in the objects themselves, not in
> some far corner of the universe, and that the world as we see it is
> complete: there is nothing outside of it.

He returned to his apartment and read William Blake, including his poem "The Sick Rose." "I realized once more that the last and most terrible veil had been torn from my eyes, a final shuddering glimpse through death. Then I moved across the room with the gnawing pulse of animality engulfing my body with slow carnal undulations of my frame, and shrieked and col-lapsed in silent agony, moaning on the floor, my hands grasping and hollowed in my thighs."

The Sick Rose, William Blake, 1826.

He again described what had happened one year earlier:

Suddenly, one day [July 1948] when I was browsing in the bookstore at Columbia, I experienced the first of what at the time I took for "mystical experiences," a visionary state quite unlike any which I had ever experienced before, but seemingly the consummation of all my earlier creative aspirations and longings.

I will not try to describe this as it is indescribable. It returned during that week several times. I found it, finally, frightening and fled to Paterson where I scared my father with wild talk; then I went back after a few days to N.Y. and took up my routine existence again; only this time gnawed inwardly with recollection of these experiences, which, because of their absolute and eternal nature I assumed as the keystone and reference point of all my thought—a North Star for life; much as Dante says, "*Incipit Vita Nuova.*"

He described reaching out to friends and teachers who he thought would understand what he had experienced:

I have no idea fully if what I am saying is madness or truth. I said to myself at the time. . . . My poetry began to take more body and order and clarity at this point; but it was still mystical and still clouded by the lack of all of concrete sensuous realism. I have spoken of all of this because the "Visions" have been constantly on my mind and have been monomaniacally inspiring all my conduct for the last year.

It was only recently—several months ago—after a psychoanalyst I went to dismissed them as "hallucinations" that it was necessary to forget them entirely and begin life all over in activity and real work, etc. The road to God I discover is not a leap, but work—concrete sensuous reality. Fully experienced I presume it is satisfactory. I saw my situation described in theological literature, in Kafka, Eliot, Blake, etc. Particularly the Kafkian hero who is suddenly wakened in the middle of his life and put on an unknown trial—I also realize that I am sick.[30]

In "A Confession of the Fall," Allen explained it all for his attorney, who said a client's confession could be useful background to strengthen the legal argument. Orleans was trying to make the case that Allen wasn't an ordinary criminal but was mentally ill. For Allen, this "Confession" was different from the journal writing that had absorbed him for years. One difference is that he had to turn the events of the past year into a text that would explain himself to others. Outside of a number of flourishing correspondences and his student essays, the "Confession" was the first major prose text he had ever written.

In "A Confession of the Fall," Allen also shifted the relationship between writing and life. Not only did the writing document his life, but his life itself became, more than ever before, like a novel. He was stretching the limits of self-representation, showing a new ability to use his life experiences and identity as a template for the working of a literary imagination. Life and writing were merging. He, subject and author, could draw from experience, memory, correspondences, literary texts, and poems, actively inventing and consolidating a new sense of self. Though the confession was ostensibly written for his attorney, there were important benefits in this writing for the young artist. He had much reworking to do, both as a writer and as a young man.

"A Confession of the Fall" describes the visions and then tells the story of Allen's dark night of the soul. How after making contact with the divine in the visions, Allen was thrust into the second night. He exposed himself to harsh conditions that were intended to rid him of the burdens that were holding him back from making contact with God. Living with Huncke and his gang would help cure him of the sin of spiritual gluttony. He had to suffer, to feel distress, to be stripped of the impurities that society had put into him.

"A Confession of the Fall" also has an affinity with the classic myth of the American hero. Mired in a state of impurity and sin not of his own making, the American seeks rebirth as a self-made man, embodying innocence, order, and truth. It is not through work but through faith alone that salvation may be attained. In Allen's case, this meant dedicating himself to the visions and to Herbert, whom he saw as possessing the true qualities of saintly innocence and purity.

But the hero cannot totally separate from society, and with his arrest he was reminded again that failure was certain. He was thrust back into the actual world, which in this case meant facing the law and the madhouse. He became the American Adam, as described by R. W. B. Lewis: "An Adamic person, springing from nowhere, outside of time, at home only in the presence of nature and God, who is thrust by circumstances into an actual world and an actual age."[31]

In the summer of 1948, Allen turned twenty-two and was still a college student. In order to graduate from Columbia, he needed to complete one course in Victorian literature and finish a few papers. In "A Confession of the Fall" he wrote: "I settled down for a quiet and lonely summer in an apartment in East Harlem which I had sublet from a school friend."[32] He worked part time as a file clerk at the university and recalled being "deeply depressed over my inability to write poetry" and a "growing sense of futility of my thoughts and doings and the ineffectuality of various half-assed schemes for homosexual orientation." This was a "limbo period." He was close to finishing college but felt directionless and without any well-defined career plans. Thus far he had fallen short of his goal, which was to become a writer of poetry or novels. He wrote, "My desire was black—I had no plan. I was deeply depressed."

Next, he wrote, "I had been aware of a 'problem,' as I shall call it, which had haunted me ever since childhood . . . a strain to settle what seemed unsettled." The problem's effects varied over the years. From fourteen to sixteen years of age the problem played out in "political forms," leading him to want to study law at Columbia and to become a labor lawyer. Then it was channeled into "aesthetic, psychoanalytic, anthropological, and criminal (jazz music and drug) areas."

In spring 1947, he discovered something important in unfinished manuscripts of Kerouac's novel, *The Town and the City*, in which he was portrayed as a character named Leon Levinsky:

> I felt all the turmoil and frenzy of the last five years had been somehow justified because I saw expressed in his novel a peace and knowledge and solidity and say a whole recreated, true and eternal world—my world—finally given permanent form. And so I felt my own failure as an artist to conclude a large and, if not mature, at least complete and internally perfect work—or personality for that matter. I was still trying.

Here Allen articulates how closely related were his artistic project and his personal development. Art had the potential to remake and redeem a life of hardships. After reading Jack Kerouac's novel *The Town and the City*, Allen wrote "Two Sonnets," which stated: "I witness Heaven in unholy time,/I room in the renowned city, am/Unknown."[33]

Where you might expect Naomi to play a large part in "A Confession of the Fall," she comes up surprisingly little. Instead, a large part is a response to the question: "Who is Herbert Huncke?"

> I saw him as a self damned soul, but a soul nonetheless, aware of itself and others in a strangely perceptive and essentially human way. . . .
> I see that he suffers, more than myself, more than anyone I know perhaps, suffers like a saint of old in the making, and also has "cosmic" or suprasensory perceptions of an extraordinary depth and openness.

Huncke was thirty-nine years old, a drug addict and "thief by profession." Huncke showed up on Allen's doorstep in February 1949, and Allen offered him a place to stay if he would get a job. Huncke had an "openness to higher ideas," which he attributed to the "depths of his rootlessness and lack of possessiveness of property and ideas, and education and social position." He was the perfect companion for Allen, who wanted to withdraw and to build "a jail for myself in the world, where I would finally come to a peaceful rest, look around, see clearly, and begin to act. Finally, I hoped that a withdrawal would bring a recurrence of visions."

Daily life didn't live up to this ideal. Allen was being drained by Herbert's dependence upon him. When problems arose, as they often did, he did not let himself get angry at Herbert or his companions, questioning why he should prioritize his problems over theirs. "I rationalized Herbert's own parasitical situation, ascribing it to mental sickness not so unlike my own that I could afford to judge him." Herbert was filling up the apartment with stolen goods and even stealing from Allen, but he could not ask Herbert to leave, because that "meant that I would have to see clearly into my own personality problems and act on that. And I was not ready."

His father and friends told him to get rid of Herbert, who was "absorbing my sustenance and money, and taking me away from real creative activity." Lucien Carr told Allen he was "tempting fate" by leaving his personal papers lying around the apartment. He gathered all his "hot manuscripts" and got a ride from Herbert's buddy Little Jack Melody to his brother's in Long Island. They never made it past Northern Boulevard in Queens.

Their car tried to run down a policeman, sped sixty-five miles per hour the wrong way down 205th Street, hit the curb, rolled over twice, and finished upside down. Allen's papers and journals were strewn amid the wreckage and confiscated by the police. He walked away from the accident scene and asked a man for directions to the city, seven cents in his pocket. He regarded this whole episode as "divine wrath."

> This catastrophe had given me the key of understanding of my own actions. I thought of the nature of tragedy and the tragic hero, and saw the parallel chain of events and logical sequence of development of understanding and fate in Lear, Hamlet, and Macbeth. I felt most closely akin to vacillating and falsely ambitious Macbeth. In this sense I refer to the accident—seemingly the result of a far-fetched one way street misfortune—as a logical and clear descent of Divine Wrath and at the time I felt thankful and began to pray that I be forgiven what I then understood as my "sin."

Later that day the police came to his York Avenue apartment and arrested him, took him down to the station, and booked him. In the interrogation they first treated him like he, with his Ivy League education, was the brains of the operation. He told them he was a writer who had banded with the gang strictly for material. The police looked through his journals and then "turned gentle" and "began to treat me as if I were some suffering angelic freakish poetic queer; a quixotic doe-like creature."

The *New York Times* reported that Allen Ginsberg "told the police that he was a copy boy for a news service who had 'tied-in' with the gang to obtain 'realism' he needed to write a story. He said he held a Bachelor of Arts degree from Columbia University, and had shared his apartment with the gang for their tutelage." This was not exactly true.

Louis thought Allen's real troubles were not criminal but psychological. Allen had been wounded by his mother's illness and its terrible impact on his parents' marriage. The attorney Louis hired, Ilo Orleans, agreed and recruited several Columbia professors who knew Allen well to write letters on his behalf. Unbeknown to Allen at the time, his world-famous professors Jacques Barzun and Lionel Trilling teamed up to help their former student out of a jam. They all agreed that Allen did not belong in jail, and that what he really needed was psychiatric help.

Years later, Allen learned from me that Professor Barzun had written to Dr. Nolan Lewis, chair of the Department of Psychiatry and director of the New York State Psychiatric Institute (PI), on June 1, 1949. He endorsed the lawyer's plan for getting Allen hospitalized, providing this rationale:

> Knowing him as a student, I came to form a high opinion of his native gifts and, long before his recent predicament, regretted that he seemed to be hampered in the exercise of his fine mind by the presence of inner troubles. If he can be saved from the consequence of his rash acts, and restored to the control of his intellectual powers, the salvaging operation will have been worthwhile, not only for him as an individual, but for the community to which he may make valuable contributions.[34]

Perhaps wisely, Barzun did not write anything about Allen's desire to become a visionary poet. You do not share that sort of thing with the grand jury. Better to make him sound like an English professor in the making, which his father still hoped for. Dr. Lewis and his PI colleagues would figure out the rest. Surely the PI psychiatrists would understand how to get a brilliant young Columbia College graduate and potential future academic back on track.

The legal strategy worked as planned. Within a few weeks, they learned that the grand jury had not rendered an indictment. The lawyers wrote to

I. H. McKinnon of the Psychoanalytic Clinic for Training and Research at the New York State Psychiatric Institute, "We are happy to make this report to you because we believe that this now paves the way for the possibility of some genuine help to Allen Ginsburg [sic]."

After several more weeks, the attorneys and doctors arranged for his admission. Allen waited out the legal and psychiatric deliberations at his father's home in Paterson, his journal entries reflecting anticipation about the prospect of entering a madhouse. On May 23, he wrote:

> Several days ago I had a dream that I was enrolled into the mad-house. I was given my bedding and bunk—much like jail or like Sheepshead Bay Maritime Training Center. I remember the colorful feeling of wonder at this new institutional monastery I had entered. I had a bunk in an enormous ward, surrounded by hundreds of weeping, decaying women and men.[35]

He next wrote that after his lawyer told him he might be "institutionalized,"

> I had a great feeling of relief and joy at the thoughts of going out and away from the East Cities to some psychoanalytic retreat, where I would joy in freedom, then doubts about my sanity, and helplessness of myself in this vast illusion I have created. Doctor and lawyer accuse me of egocentricity—egotism—thinking I am mentally 10 steps ahead of anybody I talk to. So it is, so I often feel; and in the joy of release into official irresponsibility and insanity, despite doubts and fears, I spent the day 10 steps of freedom ahead of everybody.

Allen looked forward to going to the psychiatric hospital and receiving long-sought psychoanalytic treatment. Only a proper psychoanalysis, he believed, could rid him of the unconscious conflicts that caused him emotional problems and kept him from doing the kind of writing that he aspired to and that the visions required. Besides, a bit of official irresponsibility sounded appealing. He would have lots of time to read and write.

He had already received many valuable lessons concerning madness from William Burroughs, Jack Kerouac, and Neal Cassady. Now he was set to go to the madhouse and get an advanced degree in madness. Of course, the first to teach him about madness was his mother, who did so beginning when he was just a child. He had worried tremendously about what might happen to her when she went to the madhouse. Now, about to go there himself as a patient, Allen seemed ready and curious.

Naomi was out of Pilgrim State and was living with her sister Elanor in the Bronx. Allen could see that ever since the lobotomy she wasn't the same person. He thought about a recent evening spent together with Naomi, Elanor, and Eugene. After the visit, he wrote:

> I suddenly became angry at Elanor and inwardly angry at my brother, because they patronized, baffled and fogged the natural exuberance and innocent perception of Naomi. However, Naomi too had started compulsively, blindly questioning me in repeated monotones, about my travels, which she'd half forgotten, till I became weary of all. I had earlier a sense of their great illusory conspiracy to "handle" Naomi as a machine, blind, based on habits of thought peculiar to themselves, which was out of their control and that Naomi somehow saw and I winked at her and tried to communicate my own under-standing of her baffling problem in a few terse and fragmentary state-ments to her; but with not too much response. I feel that I could start a conspiracy of the insane with her, underground—but she goes blank and mechanical too often.

Naomi's illness, the electroshock treatments, the insulin and metrazol, being cooped up in a hospital for years, and the personality-robbing lobotomy had all taken a heavy toll. How much longer could Allen possibly keep trying to rescue her? Hadn't he already done enough?

Besides, now he had serious problems of his own to deal with. This time the madhouse was for him, not for her. Would he end up just like her? The psychiatrists would tell him what was to become of him. He would visit and inhabit the scary distant world where Naomi had lived during his childhood, experiencing, learning, incorporating, or transforming what had long been threatening and unknown. At PI, he might meet others who could join him in the conspiracy of the insane. Most importantly, a degree in madness might help him become a poet.

The prospect of a deeper immersion into madness did, however, raise serious questions over whether this was either a divine or a pathological madness. "Am I face to face with the eternal, or am I the victim of fear and lethargy and all too human pride? Vanity? Am I becoming human or super-human? The analysts say human. The poets say superhuman."

Allen was determined to make art, if he could only figure out how. PI wasn't a detour; it was where he, still in descent, now had to be. Madness had caught up with him, and he needed to own it, embracing both spiritual visions and clinical madness. What would the psychiatrists see in him?

Chapter 5

The Psychiatric Institute, 1949–1950

NEARLY FORTY YEARS after being admitted to the New York State Psychiatric Institute (PI), when asked about his hospitalization, Allen told me, "I was a Columbia student with no job, nowhere to go, suffering from vocational disability. It was either go to jail or shuffle off bourgeoisie style to a bughouse. One year earlier I had the vision of Blake, a socially transcendent vision. I used it as an excuse."[1] Allen also made light of the hospitalization, calling it "my leave of absence from college."[2]

In a deal with the prosecutor, the criminal charges against Allen were dropped, and he was voluntarily admitted to PI, where he remained for eight months. Allen didn't know why his stay was so long, but being there wasn't so bad. "I had a good time. Read a lot. Wrote a lot. I went through psychotherapy for the first time, which I enjoyed, two or three times a week. No drugs. No ECT. They were doing transorbital lobotomies at the time. I saw lots of them. But none of that stuff for me."[3]

"So that's it?" I asked. He made it sound like relaxing at a retreat. After having read "Kaddish" and "Howl," I expected more suffering, more hardship. Did the man who coined the phrase "a generation destroyed by madness" really have it so free and easy in a psychiatric hospital? I also wanted to know how the psychiatrists diagnosed him, what treatments they provided, and what, if anything, was accomplished. How did their treatments or his hospital experiences affect the young writer and influence his poetry?

Maybe it was so long ago that Allen had forgotten. "You don't get admitted for eight months for nothing, do you?" I asked.

So Allen offered, "If you want to check the medical records, go ahead. My secretary will give you permission." I had piqued Allen's curiosity about what the PI records might contain.

With Allen's written permission and permission from the leaders of PI, I could examine and quote from Allen's medical record. From the first morning I sat in the medical record suite with the records before me, I was struck by its richness of stories, details, and meanings. Unlike today's medical records, which have been systematized to meet best-practice guidelines and sanitized to protect against disclosures or legal action, Allen's PI record contains an extraordinary collection of voices, experiences, and perspectives documenting the story of a remarkable young man who became an exceptional poet, during a crucial period in his personal, spiritual, and artistic development. When read alongside his correspondences and journals, I hoped it would help me better understand how Allen put mental illness and madness to work for revolutionary poetry.

After several weeks of waiting at his father's house in New Jersey, in June 1949, Allen was finally admitted to PI. Located on the cliffs overlooking the Hudson River off upper Riverside Drive in the Washington Heights neighborhood of Manhattan, PI has long been the crème de la crème of American academic psychiatry. PI is a collaboration between the New York State Office of Mental Health and the Columbia University Department of Psychiatry and also has a highly regarded psychoanalytic institute.

I know PI directly from my years as a medical student at the Columbia College of Physicians and Surgeons from 1983 to 1987. Back then at the PI library I read the 1950 "Report of the Director of the Psychiatric Institute," which documented the research activities then being undertaken. "Modern psychiatry . . . attack[s] the problem of mental disorder from as many viewpoints as possible . . . and is slowly progressing to the point of influencing all branches of medicine."[4]

In 1949, PI researchers were conducting multiple different experiments and trials. "Many patients were selected and invited to participate. Some received drugs that produced abnormal mental states, including sodium amytal, pervitin, mescaline, and lysergic acid. In addition, those patients received psychotherapy, electroconvulsive therapy (E.C.T.), or insulin to try to influence the experimentally-produced psychosis."

The purpose of this scientific work was to revolutionize psychiatry, claimed Dr. Paul Hoch, the Hungarian-born principal research psychiatrist at PI. Hoch and the other PI psychiatrists wanted to distance psychiatry from psychoanalysis and bring it closer to medicine, where they thought it belonged.

They conducted experiments using biological and surgical interventions among their patients with serious mental illness.

At the time, PI was a leading center in the study of psychosurgery. In 1950, sixty-six patients at PI underwent topectomies (surgery on the frontal cortex through a somewhat larger opening than a lobotomy) performed by Dr. J. Lawrence Pool. Many of those patients also received experimental drugs before and after their topectomies to see whether ablating part of their cerebral cortex changed their symptoms and behavior.

Dr. Paul Hoch conducted transorbital lobotomies. "Eight female patients with severe and marked symptoms of tension and anxiety, mainly in a schizophrenic setting, were given transorbital lobotomy operations by Dr. Paul Hoch." One woman showed temporary improvement, but otherwise there were not any "ultimate favorable effects whatsoever." The PI researchers were also collaborating with Dr. Harry Worthing at Pilgrim State Hospital, who had lobotomized Naomi a year and a half earlier.

Additionally, Dr. Hoch was a leader in the early investigations of "psychomimetic" or "madness-mimicking agents," which were being used as a model for the investigation of various treatment modalities. They gave mescaline to patients with mental illness and then tried to mitigate mescaline's actions through psychotherapy, electric shock, or insulin. Mescaline was given to all patients undergoing psychosurgery both before and after the procedure. Their unsurprising conclusion: "It was found that mescaline in schizophrenic patients underscores and reactivates the psychosis in patients who are apparently recovered." In conducting this and similar work, Hoch was a paid CIA consultant and a contract employee of the US Army Chemical Corps.[5]

Dr. Hoch took special interest in another area of psychiatric research that directly pertained to the diagnosis and treatment Allen received at PI:

> Dr. Hoch continued his investigations in the pseudoneurotic form of schizophrenia with a young psychiatrist named Dr. Phillip Polatin. The psychodynamics of these patients were studied and compared with cases suffering from other forms of schizophrenia. The effect of different therapies, namely, psychotherapy, shock therapy, and psychosurgery on these patients is also under investigation.

These patients were hard to figure out. They were not as floridly psychotic as those with classic schizophrenia, like Naomi, but to the PI psychiatrists they still appeared very disturbed. Some psychiatrists called them "ambulatory schizophrenics" or "early schizophrenics" because they had some psychotic symptoms but not full-blown schizophrenia.

Hoch and Polatin characterized them as having "pan-neurosis," "pan-sexuality," and "pan-anxiety."[6] They theorized that these patients were really psychotics dressed up in neurotic's clothes. The doctors noted, "A history of the existence of schizoid individuals or frank schizophrenic psychoses in the family of near relatives is important." Many of these patients would go on to become full-blown schizophrenics, they hypothesized. Exactly which ones were not yet known. But they believed it was important to get all these people early treatment. Should they receive psychotherapy or biological therapies or both? This was uncharted territory, which they were investigating on the inpatient unit where Allen was admitted.

In one publication, Dr. Hoch remarked that some with the pseudoneurotic form of schizophrenia had received ECT: "But I can tell you now that I have never encountered a single pseudoneurotic person who ever responded to this therapy!"[7] According to Dr. Hoch, "Some patients have responded very well to psychosurgery." This means that at PI, Allen Ginsberg himself was in a cohort of patients where some were being selected for lobotomy and had their lights forever dimmed. Allen was not selected, but he saw many others who were. His first therapist at PI told me he tried to protect Allen and other patients from being selected for lobotomy.

Some persons with pseudoneurotic schizophrenia responded well to psychotherapy, but Dr. Hoch cautioned that this psychotherapy required techniques distinct from the psychotherapy for either schizophrenia or neurosis. These were very challenging cases, especially for young psychiatrists in training. That's exactly what Allen would get at PI. Being part of the Columbia University Department of Psychiatry meant PI was a center of training, and treatment was provided by residents in psychiatry, who would be just a few years older than Allen at the time of his hospitalization.

In the days leading up to his PI admission, Allen journaled about his madness and impending treatment. On May 23rd he wrote: "In the hospital I hope to be cured. My images tell me that hours of truth are at hand. I am not going to die. I am going to live anew. . . . I have been reading *The Possessed*. My devils are going to be cast out. . . . I am becoming incomprehensible and false to myself and I will stop."[8] At moments he acknowledged feeling lost and needing some kind of help: "I am ill. I have become spiritually or practically impotent in my madness this last month. I suddenly realized that my head is severed from my body."

He did not recognize Naomi's madness in himself. At the time he wrote very little about her in his letters and journals. He could count on Jack Kerouac for an insightful perspective on his situation. On June 10, 1949,

Kerouac wrote from Massachusetts: "I'd say you were always trying to justify your ma's madness as against the logical, sober but hateful sanity. This is really harmless and even loyal."[9] Kerouac, who knew Allen as well as anyone, offered his own interpretation of Allen having historically defended Naomi's madness and how his attitudes toward his own madness were tied in with justifying hers.

On June 15, Allen wrote: "My life is devoted to the making of images."[10] He had to go to the hospital, but he was going as an artist at work.

Kerouac and Allen wrote several new lines that humorously deflated the gravity of the situation and depicted Allen as a trickster for whom the doctors and hospital were no match:

I had visions to beguile 'em
Till they put me in th'asylum[11]

Allen knew that in agreeing to go to PI he had Kerouac's blessing. But to Kerouac, Allen's strategy was not without risks. In America, people pay a price for opposing sanity. If that is your path, Kerouac seemed to be saying, then you should take special care. The psychiatric hospital can be a dangerous place, which Kerouac knew well, having been in a mental hospital while serving in the US Navy.

Allen had a less fearful attitude. He knew he needed psychological help and thought he might learn something of value from the professionals at PI. He and others in his circle believed in psychoanalysis. Psychoanalysts could unchain one's emotions and might help him reach the new vision he and his friends sought.

On April 21, 1949, Allen was lucky to be alive. He could have easily been killed in the high-speed car chase that resulted in his arrest. And if not that time, then maybe the next time by some other senseless means. Allen was tempting fate. He could have become another early casualty of the Beat Generation, like his friend William Canastra, who died in the New York City subway and was memorialized by Allen in "Ode to William Canastra" and "Howl."

Louis Ginsberg knew enough to recognize Allen's behavior was not normal. He traced it back to the impact of Naomi's illness upon the young Allen. Louis was an effective enough advocate to hire an attorney and to rally Allen's professors. In a sense, Allen's statement to me, that he was shuffled off bourgeois-style to the bughouse, was correct. There is no doubt that in those days, and still today, access to mental health services is much easier if you have money and connections, and many poor people with mental health problems often end up in the criminal justice system instead of in mental health treatment.

But that does not mean Allen didn't benefit from it or that others wouldn't also benefit. It means such services are offered inequitably even in rich countries like the United States. The psychiatric admission saved Allen from going to prison, which would have been a very different and much less nurturing experience, to state the obvious.

Allen did not end up at a facility anything like Pilgrim State, where his mother had been, but at the top-notch PI. The fact that he was a Columbia graduate with letters from esteemed Columbia professors opened doors for him. Allen knew that as an elite with VIP connections he was getting special treatment not afforded to all. That may be partly why he downplayed his psychiatric treatment with me and in other interviews. He recognized his privilege and good fortune, especially in comparison with his own mother, who was treated in far less distinguished state psychiatric hospitals.

On a preadmission visit to the hospital on June 28, 1949, Allen was accompanied by his brother Eugene, who was asked to sign consent for treatment. "I hereby give my permission for the following treatment in the case of my BROTHER Allen Ginsberg."[12] The form listed:

Electric Shock Therapy
Insulin Therapy
Metrazol and Curare
Electro-narcosis.

Eugene put several bold lines through "Metrazol and Curare" to cross them out, but the others were left. He signed his name under the sentence that said, "The nature and consequences of the treatment have been fully explained to me." Lobotomy would have required a separate consent form, given that it is a surgical procedure.

The first page of the admission form lists personal information. The residence was 3556 Rochambeau Avenue, Bronx, N.Y. Age 23. Height 5' 11 1/2". Weight 132lbs Eyes Brown. Hair Brown. Complexion Fair. Build Asthenic. Occupation: Copy boy—Asso. Press. CRIMINAL HISTORY, IF ANY. None.

The left-hand side of the form was dominated by a passport-sized photo of Allen. He is trim, and his hair is short. He wears a dress shirt with the top button loose to show his bare chest. His head is turned slightly to his right and his eyes are fixed on a point a few feet above. There is something intense on his mind. Why is he looking away like that? A psychiatrist does not diagnose someone solely based upon how they look. But appearance is information that informs the assessment. Is Allen fearful or paranoid?

The first psychiatrist to see Allen at PI was the admitting resident who wrote the anamnesis, a preliminary version of the case history based upon information obtained during the admission interview. This anamnesis told the story of a young man, born to a severely mentally ill woman, whose troubles began early in life.

> Soon after her marriage, the patient's mother was hospitalized in a state institution for the first in a long series of admissions with a diagnosis of Paranoid Schizophrenia. She spent the years 1932–34, 38–41, 47, 49 in state hospitals, and was recently discharged from Pilgrim State Hospital after undergoing a "prefrontal lobotomy." She was never able to perform her role as a mother adequately, had frequent violent arguments with the father, and attempted to "poison" the children's minds against him. She is now living alone in New York City.

The admitting psychiatrist's story made no mention that Allen himself had consented for her lobotomy. Nor did this fact appear anywhere in the entire PI record. Remarkably enough, in his eight months at PI, Allen never told them, and they never asked. The trauma of the lobotomy, and much of the trauma involving his lifelong exposure to her mental illness and injurious psychiatric treatments, remained out of their awareness and never figured in his care.

The story documented in the anamnesis has things starting to go awry when Allen became a late adolescent:

> He became very much interested in writing poetry and thought of himself as a character in Dostoevsky. He enjoyed college and showed a great interest in creative writing. He made a complete break from his family and seemed to be independent of his father and brother. Through association with homosexuals in college and first out of curiosity the patient began having homosexual affairs which he has continued up to the present time.

To the psychiatrists of the day, homosexuality was either itself a mental illness or a symptom of other types of mental illness. The present illness began a couple years ago:

> He seemed to drift from one place to another and eventually became associated with "queer" people in Greenwich Village. He had several homosexual affairs of a rather intense nature and spent about a year

and a half until several months ago using such drugs as marijuana, heroin and Benzedrine. He became intensely interested in crime and spent much time with members of the underworld. He expressed feelings of inadequacy, of his inability to make his contribution to the world, or a lack of vocation, and a feeling of being uprooted. He spoke in expansive terms and often stated he "saw God."

Here the young psychiatrist was giving an account of an emerging psychiatric disorder. Perhaps because this was only the first telling of that case history, by a psychiatrist in training, it reads more like an early draft. It is loose and incomplete, but still there are some themes that come through: psychosis, homosexuality, antisocial behavior, a significant family psychiatric history, and worry that he may acquire paranoid schizophrenia from his mother. The case history contained more than enough evidence for the psychiatrists to reach a diagnosis.

On top of the admission form next to the title "psychiatric classification group" somebody typed "Dementia Praecox." Next to "TYPE" was "Paranoid" (which was Naomi's diagnosis), with a line placed through it and the words "Other Types (Pseudoneurotic)" written in its place. This indicates Allen was diagnosed with Pseudoneurotic Type Schizophrenia.

One long passage from the anamnesis describes Allen's grandiosity and anticipates the dilemmas his doctors would face in treating Allen:

He expressed the idea that he is probably intellectually endowed with the ability to understand the ultimate truths about life given to no one else. Spoke of himself as "the resurrection and the life" come to save the rest of the world. One year ago he stated he had ecstatic "visions" of momentary duration in which he experienced the world as an exhilarating phenomenon that was revealed only to him—that he had finally seen the "light" that was revealed to him as a chosen individual. He feels that inanimate objects have an intelligence and souls, and often would sit for hours trying to feel emotion towards such things as a chair or lamp, in which he was sure was a soul and intelligence. He feels that he was sent to the world to reveal its mysteries and to him is given the power to experience feelings denied to others. During these "visions" he felt that he had at last seen the world as it really is, and that what is considered reality is just blindness. He has made great efforts to experience feelings and sensations that will reveal to him the transcendental and divine. He identifies with Christ, feeling that he is fixated with the latter's attributes, and will admit those of his liking to the rank of angels.

Was the new patient a mystical genius, a megalomaniac, a psychotic, a prankster, or some part all? To further assess Allen and to begin applying the indicated treatments, they put him on an inpatient unit. The psychiatrists wanted to see how he related to his visions not just on the first day but in different situations over the coming weeks and months. Were the visions all he was going to talk about? How open or insightful was he? What would happen if someone challenged his visions? This could indicate whether he was delusional and perhaps on the path to full-blown schizophrenia or could still be saved by bolstering his ability to distinguish fantasy from reality. The psychiatrists spent the next eight months completing their assessment and then treating their brilliant but disturbed young patient, in part for his fixation on these visions.

The social worker met with Allen and also with his brother Eugene. The social worker wrote how Eugene told her Allen's illness was first noticeable last year:

> He was up in the air with visions of spiritual rejuvenation. . . . He had always had a kind of superior attitude. He had been interested in leftist politics and the unrest of the world. He was not a Communist. But he was influenced by his parents' politics. His mother was a Communist and his father a Socialist. They argued about politics all the time. Actually, neither parent was wholly realistic. Father was very academic. Mother was mentally ill.

The social worker wrote of how when the patient went to college he fell in with some unorthodox friends:

> These friends represented the kinds of logic against current governmental and legal controls and systems, based upon false premises. One fostered ideas of homicide, another revolution, another was a sexual misfit with a philosophy to support it, etc. . . . Patient also nursed bizarre concepts of himself through the past year—inclined to follow a Jack London philosophy, or to carry through the "Gustavsen" theory of picking up with any stranger just to see what they were like. He wore a beard and slouched around in true "Bohemian" abandon.

The social workers on the team discussed the case and then wrote: "We think he is a paranoid schizophrenic. But some of his grandiosity may be real. That is, he just may be a great poet. Mark Van Doren is looking at his stuff." Compared with their typical patients, it was possible Allen's grandiosity was justifiable and not delusional.[13]

The multidisciplinary treatment team looked to the psychologists and their tools of psychological testing to make more precise determinations about Allen's level of psychological functioning. Allen scored 17 points on the Wechsler-Bellevue Vocabulary. This put him in the brilliant portion of the population. "His answers on the Vocabulary were quite obsessively precise and lengthy. He apparently places great value on his brilliance."

The examiner asked him to do drawings and thought they were "most unusual." The figures were nude, with the heads of adults, the bodies of children, but the genitalia of adults. "The eyes and ears are so large." "Why?" "Those are listening ears," he said. The psychologist wrote: "The drawings give the impression of a psychotic condition with extreme sensitivity to what is happening in the environment."

As for the Rorschach test, the psychologist wrote: "The Rorschach is the production of an ambitious, brilliant person whose creativity, unfortunately, is highly autistic. The patient would appear to be a schizophrenic who has ideas of omnipotence and greatness. He apparently feels he knows the meaning of life and that he feels things more deeply than others." As was common practice those days, a person's way of interpreting the Rorschach's ambiguous inkblots was used to help make the diagnosis of schizophrenia. The psychologist concluded:

> The patient is a brilliant, but autistic schizophrenic, probably of the catatonic type who has religious ecstasies and occasional agitated periods in which he can be destructive. He feels alternatively crushed by the world and in command of the world. His "unconscious" seems to be extremely conscious. He has much bizarre sexual fantasies and may actually be perverse sexually. There are marked regressive trends present. Thinking appears to be eroticized, although actual intellectual deterioration has not taken place. Prognosis is difficult to judge on the basis of the projective tests in this case.

The psychologist detected both brilliance and severe illness; he diagnosed schizophrenia but could not make a prognosis. The idea that Allen feels "crushed by the world" is framed as him being on the verge of a psychotic fragmentation, rather than being traumatized by adverse life events, such as his mother's mental illness and lobotomy. Nowhere does the psychologist remark on Allen's poetry, but the testing demonstrated how Allen was accessing inner experiences that could potentially be put to creative use, if he were able to survive his troubles and not be harmed by psychiatric treatments.

When in 1986 I told Allen his diagnosis at PI was "pseudoneurotic-type schizophrenia," I was surprised to hear he thought the diagnosis was accurate and to his liking. Allen said the constructs of pan-neurosis, pan-anxiety, and pan-sexuality were fairly apt descriptions of his situation, although he said he was not having much sex in those days. He really liked the idea that psychosis is near and accessible, which, notably, he saw as a good thing.

At PI, Allen had the amazingly good fortune to meet another patient named Carl Solomon, a young Dadaist from the Bronx who had read Genet, Artaud, Breton, Rimbaud, and Gide. They first met in the clinic, a week before Allen's admission. Allen wrote in his journal, "This is a real madhouse—what a weird feeling," and was taken by "a secret conspiracy of the great dichotomy—the lunatic v.s. society."[14] He then talked about:

Carl Solomon, 1953. © Allen Ginsberg Estate.

Solomon a twenty-one yr old Jew, an intellectual—said that they, the doctors, make no attempts (even encourage in sublimate activities) the abstract madness; as long as behavior is socially acceptable. It is only when abstract systems are carried out (particularly Solomon's absurd sense of them) in flesh does society object: i.e. yesterday he gave his doctor a handful of marbles in hope that he would swallow them and kill himself.

Solomon was perfectly suited to join Allen in launching the "conspiracy of the insane." He was rebellious and political in ways Allen was not. He despised psychiatry, which he later wrote was incompatible with literature, and affirmed the position of the "lunatic, who in Artaud's words 'is a man who has preferred to become what is socially understood as mad rather than forfeit a certain superior idea of human honor.'"[15] Allen hadn't yet gone that far in critiquing psychiatry or defending madness, but he was happy to tag along.

Allen had been learning to deploy his madness to be provocative more along religious lines. After admission to PI, he picked up painting in occupational therapy and with it kept going down the religious path. Two weeks after meeting Solomon, he signed one of his paintings "Jesus Ginsberg." This was Allen's way of being outrageous for his Jewish doctors and his father. But Jesus Ginsberg was not just a slap in their faces. He was serious about spirituality, sainthood, and Christian icons, and over many years kept working on developing images to have the impact he desired.

On the day of Allen's admission to PI, Jack Kerouac wrote to him: "I admire you for delivering yourself to the actual bughouse. It shows your interest in things and people. Be careful while convincing the doc's you're nuts not to convince yourself (you see, I know you well)."[16] Allen knew he was fortunate to have a friend like Kerouac who was so perceptive. Kerouac seemed to believe Allen could have it both ways: learn something from the doctors and the other patients but also not forget who he was and the artistic path he was traveling. Allen knew he needed help. On his first day in the hospital he wrote: "Why not live for the secret well springs of beings outside of formulations, synthesis—but where are my wellsprings now?"[17]

He spent most of his stay on the fifth floor, nicknamed the "genius ward," which also had a tradition of offering long-term psychotherapy to young, intelligent patients. Other patients on the ward were getting electroconvulsive therapy, insulin therapy, and lobotomy, but not Allen. The treatment prescribed for him centered on individual psychotherapy provided by psychiatry residents, not an experienced psychoanalyst. The psychiatrist resident who completed the initial interview was assigned to be his psychotherapist, and two other residents came after. They met in psychotherapy three or four times per week during his eight-month stay. Once a week or more, his psychiatrist wrote a detailed progress note. These include many quotations, but they are not verbatim recordings of sessions. These notes provide a close-up view of Allen the patient and the psychotherapeutic treatment he received at PI. Let us listen in on these sessions and try to understand Allen's experience as a patient in psychotherapy. How, if at all, did the psychotherapy help Allen either with his alleged mental disorder or his relationship to the visions? How was the therapy supporting his development as a young man and a poet? *My reflections are italicized.*

Psychotherapy should be driven by theory, best practices, and scientific evidence. Although informed by science, as a practice psychotherapy introduces tremendous variability in terms of each therapist's personality, approach, values, and skills. At PI, the psychiatry residents were supervised by more senior clinicians. Reading the psychotherapy progress notes shows how different the three psychotherapists were from one another. I will not reveal their identities, because learning about them was never my goal. Readers can detect the first therapist's cautiousness, the second therapist's boldness, and the third therapist's doggedness. To his credit, Allen found ways to derive something useful from his work with each of them.

Allen was eager to get started in psychoanalysis. In their first session, he grilled the therapist about his qualifications. "Where did you do your training? Who was your psychoanalyst? Are you a Freudian, a Jungian, or a Reichian?" When Allen was told he would not be getting psychoanalyzed, he was very disappointed. He had read a lot about psychoanalysis and thought it was what he really needed. He wanted a senior psychoanalyst who was well schooled in visions and poetics. Not a wide-eyed trainee who hadn't even heard of Artaud. However, he would cooperate with the treatment being prescribed. He knew he needed to make changes in order to steady his life and become a poet.

The therapist gave him the standard instructions. You sit in this chair, and I sit over there. Talk openly about yourself. Tell stories. Don't censor yourself or hide your feelings. Say everything. Allen said his main problem was homosexuality. His lifestyle was no secret and no problem to his friends. But when his father found out the year before, he was aghast. *Allen abided by the dominant psychiatric view of the day that homosexuality was an illness.*[18] *Psychiatrists believed they could cure homosexuality and in Allen's*

7/1/49

The patient began ~~interview~~ talking of a change that occurred
in his life at about the age of 17, when he thought of a "new
vision of reality", and that "the whole world had an intelligence running through it". He began to be interested in Freud
and Spengler, and wondered if "the health of man might trans-
cend society." At 19 he began a search for a new vision
outside of society, and turned to antisocial activity, such
as drugs, free sexuality, and criminal behavior. In speaking
of his feeling during drug usage, patient states, "It awakened
new feelings and broke up the stasis. I began to see people as
individual souls and lives--saw them for themselves and not as
a system. I had fantasies of the healthiness of criminality,
and began to feel that criminals were liberated and healthy."

Patient spoke of his feelings about inanimate objects, stating
that he felt that all objects were "beings" and had intelligence and souls, and that he would spend long hours staring at
objects in the room in an effort to sense their souls and feel
emotionally toward the object. Patient states that trees have
souls as humans. Patient is being allowed to talk without
interruption, except when therapist attempts to paraphrase
patient's ideas to confirm his understanding of them.

Patient relates well with therapist and is willing and anxious
to talk continuously throughout the interviews.

1

Psychotherapy progress note, New York State Psychiatric Institute, 1949. © *Allen Ginsberg Estate.*

case saw it as one dimension of his pseudoneurotic-type schizophrenia,
which they were treating.

Allen recalled his first day of school, when he had a temper tantrum and
refused vaccination. The therapist wrote: "He always felt superior to the
other children." On the unit Allen tried to get along with the others but the
therapist noted Allen carried himself like he was not one of them. Allen
expressed concern: "I don't think I'm feeling as other people do." He didn't
mean to sound superior, but he was being honest. The therapist wondered
what exactly was so different about how he felt.

Allen began the subsequent session by relating that when he was seventeen, he started to have a "new vision of reality." At nineteen he took this
vision a step further and "began a search for a new vision outside of society."
He turned to what the therapist called "antisocial activity, such as drugs,
free sexuality, and criminal behavior." Allen told him, "I had fantasies of the
healthiness of criminality and began to feel that criminals were liberated
and healthy." As Allen kept talking, he got more intense and started to sound
more grandiose and bizarre in his thinking. Trees have souls. Even inanimate
objects have souls. I sit and stare at them for hours to feel their intelligence,
said Allen, echoing words he had said in his admission interview and had
written in his journal a few weeks before his admission.

Allen also said his sexual feelings had always been homoerotic. His first sexual contact was at age nineteen, when he had a "short intense love affair" with a man he met at school (Neal Cassady). When this man chased after women, it made him jealous. Allen went out west to meet him, but things did not work out.

The therapeutic method called for the therapist to mostly listen, not to confront Allen, who may be too psychologically fragile, and according to the approach to pseudoneurotic-type schizophrenia, could become floridly psychotic if his grandiosity was challenged. For now, just let him talk. At least Allen felt comfortable enough to open up.

A few days later, Allen wrote to his former professor Lionel Trilling. He was getting psychotherapy daily and although it wasn't psychoanalysis, "I expect this to be sufficient and helpful, or hope." He thanked him for his help and offered this postcard as a token of gratitude. "I like it here. I finished cleaning up and selecting forty poems for a book just before I came in."[19]

On July 4, a quiet day at the hospital, Allen stared out the window at the George Washington Bridge and wrote about his dilemma:

I am torn between putting aside my loyalty and love directed to the past (the underworld, the mythical symbols of tragedy, suffering, and solitary grandeur) and the prosaic community of feeling which I might enter by affirming my own allegiance to those bourgeois standards which I had rejected. Yet what do I know of the reality of these bridges and ideas which make up the visible and invisible world? And why am I in the madhouse? How easy is it to reverse these values entirely and consider myself Ginsberg and forbearing wiseman in a nation of madhouses. Neither of these are true. I tire of this thought.[20]

Something about the awesome bridge captured his imagination. A bridge connecting the two worlds of New Jersey and New York reminded him how he was caught between madness and normality. He had to choose, but which would it be? Neither was entirely satisfying, so why choose? Or why not choose the bridge? It appears his thinking was flexible enough to sensibly imagine these different positions and to move between them. This was an indicator of his overall healthy mindedness, as opposed to more rigid or disorganized psychotic thinking. He even painted the bridge in art therapy.

At the next session, Allen said he was surprised at how kindly and considerately people on the unit were treating him. It wasn't nearly as bad as he expected it to be, based on his real and imagined experiences of Naomi at the state hospitals.

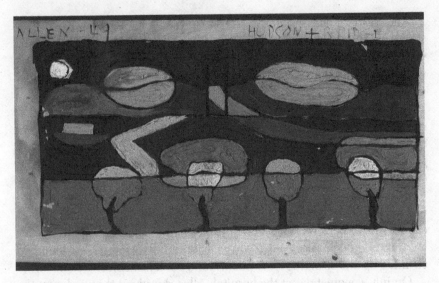

Hudson + Bridge, 1949. © Allen Ginsberg Estate; Courtesy Stanford University Libraries.

He talked about his sexuality. "Patient states that he masturbates almost daily and that his fantasies are of complete submission, self destruction and annihilation on his part." He tried sexual relations with women but couldn't have an erection, and his true feelings were not for them.

He spoke of his mother who is a "paranoid schizophrenic." He said, "She weaned me to her side of reality and I began to hate my father. She spoke against him to me. He treated me like a mother, babied me, and I used to sit on his lap until I was fifteen." Naomi's paranoid delusions, combined with the marital conflict, were very hard on Allen. "She is a hateful fat old bag. It's because of her that I can't feel sexually towards women."

Sexuality comes up a lot in the psychotherapy notes, which in part reflects the overall culture and therapy practices of the day, which were highly influenced by Freudian theory that sexual energies underlie many aspects of human behavior. This includes formulations explaining homosexuality as psychopathology, which Allen went along with. Beyond that, was Allen excessively focused on sexuality?

At the following session, Allen spoke of feeling competitive with his brother. They usually slept together. At ages fifteen to seventeen, he slept with his father, had erections, and masturbated. When his brother went into the service, "he adopted 'blood brothers,' with whom he signed covenants with their own blood." When his mother was acutely psychotic, it was he who had to take care of her.

In a session a few days later, Allen said he regarded neurosis as a sin, a free-will choice of behavior. To change, Allen had to confess. Full responsibility rested within him. Allen said he tried to gain control over a man he likes and get him into a position of submission and dependence. *Allen demonstrates some good insights into this interpersonal pattern, which was not working well for him.*

Allen began occupational therapy and chose oil painting. The occupational therapist noted Allen "wants to produce a perfect, artistic picture with his first try. Hesitates in starting as, 'It doesn't come out the way I picture it in my mind.'" This was also a problem in writing poetry. Would he ever be able to write about more than the ideas in his head? Once he thought the visions had cured him of that, but he was wrong. Now he was seeing if being in the hospital, getting psychotherapy, and facing his own madness would help him descend from such a conceptual position and to write something more alive. Later the same day, Allen discussed with his therapist his frustration in occupational therapy. "He is irritated when his superiority and omnipotence is questioned or threatened." *He appears to be gaining insight into the negative dimensions of his grandiosity.*

Five years ago, Allen met an older man (William Burroughs) who psychoanalyzed him for several years. This man led him into homosexual activity, drugs, and "the underworld." He used morphine, heroin, pantopon, dilaudid, and marijuana; these drugs made him "feel relaxed, extended his fantasies, enabled him to have telepathic communication with others, and sexual frenzies when playing the drums, almost to the point of orgasm." At PI, he thought it was better not to mention any names, given that the FBI was investigating them. Allen also became interested in someone nicknamed Hunky (Herbert Huncke), a burglar and dealer whom he fed, housed, and looked to for ideas.

A few years back Allen was expelled from Columbia for some provocative incidents, "writing obscene words on the buildings, homosexual affairs, and finally association with a homosexual group in which there was a murder." He was readmitted only after seeking psychiatric help. He saw a psychiatrist, but this doctor fired him when he became aware he was doing drugs. In 1948, Allen stopped using drugs after realizing "where it was leading to." He wasn't sure he could trust the PI psychiatrists.

At the next session, Allen reported going out on pass and seeing his brother and mother. He told her he wished she were dead and that he wanted to hit her. He resented her for betraying him. *I don't know any other example of where Allen expressed such aggression toward his mother. But behind the aggression was accumulated hurt and loss as a child injured by her extreme behavior.* "Mother had a contempt for father from the start. She told him he was an ugly duckling. I have a desire to be a little boy again. It's all a matter of the right relationship with my mother. There is a yearning for the lost mother and lost son."

As a child he often wanted to expose himself in public. He didn't know why he did that or what it meant now. *This is a common response in persons who as children were exposed to too much adult sexuality,*[21] *as was the case with Naomi walking around their apartment nude when Allen was young.*

The therapist noted on the ward and in the session that Allen was playing the role of the "model boy" often, "trying to elicit an approving remark or smile from the therapist."

A few days later, Allen told his therapist he had been playing with him. He was intentionally trying to frighten him. But he couldn't get anything out of this therapist. He told the therapist he was not inspired by his "rock like confidence." Can't you be more human? Or are all psychiatrists really so square? The therapist stuck to his rock and offered an interpretation directly challenging Allen's grandiosity. He told Allen he acted this way because otherwise Allen would "be defenseless against 'the world of reality' from which he fled to his world of mystical fantasy."

Allen then said his mother often exposed herself. At age ten he remembered feeling tempted to look. He felt this was a seduction and "that she demanded 'husbandly' responses from him." *Experiences like this are very disturbing for children and can lead to lifelong pain, confusion, and problems with intimacy and sexuality.*[22] *On the other hand, they can be channeled into desires to perform, to please, to provoke, or to command, in ways that can be of personal and social value.*

On July 13, Allen wrote a letter to Jack Kerouac introducing his new friend Carl Solomon, who was "responsible for the disparaging and humorous line: 'There are no intellectuals in madhouses.'"[23] Allen and Solomon became buddies. Solomon turned Allen on to Jean Genet, regaled him with stories of actually seeing Antonin Artaud in Paris, and told tales of a madness far more connected with literature than anything Allen ever heard from Naomi. Allen wrote to Kerouac that Solomon had committed himself to the madhouse at age twenty-one, "present[ing] himself practically at the front door demanding a lobotomy,"[24] a line that would later appear in "Howl." The nurses were miffed with Allen when "he and C.S. go into gales of laughter for no apparent reason." *Solomon's absurd, piercing critique of the madhouse and psychiatry was apparently just what Allen needed.*

Allen and Solomon collaborated on a letter to T. S. Eliot from PI, which read:

> We send our regards and highest genuflections to Mrs. Literary dictator and all the little literary dictators. We are waiting for our marching orders. I may be permitted to speak of myself as a young poet who though passing through a position of temporary and purely transitional sterility, as far as productivity presently counts, will soon be bigger than you.[25]

At PI, Solomon was reading "Hoch and Kalinowski's SHOCK THERAPY (a top secret manual of arms at the hospital) quite openly, after I had put it in the dust-jacket of Anna Balakian's LITERARY ORIGINS OF SURREALISM."[26]

Before the next therapy session, Allen had just completed the Rorschach test in which he had stated "I am the resurrection and the life, come to save the world." The psychologist interpreted this as schizophrenic grandiosity. *Was it really, or was he just playing? Could the clinicians tell the difference?*

In the next therapy session Allen talked about his visions. Each lasted a few minutes. At first he felt on trial.

> I had to break through the wall and take action. I felt something had changed in the physical and mental life of the universe. I was afraid of hurting someone, and of going insane, and wanted to go to an asylum to express myself without hurting anyone. I felt that in the moment of discovery of my own identity I would act blindly. A voice emerged from the writings of Cezanne with the absolute fact of eternal truth.

This is the only mention of a voice before 1958, and it is not at all clear this was a voice he heard so much as read. It is also not the voice of William Blake, which years later Allen would claim he heard. In therapy sessions, Allen said while at PI he was feeling "vague tremblings" and thought another vision might come imminently.

Allen said he didn't want to get admitted to the psychiatric hospital. Instead, he had a "longing to go to jail." There he could get punished and simply rebel. At PI, he was finding things more complicated. He wasn't so sure what to make of this place or of himself any longer. *The therapy was working. Allen was starting to gain some perspective on his grandiosity, learning to take responsibility and work with it.*

A few days later, Allen confessed in psychological testing he had tried to frighten the psychologist by producing bizarre fantasies in his drawings. "They show that human and super-human are the same. There are large genitalia on both male and female to make it a good omen instead of evil. There is ground under to show they were on earth. Adam and Eve in the garden of Eden before the fall with navels and no fig leaves. It was a challenge to draw figures without fig leaves." *Allen could be as provocative as he or they wanted him to be. But he knew he needed more than just being provocative to actually make transformative art.*

At the next session, Allen shared adolescent fantasies of sexual relations with his father as a preadolescent up until age fifteen. He then talked about his paintings in occupational therapy. One pictured the crucifixion. Allen was Christ, and the angel watching him was the therapist.

> I don't know how to choose a theme out of reality. This is me being crucified by psychotherapy, jail, time, from a creature of fantasy to a creature of fact. I see myself worn down by time. I don't feel the present—memories, thoughts, abstractions, fear. Nothing is coherent. I don't feel like doing anything. Just sit here and take no action. I don't know what I'm looking for.

Allen was feeling empty and bored without his so-called fantasies, which occupied him and made life more tolerable.

During several of the following sessions, Allen talked about his visions and how he has used them. He was starting to see the visions as "his defense against his underlying feelings of insecurity and fear of competition." *This was a major insight. He was beginning to change his relationships to the visions.* That same week in occupational therapy, "Ginsberg complained that he didn't like his painting," and "halfway through class he completely smeared out the objects with black paint."

At the next session, Allen brought up a new topic. He talked about practical issues regarding the future. He wanted to get his book of poems published. But he wasn't sure if it was good enough. He wanted to get a real psychoanalysis, which meant he needed a real job and a steady income. He wanted to teach English literature at a university. He was embracing a new and more conventional path into adulthood.

Allen held a male patient's hand on the unit, which frightened him and made him feel guilty. Was something happening here? He wondered if his guilt was a signal he was prepared to change his homosexual feelings and practices were it possible.

At their next meeting, Allen talked about writing a long prose work to establish him in the literary world. When the therapist left the room to answer a phone call, Allen read his note, which said, "I am the greatest poet of my age." When he returned, Allen said, "That sounds pretty paranoid the way you have it there, doesn't it?" *This inadvertent interpretation uttered by Allen was better than anything the therapist could have possibly said. Here, Allen directly challenged his own grandiosity. He was recognizing he had to take responsibility for himself as a madman or poet or whoever he claimed to be. It had taken this therapist and patient over a month to get to the point where this kind of exchange was possible. No doubt the therapist felt bad about what he had to say next.*

"There's something I have to tell you." The therapist would be leaving in two weeks and Allen would be transferred to another therapist. Allen asked for a female therapist. He had never had any contact with an ordinary woman. Just "prostitutes or extremely maladjusted Bohemians."

At their next meeting, Allen talked about his money problems. He didn't have money and felt guilty asking his father for an allowance. He talked about visiting his old friends, with whom he didn't feel as fearful and over-whelmed as previously.

Allen said he was surprised he was not having erotic feelings toward the therapist this week. They superficially discussed Allen's attempts to manip-ulate the therapist. *But no serious attempt was made to analyze or interpret Allen's feelings toward the therapist, which could be too risky.*

In his last week with the first therapist, Allen said he looked forward to working with a female therapist. He even dreamed of having intercourse with a woman. "The woman was the wife of the man who had attempted to psychoanalyze him several years ago" (William Burroughs's wife, Joan Voll-mer). This was his first dream of this sort, and it encouraged him. The therapist chose to not analyze the dream.

After several months of not getting much writing done, Allen had resumed working on some poems and was waiting for the reviews of his first book manuscript.

At the last meeting with the first therapist, Allen was looking forward to beginning with the female therapist. Over the weekend, he saw one of his homosexual friends and they slept together. He was not satisfied and bored. He did not want to be "involved emotionally" with him anymore. "Since this is the first homosexual contact Ginsberg has had since hospitalization, it is felt that perhaps he was in part testing the therapist's reaction to the situation. The therapist remained noncommittal about the relationship and left Ginsberg's conduct to his own discretion."

Allen liked his first therapist the least of all three. He was a straight, young guy, rigid, square and said little back to Allen. Allen later said: "In our first conversation, I was trying to explain to him where I was at and I said, 'It's like the telephone is alive.' Now, had he been a doctor of any kind of wit, like they had in the old days, he would have said, 'And what does the telephone say, Allen?' But instead he got annoyed and stamped his foot and said, 'The telephone is not alive.' So he didn't know where I was at at all."[27]

I had the opportunity to speak with this psychiatrist. In his defense, I believe he was trying to let Allen speak and to prevent himself from being provoked or manipulated. He feared if he got provoked by Allen and said something wrong, it would only amplify Allen's psychological fragility and lead to a marked deterioration in schizophrenic symptoms. He thought psychosis underlay Allen's preoccupations with criminality and art, and he didn't want to push him further into psychosis. It took over one month for the therapist to enable Allen to deliver, quite inadvertently, an interpretation regarding his grandiosity. Sometimes accidents like these are better than anything the therapist could have intentionally said. They didn't have time to see what more they could achieve in the therapy, but it was a promising start in terms of Allen taking some distance from his visions and grandiosity.

Allen wasted no time challenging his second therapist. He asked about her qualifications and said his main problem was his homosexuality. He did not feel she could help him very much. He needed someone older and more experienced because of his "psychotic breakthroughs." Was a young woman doctor really up to the task? Allen wanted to be changed from his homosexuality. He wanted to be more of a "human being" and to have systems that did not shift. "I've been building systems. There have been moments of ecstasy. But I think too much. I don't feel." "I expect a panacea," he said, laughing at himself. Alright, he would accept the therapist and her therapy. *He was learning to back down from his grandiose expectations of himself and others.* He told the therapist about what he was writing. "It's a great book," Allen proclaimed.

At their second meeting, Allen discussed his docility. His father often praised him for being sensible and said he should not show his reactions to his mother's psychotic behavior. In the therapy, Allen turned this dynamic on its head. Allen tried to bait the therapist about her manners. Like the prior therapist, she was not easily provoked.

Instead of sharing something he wanted to say, in the therapy he tried to force the therapist to determine what they talked about. But unlike the prior therapist, she talked back and offered interpretations. The therapist told Allen about these behaviors. This is your space to talk about what you want, how you want. Take responsibility instead of pretending you have none. "He offered to show the therapist his poems, then hesitated, and finally was able to discuss his need to impress her. He realized the inconsistency of wishing to explain and deny his illness at once."

At their next meeting, Allen spoke of his "psychotic mother" and "patronizing father." They put conflicting demands on him, personally and politically. He was a socialist. She a communist. He a responsible professional. She mad and unemployable. "I had a messianic complex. To be president, run things." He said he couldn't feel. He thought this was because of the disapproval of emotional expression at home. As for his homosexuality, Allen linked it with his mother's sexual demands on him. He had tried lots of things to feel more settled. Intellectualization did not help, and drugs made him even "more perplexed." Allen asked: Could he see the therapist more often?

At their following meeting, Allen was less hostile and talked more freely. He spoke of an intense homosexual relationship. He described his passivity and his provocation of humiliations from Neal Cassady. He found in his partner the qualities he lacked in himself: aggression and irresponsibility. The relationship was very unsatisfying.

Allen recalled childhood scenes in which a playmate taunted him over his mother's madness. Just then he challenged the doctor, "What do you want? I feel we're not getting anywhere." They talked about it and agreed he wanted her to call his bluff but was afraid she was not smart enough. *He projected his own insecurity onto her.*

Allen showed the therapist his poetry. The therapist thought it demonstrated technical skill but tended to be obscure and pretentious. Allen admitted these shortcomings. But he felt the virtues of the work should cause the readers to overlook the defects. Was this growing confidence or a return of grandiosity? His poems were being considered by a publisher this week.

Allen spoke of his mother's illness. "He made it clear at the start that he looked upon mental illness as a definite entity; that for him everyone in the world is sane or insane; He is having a little trouble placing himself in this scheme. He described his 'visions,' stating clearly that these are the experiences which previous therapists labeled 'mad.'" *His view of madness was still limited by binary and individualistic approaches.*

He recounted an episode that had occurred several years ago. After some weeks of living all alone, he went into a bookshop at Columbia, and suddenly the quality of his experience changed. "Everything had significance. The universe opened like a rose." He felt able to understand the nature of things and to experience them directly. The ecstatic condition lasted only a few minutes. "He did not find the episode unpleasant. But in discussing it he was concerned that it should be so transient." The therapist pointed out that "there was nothing unacceptable to others in the fact he occasionally experienced things in a different way from other times." Allen became angry and pointed out he did expect some kind of response to the very mystical manner in which he described it. "Yes, I want everyone else to accept it too."

At their next meeting, Allen and the therapist continued their discussion of the visions. Allen amended his statement that they had all been pleasant. At times the world had changed not pleasantly but frighteningly. He asked, "What am I doing here?" and felt terrified. The therapist recorded: "Again when it was suggested that the unusual intensity of experience may be a state in which his usual intellectualizing defenses were not operative, Allen was disappointed. He wanted these to be considered special and prophetic states." Special states, not just explainable psychological phenomena.

The therapist then confronted Allen on his need to feel different. In response, Allen began an account of his "antisocial" friends and experiences. The therapist noted that when she pushed him away from psychosis, he would shift more into antisocial behavior. *This reflected her formulation of pseudoneurotic-type schizophrenia, which said Allen was using antisocial defenses against an underlying psychosis.* Perhaps, she thought, this was also provoked by the FBI, who had come to the ward to interview Allen.

At their next meeting, Allen told more stories about his relationships with his "antisocial" friends. One was "a kind of father to him." Another couple was a "kind of mother and father." He spoke of the friend who systematically "psychoanalyzed" him (William Burroughs). He admired the independence and self-affirmation of his friends and delighted in his college experiences. He got into trouble with the authorities at school. It sounded to the therapist as if Allen had been seduced and exploited by his friends and needlessly punished by authorities. She kind of liked him.

The therapist was struck by how he described his admission that "I was queer," as though his homosexuality were an inherent quality. She was taught by Dr. Hoch that homosexuality was a symptom of some other disorder, but she wasn't sure if she really believed that. Allen spoke of his father's horror at his sexual orientation. His father couldn't accept that his being queer involved anything more than perverted sexual acts.

Allen was interviewed by the chief of service in preparation for the upcoming case conference focused on him. He resented the chief questioning him about his "antisocial" activities, which the chief seemed to consider his primary symptoms. The therapist and patient talked about this at length, trying to steer past his intellectualizations. Call them what you want, said the therapist, you really have been engaged in criminal activities.

Allen discussed several vivid dreams of homosexual contact. In one, "he was in an airplane with a prominent critic, a friend of his: they were lovers though no act took place. 'He told me I would have to choose between society and my career . . . like my father.'" He called these "crazy" dreams. The therapist confronted him on his use of terms. She said he uses "crazy" and "psychotic" as labels and as weapons and shields against his doctors and against understanding what the dreams could mean. She was trying to help Allen to get a perspective on and abandon his defensive use of madness.

That same week, the nurses reported that Allen "attended party and seemed to enjoy it—nurses got him to dance and he did fairly well, except in a very exaggerated feminine way slowed way down, dancing on tips of toes, etc."

In the following session, Allen talked about concerns over his relationships with his brother and father. His brother had told his father about Allen's activities and relationships. His father demanded he give up his friends and homosexual behavior. This was unworkable, but the therapist discussed with Allen that he too was making the situation impossible. He wanted not only his father's help and love but also his approval, while he was unwilling to give up anything to obtain it. Allen declared, "I guess I want to be the Queen of May!" The therapist said back to him: "Does being homosexual mean having to take the extreme social risks you have taken?" Allen said he knows he doesn't get any real satisfaction from it. Well then why can't you find another way to be gay?

A few days later in therapy, Allen tried to work out some acceptable arrangement with his father. He wanted his father's and the therapist's approval. But he approached both with a refusal to compromise, only seeing what he himself wanted. The therapist said, if it were her, she might allow some activity, but it didn't mean she condoned it. Don't expect any more than that from your father.

Allen spoke of family life. In childhood he felt close to his father and disloyal when he sided with his ill mother. It was all or nothing. He said that's just the way it is with him. His father would never approve of his homosexuality but might tolerate it under certain conditions. He needed to figure out what the conditions might be. But it was not only his being gay but also the conflict between his parents, which had complicated his relationship with his father.

The therapist recorded: "He somehow felt responsible for his mother's attack on his father, and felt very guilty and desperate when he saw his father cry. His father would weep for sympathy but he never knew quite how to give it. He would sit on his father's lap and feel an emotion he now regards as sexual. When, at about ten years, he discovered his father was unfaithful to his mother, he felt personally betrayed."

He asked the therapist to see his father and to advocate for him. "OK, you two fight it out. I withdraw." Allen calmed down and discussed the terms he was prepared to offer his father: "to stay out of trouble with the law, to not make financial demands, and to sincerely attempt to work out the sexual problem. He asked that his father not make demands he can't fulfill, that is, not prescribe his friends or sex life."

In their next meeting, with Louis joining them, Allen succeeded in making a bargain with his father. Allen could live in his father's home after he remarries. His father will support him for a year while he tries to write his novel. He has to take his work seriously and stay out of trouble. Allen was proud they had worked this out and asked for more privileges on the unit so he could start writing immediately.

In their individual meeting, Allen began, "Let's talk about sex," as though his family problems were solved. All his sexual fantasies were with men. He recalled several early sexual experiences. "He remembered too that once his mother offered to mend his trousers. To bend him over her knee. He refused with great embarrassment, feeling that this was a sexual situation." This was, unbeknownst to either Allen or his therapist, their last meeting.

The therapist then met with Allen's father individually, with Allen's consent. Louis was told his son had a serious mental illness. The therapist gave no specific diagnosis, since he would probably identify this with his wife's deteriorated paranoid schizophrenia. He was told his emotional problems showed in many ways, including the behavior disorder and the symptom of homosexuality. Louis' main concern was his son's "homosexualism . . . did you tell him how degrading it is?" The therapist told Allen's father he had to accept his son's homosexuality, even if that meant knowing he put penises in his mouth. The therapist noted: "Finally he openly asked and received reassurance that the perversion was not his fault." Allen's father was very critical of the hospital and the therapist. The therapist wrote he had no insight whatsoever into the nature of mental illness.

Allen liked the second therapist best. He never forgot what she did with his father, how she stood up for him and insisted that Louis tolerate Allen's homosexual behavior. "That was really quite out there for those days," Allen recalled with me. *She took Hoch and Polatin's teachings that homosexuality was a symptom of something else—and therefore must be tolerated—a step further by insisting his family learn to live with it.*

She was also unsparing in her observations of Allen himself. She drew his attention to his attempts at manipulating interpersonal relationships and his insufficient awareness of his own feelings and behavior. She was steadfast in her confrontation regarding the visions and madness. She told him the mere fact of having this experience was not enough; it was what he did with it. That was hard on him, and she sensed it. She accepted his request to stand up to his father regarding his homosexuality. She helped Allen through confronting both him and his father. It got her fired from the case, but it was worth it.

In the next session, Allen was told he had a new therapist. There is only one plausible explanation: Louis Ginsberg had the female therapist taken off Allen's case. He was so upset by the meeting with the therapist that he immediately complained to the unit chief, who made the reassignment.

Allen immediately undertook evaluating the new therapist by plying him with questions. Allen said he had been involved in "mystic symbolism" but that "after some therapy he is much more at peace, does less subjective living and more objective living and is generally getting along much better." He wanted to write but hadn't yet written anything significant. He planned to start by writing a novel. He wanted to be analyzed so as to be libidinally redirected and to have more peace from neurotic symptomatology.

In their second session, Allen went over more of his history and showed the doctor some of his paintings and poems. The poem he shared was a "long totally abstract, incomprehensible poem about his relationship with his father." The therapist tried to "get" them and liked the "language" and the "figures" but found the poem to be "lacking in continuity" and "meaningless."

At their next meeting, Allen reviewed his life history from adolescence through college. He was always a misfit. In high school, he had no friends so would sit home and read. He transferred schools for his junior year and ran for school office. He was attracted to men. He went to college in the city but was expelled because of trouble with homosexual characters and entered the Merchant Marines. As a merchant mariner he started to have "cosmic feelings in which he would identify with the clouds and the sea and would read unusual meanings in these objects." In Dakar he took heroin and would "get the pimps to procure opiates or small boys for him." He returned to school and eventually graduated.

His major problem at the present time (according to him) is that he wants to write his novel but he has difficulty composing it. In each of his creative acts he tends towards the fantastic rather than the objective: for example, his paintings are almost entirely fantastic and he shies away from copying or drawing real objects. Same is true of his literary accomplishments in which he shies away from objective narrative tales towards poetic imagery and magical creations. Consequently it's not surprising he's having difficulty writing an autobiographical novel which would require considerable more objectivity than this patient has. He realizes this problem and his approach to the solution of it is to procure a private room where he can be alone in order to write.

The therapist thought Allen had transferred well to him. He shared his paintings, of which he produced one or two a day. He also shared some poems.

Ginsberg's poems were unusually good and were fairly short, introspective poems dealing with his own personal problems or with the central theme of "unity of being." This is the first poetry which the examiner has seen in this patient which seems to be reasonable and well thought out. Allen seems deeply pleased the examiner would listen to his poetry and much of the interview time has been spent in discussing the content of the poetry as relating to his sickness.

Next, the therapist and social worker met with Allen to do long-range planning for his eventual discharge. He had been telling the social worker he wanted to write a novel and needed the time. His father had agreed to support him, but the doctor wanted Allen to get a job. They decided he should try to get his old job back at the Associated Press. The plan was for Allen to go live with his father and stepmother as soon as they moved into their new house in March.

Allen was rumored to be in the company of his homosexual and criminal friends, and this led to a reconsideration of his status on the unit. Further investigation showed he had only been with his homosexual friends but not his criminal friends, so his status was not changed.

Allen spoke of his plans for attacking his "homosexual symptomatology." It involved a plan for a threesome with the woman friend of his bisexual friend O'Neil. First have sex with her, then transfer that skill to other women. Allen then spoke of his "relation to his psychotic mother," and the therapist noted: "There seem to have been a number of unusual genital shocks by the mother. Ginsberg early identified with her for reasons which we are not able as yet to ascertain. His father does not seem to be a very moving force in Ginsberg's early life." *Genital shock appears to be an archaic term from psychoanalysis relating to trauma of a sexual nature, such as how a child might adversely respond to exposure to adult sexuality.*

Allen was now writing three to four hours each day and claimed to be making progress. In the next therapy meeting, Allen's dreams were explored. One dream showed strong homosexual attachments to the therapist and incestuous feelings toward his mother.

Allen and the therapist discussed the changes in his art. When his freedom on the unit was threatened, he produced "very dark, black, depressive works, one of which was a crucifix of black with a black figure on it in a small halo light, surrounded by darkness and gloominess. Ginsberg made the spontaneous association of intrauterine existence, the crucifix in the uterus. The therapist interpreted this as a symptom of regression." *Allen was able to respond to the therapist's interpretation, thus showing he could stop backsliding into psychosis when faced with frustrating reality.*

On October 24, 1949, Allen wrote in his journal:

> The whole bare world of smoke and twisted steel around my head in a railroad car and my mind wandering past the rest into futurity. I saw the sun go down as if in a carnal and primeval world, leaving darkness to cover my railroad train because the other side of the world was waiting for the dawn. Later I saw a rainbow which is a rare form of God. I want to live in a rainbow, in will and in womb.[28]

Allen had a difficult week with several setbacks. Jack Kerouac's mother called him a jailbird and told him not to come around anymore, and his book of poems was rejected by two publishers. He became more depressed. "Felt that life really had very little to offer for him. Wished actively to become schizophrenic so that he would not have to face reality, stopped writing, stopped producing in therapy, and in general regressed and slipped back." He then started getting openly hostile toward the therapist. "Soon he began to blame the therapist for his own incurability."

The therapist discussed Allen's transference. "Eventually Ginsberg began to realize that he was primarily a very passive person whose aggressive urges were markedly frustrated and inhibited." *Instead of taking responsibility, he blamed others, such as the therapist.*

> It developed that he was actually in love with the examiner and that he was ashamed to tell the examiner about his feelings and that since he felt that the examiner could not reciprocate this love that he,

Ginsberg, would then punish the examiner for not loving him. The masochistic nature of Ginsberg was discussed at length and he was showed how a patient may by projection provoke injustice or provoke mistreatment by the examiner in lieu of the expected love feelings. By Friday Ginsberg was out of his depression, was more positively related to the examiner and treatment was progressing rapidly.

It is a positive indicator that Allen responded to interpretation. "He wrote a long creative poem which is quite good and the poem was analyzed to show its components of incestuous ideas coupled with castration fear, which Ginsberg spontaneously produced." Handwritten notes on the bottom of the progress note page mention "genital shock," "castration," and "Shrouded Stranger."

The next session's notes I quote in full:

Today Ginsberg brought up memories of his mother, naked, wearing a "G-string" [Kotex belt], fat, and with long breasts. He describes the memory as very vivid and goes on to add that she was menstruating, using a thin inadequate pad which did not cover her vagina. Blood was on her knees. He saw his mother this way five years ago but feels he has seen similar scenes earlier.

He felt anger and disgust at this "violent, womanly process." He associated bandages with Kotex and then began to talk about his appendectomy at age 7. He equated menstruation with his own operation. He described his aunts showing him their abdominal scars in an effort to persuade him to be operated.

He described his preoperative memories, enuresis in bed with father and operation as result of investigation re: enuresis (retaliation?) He described pleasurable erotic feelings when being examined per rectum by surgeons. He remembers being examined post operatively and regarding his "appendix scar" as a bandaged wound "like mother's vagina." A surgeon snipped off granulation tissue from the incision site and Ginsberg felt hurt and punished. He equates "incision" with "vagina" and "operation" with "castration."

"He felt betrayed by father and regarded the surgery as punishment. The surgeon he regarded as a punishing father, saying "he castrated my operation." . . . He ended the interview saying, "This operation made me like other women. It gave me a vagina."

Psychosexual material like this would be of high interest to the therapist in an era dominated by Freudian theory. Allen described memories of exposure to maternal and other female sexuality. Allen also offered his own analysis of what made him a homosexual and shaped his sexual identity. These are described in a vivid, though not psychotic manner. Did sharing these memories of exposure to female sexuality somehow unburden Allen? It is impossible to know, but for whatever reason something shifted.

At the next session, "Patient feels much more 'real' and announced he has decided to abandon the pursuit of the 'unity of being' and the 'visionary world.'" *Allen was making a big turn away from madness and visions, and towards reality, but as a poet.* "He volunteered that a job was a good idea and seemed to actually want to seek one. All in all he seemed better motivated and more normal today than ever before." *Getting a job was one part of what the psychiatrists and his father had wanted from Allen. But what of his writing?*

On November 15, 1949, Allen journaled: "This is the one and only firmament; therefore it is the absolute world; there is no other world. The circle is complete; I am living in eternity. The ways of this world are the ways of Heaven. The work of this world is the work of Heaven. The love of this world is the love of Heaven."[29] A few days later, Allen said he now enjoyed "living in reality." He was following real pursuits instead of "fantastic ones." He was actively looking for a job.

"He still holds hope of finding a woman who will lead him into heterosexuality . . ."

"Psychotherapy proceeds regularly and Ginsberg by now has great insight and is very cooperative."

The therapy was well underway. Allen was focusing on "who is the shabby stranger, who were his major psychic identifications with, and why were his fantasies so often about his father, whom he feels erotic toward." "In general Ginsberg is very taken with the idea of living in reality now and in general spends a great deal of time talking about his new found pleasures." Still, he hadn't tried to change his homosexual behavior or give up his drug use.

The social worker noted she had met with Allen six times thus far. He was less anxious about his mother and more focused on finding a job. The social worker helped him make contact with his old employer, but they did not want him back. She also helped him make inquiries about the papers of his that had been confiscated by the police. "These papers contain patient's deepest doubts, fears, extreme ideas, etc.—including suicide notes which patient wrote over a period of time. Patient is anxious about these papers being in the hands of the police."

In mid-December, Allen was planning to go home for the holidays. He hoped to find a job. His father was contacted and told to be more tolerant "of the patient's wishes toward homosexual desires." His father said he feared he would go to bed with boys "in his own home." On New Year's Eve, 1949, Allen was out on pass and able to control acting on his symptoms.

A few days later, Allen became very interested in the prospect of taking mescaline and mentioned it several times to the therapist. Mescaline was being offered to patients as part of a study being conducted on the ward. "This has been interpreted as a wish to return to his previous unreality state and as a general wish to resist therapy. Ginsberg showed some resentment towards this interpretation but accepts it." At their next session, Allen focused on the mescaline issue and used it to resist freely associating in therapy. He hadn't yet found a job. His book had been rejected by several publishers. In retaliation, he took a copy of someone else's book from one publisher.

At the following meeting, Allen resisted getting a job and moving to Paterson when his father remarried. "He equates this with a return of conventionality which he deeply loathes." "It is the aim of the therapist at the present time to get him out of the hospital and into a job of some sort so he can begin to write in his spare-time. After his exit from the hospital he will be asked to give up his symptoms of homosexuality while he can be treated for it."

A new social worker started on the case, and Allen interrogated him. Have you read up on my case? Yes, I have. The social worker asked Allen about his plans for writing. Allen said it might be difficult because he didn't have much drive to write. The social worker asked, "Are you regretful for getting rid of your problems?" Allen laughed. "I miss heaven and the spirit, but I had to choose. I would rather lose these things and be accepted."

Allen was behaving jealously of the therapist's other patients on the ward. The therapist believed this was related to his father's imminent remarriage and "to his actual reliving of a semi-oedipal situation." Already, Allen was calling her "mother."

By early February 1950, the team decided to discharge Allen within the month. Allen expressed feeling rejected by the therapist and the hospital. The only area of present symptoms was homosexuality. He was not asked to give this up, though he said he wants to eventually. "One of his homosexual friends, an ex-patient here, has recently decided to be married. This gives Ginsberg a great deal of hope and he believes he himself will eventually be able to make the transition." Allen agreed to continue seeing the third therapist as an outpatient after his discharge.

The therapist wrote his final progress note:

Allen Ginsberg, age 23, was admitted June 29, 1949 because of anti-social behavior involving drugs, homosexuality, and involvement in a gang of thieves. He was found to be of high intelligence with marked artistic abilities and somewhat unusual philosophical beliefs. He considered himself one of the greatest living poets with marked feelings of superiority. He also had visionary experiences of a schizophrenic nature. He made progress with psychotherapy and at the end of his hospital stay had no schizophrenic symptoms, drug habits, or criminal associations although he did continue to have homosexual relations.

The third therapist was more like the second therapist than the first, extending and deepening the exploration and confronting Allen where he needed to be confronted. Allen may not have been as impressed with him as with the second therapist, but he agreed to keep seeing him after the hospitalization. This therapist appeared to have a more conventional view of homosexuality as symptom needing treatment, but at least he didn't undo the helpful arrangement with Louis. In their sessions, Allen spoke about his early life history and experiences with Naomi, especially in one particularly revealing session. These were interpreted from the point of view of "genital shock," which was as close as any 1950s Columbia-trained psychiatrist was able to come to the phenomenon of childhood trauma.[30]

What seemed especially productive about Allen's meetings with the third therapist was their focus on his paintings and poetry. The therapist was genuinely open to and interested in Allen's artworks, trying to understand his work and respecting him as an aspiring poet, and he appeared honest with Allen about his opinions. Then one month into the work with the third therapist, Allen suddenly announced he had given up on the vision world (but not poetry), which was a major step forward. Whether or not this was attributable to his sharing his traumatic memories of female sexuality cannot be known. With the encouragement and advice of this therapist, Allen also made some productive starts in the "Shrouded Stranger" poems, which I will discuss later in this chapter.

Allen said he appreciated how the third psychiatrist "had my diagnosis changed from psychotic or schizophrenic or something terrible like that to 'extreme but socially average neurosis' which gave me a lot of confidence, because since then I've had formal credentials of not being insane."[31]

On February 27, 1950, Allen was discharged from PI. He left feeling positive about his hospital stay. Living in Paterson was not going to be so bad. His therapist would help him settle into a new routine and, most importantly, to keep working on his writing. They apparently met for more than two years, until the doctor moved his office to Park Avenue and raised his fees from $5 a week to $450 a month.

Looking back forty years later, Allen said he didn't think much had happened at PI. Based on my review of his medical record, my opinion is that much of consequence did happen, mostly in the psychotherapy. Allen might have shuffled off bourgeois style into PI rather than Rikers and certainly did not suffer anywhere near as much as Naomi. Yet there was a gravity to his personal and mental health problems and his challenges as an aspiring artist, and these matters shifted as a consequence of being at PI.

At the time, all the professionals involved in Allen's treatment, as well as his family and his friends and certainly Allen himself, felt much was at stake. All were thinking he was having serious life problems and quite possibly a serious psychotic illness, for which mental health assessment and care was urgently needed. Even Allen, who at times thought he had broken through with his visions, wasn't entirely sure this wasn't the first sign of an impending psychotic illness.

The psychiatrists telling him he was not becoming schizophrenic like his mother was very helpful to him. Because he really feared this possibility, this alone made the psychiatric admission worthwhile. "They certified I was not mad," Allen told me. "More of a real neurotic who was pseudopsychotic, you might say."[32] By the time of his release, reassured about his prognosis, he was in the advantageous position of having come very close to mental illness, madness, and the experience of the psychiatric hospital, such that he could rightfully claim to be their witness.

Yet the psychiatrists also appeared to be in agreement that eventually Allen would decompensate to become a full-blown schizophrenic, even though they didn't tell him so. I think this is in part because his clinicians, like me in reading the record years later, were so impressed by Allen's abilities to express inner experiences of a near-psychotic nature. The clinicians thought they were accurately getting an early glimpse of Allen's emerging psychosis. Perhaps instead they were falling under the sway of his brilliant expressivity.

Some creative artists have unique access to inner experiences denied to most others. When they express them, it can seem as if they are expressing the inner turmoil of mental illness when in fact they might not be. This puts creative artists at heightened risk of being diagnosed with a serious mental illness they do not have. Several more recent well-designed studies have shown among creative artists a higher prevalence of some types of mental illness, including depression, bipolar disorder, and trauma-related disorders.[33] Given that at the time Allen was not a recognized poet or artist, it is hard to blame the psychiatrists. In diagnosing a serious mental illness, they erred on the side of caution. There is something to be said for that practice, provided of course that you don't subject such persons to lobotomies or other injurious treatments—a very big "if" in an inpatient psychiatric hospital in the late 1940s.

The psychiatrists and other staff respected his literary ambitions and, though no literary experts, used what knowledge and skills they had to be of some help to the aspiring writer. Despite Allen telling them he was the greatest poet of his age and them acknowledging his brilliance, it seems safe to say they never imagined how far their patient would go in his literary achievements.

But are psychiatrists supposed to unconditionally believe every patient's boasts or delusional grandiosity? Just because they didn't recognize their admittedly brilliant patient as a literary star does not necessarily mean something helpful wasn't achieved there for Allen in the psychotherapy or the experience of hospitalization.

The professionals involved in Allen's hospitalization also did not have the luxury of retrospection or years of reflection and study to commit to their own understandings. They had to act immediately to be of help in Allen's real-life situation. They were thinking of the patient before them and how to be helpful, not about his possible place in literature.

The psychiatric record indicates Allen did valuable psychological work in his hospitalization in a number of areas. Without psychiatric hospitalization, it is quite possible Allen may not have survived his self-destructive tendencies. Being in the hospital and receiving psychotherapy enabled Allen to make substantial changes to the place of madness in his identity, to his grandiosity, and to how he managed his life as a young adult.

Allen's achievement as an artist was not simply having visions. It involved an ongoing, highly difficult, and risky process of learning to rework the visions and other experiences with madness and mental illness, to adopt and live with mad muses, and to find the language to communicate all this through poetry. This included a helpful assist from psychiatry to keep from being swallowed up by the destructive dimensions of madness while courageously and brilliantly accessing and witnessing it.

Allen was interested in psychiatry and involved with psychiatrists and organized psychiatry in various ways throughout his lifetime. That is part of the reason, I believe, he welcomed and encouraged my project and provided me with mentorship. Having been given the opportunity to review his psychiatric records, I was able to develop new perspectives on several key issues: the rationale for hospitalization, the assessments and diagnoses, and the course of treatment.

The hospitalization helped Allen keep in check a tendency toward risky and potentially self-destructive behaviors. This was one of the most helpful aspects of the hospitalization, although the psychiatrists at PI did not explicitly focus on this problem. They were much more focused on the problems of psychosis, homosexuality, and antisocial behavior. They hypothesized that all his problems were driven by an underlying psychosis. On the other hand, one of Allen's biographers detailed his preoccupations with death in his late adolescent and early adult years.[34] None were too sure about what drove this behavior. But being at PI helped put a stop to his tendencies toward criminality and suicidality.

In 1962, Hoch and Polatin published follow-up research on pseudoneurotic-type schizophrenia.[35] Only 10 percent of diagnosed patients went on to have chronic schizophrenia, and 44 percent had good outcomes. Allen, whom the doctors predicted would be in the worst 10 percent, was in fact in the best 44 percent. We do not know whether creative endeavors were also present in some of those other 44 percent and what other factors seemed to play a role in their survival and recovery.

Currently nobody uses the diagnosis the PI doctors gave to Allen. Today psychiatrists have new ways of thinking about diagnoses lying between psychosis and neurosis. They do not think these are all schizophrenics in the making. Instead, they regard this as a heterogeneous group composed of several different subgroupings, including trauma-related disorders and personality disorders. If Allen presented today like he did at PI, he would most likely be given several provisional diagnoses. Those would likely include some kind of psychotic disorder, such as schizophreniform disorder, which presents with psychotic symptoms of a relatively short duration.

He likely would not be given a specific trauma diagnosis, such as post-traumatic stress disorder (PTSD). That is because it is widely accepted that trauma in childhood and adolescence often results not in classic PTSD or any other diagnosis but in behavioral, interpersonal, or personality characteristics beyond what current diagnoses capture.[36]

Yet diagnosis is very important in psychiatry because it directs the course of treatment. In Allen's case, the diagnosis caused the treatment team to prioritize psychotic symptoms in the first place, as well as antisocial behavior, homosexuality, and drug use, which were considered his other symptoms.

Was he psychotic? In a way no, given that he didn't hear voices where there was no speaker and didn't have delusions; that is, he did not hold false beliefs. Yet in another way, he was psychotic, given how he experienced what is called a "delusional atmosphere"—a marked transformation in the perception of the world and of himself, experienced with "uncanny particularity."[37]

The PI psychiatrists' diagnosis did not lead the treaters to prioritize trauma or grief, which in my opinion were central issues for Allen at the time. Their diagnosis also limited the amount and type of family-focused work with Allen's family. His problem was viewed as largely an individual and not a family matter, which is different from how schizophrenia later came to be seen. At PI in the 1980s, William McFarlane developed the psychoeducation family approach to schizophrenia, which had a major impact on psychiatry's ability to treat serious mental illness.[38] This approach works with families to strengthen their capacity to support and advocate for their loved one. But in 1949, Allen's treaters did not have the benefit of another half-century of psychiatric knowledge—and of the cultural impact of Allen's poetry upon psychiatry itself.

When I first read the psychotherapy notes from the PI record in 1986, I didn't know what to think, because I was not yet trained or experienced in psychotherapy. I dedicated myself to learning the theory and practice of psychotherapy in part so I could understand what happened with Allen, which took me at least ten years. When I later assessed the notes, I did so from the vantage point of experience in practicing, researching, supervising, and being in psychotherapy. From this more experienced position, I must honestly say I have mixed opinions about Allen's psychotherapy treatment at PI. On the one hand, I believe the psychiatrists can take credit for some treatment successes. On the other hand, there were clear limitations to their approach.

Here's what they got right. The psychotherapy helped Allen back away from but not totally reject the visions. His preoccupation with the visions had gotten to a point that was unhealthy, unproductive, and veering too close to a paralyzing psychosis. Many years later, in the poem "The Change: Kyoto-Tokyo Express" from 1963, Allen would again renounce the visions, another effort to push back against a preoccupation he regarded as problematic.

The psychotherapy also helped Allen distance himself from antisocial behavior—his involvement with criminals and drug addicts, who were potentially dangerous for him. Although he remained lifelong friends with Huncke and others he didn't again live with or tie his fate to them.

The psychotherapy also helped Allen be better aware of and more responsible for his own emotions and behaviors. He showed some signs he could better manage relationships and his own priorities and commitments. He became less invested in his own grandiosity.

The psychotherapy also helped motivate Allen to get some poetry written, which I will discuss shortly.

Finally, the psychotherapy helped his father and stepmother tolerate, if not eventually accept, his homosexuality. They didn't have to love it as long as they let it be.

There were several major limitations to the treatment. The psychiatrists were too focused on psychosexual issues and widely regarded homosexuality as a symptom of psychiatric illness. This reflected the narrow and bigoted opinions of the day.

The psychiatrists were completely unaware Allen had signed consent for his mother's lobotomy and therefore did not address his traumatization from the lobotomy, let alone from being a home caregiver to his psychotic mother. This is a consequence of psychiatry's then extreme ethical lapse regarding lobotomies and insensitivity to the impact of real-life adversities and traumas upon their patients.

The psychiatrists also paid far too little attention to family issues in the wake of his mother's serious mental illness, including his relationship with each parent. Psychiatry has had a tendency to focus almost exclusively on the individual and not enough upon the family dynamic, which itself can dramatically change when a family member has serious mental illness.

If Allen's treatment team had said his homosexuality was normal and not part of an illness, this could have saved Allen years of trying to get himself to be something he wasn't. As it was, five years later in San Francisco, his psychiatrist Phillip Hicks told him to go ahead and be gay, and this was a major relief for Allen.

When I read the psychotherapy progress notes from PI, I note innumerable times where the therapist or the patient shifted the focus to a sexual issue. For example, their concern about his mother's psychosis became limited to a concern regarding its impact upon his sexual identity. The therapists' preoccupation with sexual issues in the therapy followed from their assumption that homosexuality was an illness and that pansexuality was a key problem for the pseudoneurotic patient. If the therapist and the patient hadn't been talking about sexual issues so much, they likely would have been focused more on other dimensions of the experience of being raised by a psychotic mother. This could have been very helpful to Allen, who later in life had much turmoil and conflict with Peter Orlovsky, another person beset by madness, whom many thought Allen put up with for far too long than was good for either.

In the psychotherapy Allen often blamed his mother. There was little sense of him trying to understand her, her illness, her treatment, and their impact upon the family. I see this as the responsibility of the therapists to reframe, redirect, and educate their patient. This was an important missed opportunity. Of course, despite this lack of focus in the psychotherapy, Allen was not done with her as an actual person in his life or with her as his muse. She would come to be a huge presence in his writings, unnamed yet enlivening "Howl" and as the main focus of "Kaddish."

A key element missing from the accounts in the medical record is an understanding of Allen's experiences of traumas and losses from his childhood through young adulthood. In my opinion, we cannot adequately understand Allen's involvement in criminal and drug behaviors and preoccupation with suicidality and death without understanding his difficult life experiences with his severely mentally ill mother.

What we know from other children raised with psychotic parents is that these experiences likely left the young Allen with deeply troubling feelings: It was all his fault; he had no right to a good life; he should live and suffer like her.[39] These emotions could drive him to involve himself in more and more extreme situations. For many exposed to traumas like these, life can become a downward spiral through misery, self-loathing, risk taking, and self-destruction, leading toward horrible outcomes including untimely death.

Admission to the psychiatric hospital and interrupting this spiral was the right thing to do. However, the psychiatrists working within the paradigms of the day were too narrow in their focus. The driving question should not only have been "Is he schizophrenic?" but also "Was he traumatized and if so how?" and "How can he stay safe, recover, and become stronger?" In those days, psychiatrists lacked a way of formulating the case around maternal psychosis leading to childhood trauma and further mental health consequences as an adult. Admitting him to the hospital was more important than the accuracy of the reason for admission.

If Allen had received trauma- and grief-focused psychotherapy, how would this have changed his condition or his poetry? I cannot help but think it would have helped him be less troubled as a person, a friend, and a partner. He would have likely been more on top of the "madness" he let into his personal relationships, sometimes with unfortunate consequences. Many years later, I was talking about this with Bob Rosenthal and Peter Hale, who both worked closely with Allen for many years. Rosenthal said, "You know, Allen created a lot of madness in his life."[40] Hale chimed in, "Allen surrounded himself by madness and tried to take care of it." They were especially referring to Peter Orlovsky, who had major problems with mental illness and substance abuse and in one frightening incident stabbed Rosenthal in the groin with scissors. Perhaps the therapy could have helped change this pattern, make him more effective in helping those in his life, or lessen the distress it caused him. I will discuss this more in Chapter 8.

As for Allen's art, unpacking his experiences of trauma and grief in psychotherapy would have risked depriving the poet of the intense conflagration of emotions, memories, ideas, and dilemmas that drove his creative process. I do not say this from the position of a belief in the romantic suffering artist but to acknowledge how Allen's art depended a great deal on his experience of his mother, who was his muse but also the source of much trauma and grief. Had that experience been changed in some fundamental way through psychotherapy or an antidepressant medication, it certainly could have altered the brew, the relationships, and the processes that Allen pursued in his journals, correspondences, and poetry for years.

What we experience today through his art, especially "Howl" and "Kaddish," is a product of Allen's own ways of approaching, containing, and expressing that relationship and those difficult life issues. Going to PI as a patient helped him claim part of that experience as his own. His creative way of claiming it was entirely different from how it likely would have been claimed had his doctors worked differently with him in framing this experience as trauma and grief.

Allen was learning to take responsibility for his feelings and behavior. But he was learning it his own way. It was less about what his mother had done to him and more about how he saw himself, his visions, his libertine gang, and his entire generation—and how he could, as a poet for these times, write something that would incorporate the madness within and around us and give the sense we can make ourselves into something new.

Allen left PI with improvements in symptoms, especially of the psychosis he feared the most. Still, he had not given up on what the doctors called homosexual behavior, and though he wasn't doing drugs, he was no less interested in them. He did have an acceptable plan for living at home and dedicating time to his writing. He had agreed to participate in outpatient psychotherapy with his last psychotherapist. He had not yet succeeded in finding a job but would in time. On the psychiatrist's terms, these changes were enough to justify declaring his treatment a success.

What about his prognosis as an artist? No predictions were made by the PI psychiatrists. My assessment is that upon discharge his prognosis as an artist was excellent but by no means guaranteed. Allen was one of those persons who had access to aspects of inner experience that psychiatrists have called "unconscious," "prepsychotic," "psychotic," or "traumatic," which are denied to most people. One might say there was great artistic potential in a nearly psychotic mutability and trauma survivor's intensity and clarity. Through his dreams and visions, journaling and poetry, he could express in words what others could not and be a palimpsest for a fast-changing world.

He could verbally and visually express those experiences, and just as importantly, he was willing to receive and utilize criticism. He was willing to commit to a lifestyle conducive to being a working artist. He was well read in literature and the arts and deeply invested in literary and spiritual traditions. He could follow the advice of his psychiatrists, even if they were not nearly as well read. They said not to be overly devoted to the visions but to draw from them and make communicative art, and so he did.

Allen had a set of experiences, interests, memories, and ideas that would appear to lend itself to a literary project. It was no longer about trying to promote visions, as it was when he was first admitted, but how to live with a madness that could be an inspiration, or an illness, or both. Under such circumstances, how do you salvage madness, not just for yourself but for your loved ones and your times?

At PI he also became friends with Carl Solomon, who became the protagonist of "Howl." Solomon, who was discharged not long before him, sent a postcard to Allen on PI Ward 5 North. It read simply, "Play poet, play!"[41] Solomon got it right: PI was where Allen got serious about playing poet.

Yet later on, Allen made substantial literary use of his PI experience. The sense of being proximate to but not necessarily as bad off as others with mental illness and madness was a key position and a feeling he remembered and later put at the center of both "Howl" and "Kaddish." It enabled him to become a direct witness to mental illness and its treatment without completely surrendering to it.

Although Allen did not write very many poems while at PI and none were about visions, PI was where Allen worked on many of the poems eventually published in *Empty Mirror* and where the figure of the shrouded stranger first appeared. Both he and his psychotherapist thought the "Shrouded Stranger" poems were an important step ahead in his writing. So at PI Allen kept working on the image of the "Shrouded Stranger" and wrote a number of poems that put this imaginary figure through several transformations.

In the first version, a shrouded stranger wanders through the city in the dark of night. He moves down the avenues, past mansions, churches, and a funeral home where the dead are handled. At a waterfall, he passes through the curtain of white water and enters the light of eternity. Then the shrouded stranger, dead and entombed, beckons a child to be his lover. A child's love will put life back in his body.

In the next iteration, the shrouded stranger is a tramp wandering the railroad tracks and waterfront of a city. He calls for someone to walk with him, lie down with him in the night, and satisfy his most intimate desires.

In another poem, the shrouded stranger is a more ghoulish, urban bogeyman who teases and frightens the citizens. The successive versions shift perspective. The initial poem gives us the shrouded stranger from the outside, whereas subsequent versions give the shrouded stranger's views of himself. When Allen lets the shrouded stranger speak, the voice has a singsong tone that reveals this menacing figure as also sympathetic. The result is a poem with a character more lifelike and emotionally charged than any poem he had yet written. Allen thought he had finally written a poem with a strong poetic voice.

The shrouded stranger is a castrating figure, thought the third psychotherapist from his psychoanalytically oriented perspective. To the therapist, the poem seemed like a breakthrough because the central figure corresponded with the experience of his psychotic mother that Allen had been describing in their sessions.

Within several months, the "Shrouded Stranger" series fizzled out and did not prove to be the poetic breakthrough Allen hoped it would be. But the creation of this devouring but affectionate figure was an important achievement with respect to representing madness. I am tempted to agree with the psychotherapist that the shrouded strangers were imaginative riffs on the psychotic, seductive Naomi of his childhood, scary but paradoxically also intensely appealing. This figure gained in details and humanity over the years as Allen built on the image ten years later in writing his greatest works, "Howl" and "Kaddish," and forty years later, in "White Shroud" and "Black Shroud."

Another poem from the PI era, "Paterson," which I described in the Prologue, produces the figure and language of a liberated madman, a wild modern American Christ, in "hideous ecstasy."[42] The madness being celebrated is also clearly paid for in blood and guts. The poet has gone farther than he has ever gone in picturing madness. He has not only descended but also found a language worthy of someone putting it all on the line. If that figure were to make up a song to sing to himself, then it might sound like "Bop Lyrics," another poem from the PI era, where Allen wrote, "I'm so lucky to be nutty."[43]

At PI, Allen learned to write poems that showed two very different sides of madness: the damaging and the liberating. The poet was capable of producing not one but both. The figures were rendered with enough complexity and nuance to indicate they are not one-dimensional caricatures. Nobody knew what was possible if the poet could learn to put them both in one poem and let them talk and listen to each other. That would take years.

In July 1967, the Summer of Love, Allen was invited to speak at the Congress on the Dialectics of Liberation in London. The conference was convened by R. D. Laing and David Cooper, the psychiatrists who coined the term "antipsychiatry."[44] They became known as antipsychiatrists because they strongly condemned mainstream psychiatric practices of labeling people as mentally ill, confining them in institutions, and giving them harmful and degrading treatments including shock therapy and lobotomy.

Because his poems "Howl" and "Kaddish" presented a humanistic view of madness so different from conventional psychiatric formulations of the day and because of his public comments regarding madness, Allen became a hero to the antipsychiatrists, especially the Scottish psychiatrist R. D. Laing, who was regarded as their leader. Laing later discussed how he'd read Allen's "Howl" and "Kaddish" at an early stage in his intellectual development and cited them both as being highly supportive of his efforts to rethink schizophrenia as a consequence of a sick society.[45]

For the Congress, the antipsychiatrists also brought together philosopher-scholars including Gregory Bateson, Paul Goodman, and Herbert Marcuse and the radical activist Stokely Carmichael. Allen presented a talk entitled "Consciousness and Practical Action." Allen called for a new behavioral code of "flower power": "You make friends with everybody you possibly can. You control your temper completely; you never say a harsh word. You listen very carefully to trace back along the lines of words and feelings of their reactions."

Allen proposed expanding the self through LSD and achieving an ethics of caring for the natural world. He described the oceanic feeling of an LSD trip as a "unitive experience of One, of all of us being one—not only ourselves with varying color of skin and mysterious ego-origin or whatever we are, also one with flowers, also the very trees and plants." Allen sought the "beginning of a friendly communism, or communion, or community, or friendly extension of self outward."

Allen shared a general affinity for the antipsychiatrists, who refused to rule by lobotomy and wanted to change the world through radical politics. Yet Allen and antipsychiatry could only go so far together. The antipsychiatry movement argued that the practice of psychiatry was oppressive and inhumane and should be radically changed. Allen, whose own mother had been lobotomized along with tens of thousands of others in an abomination of science and patients' rights, was not quite with them politically. Yes, some of the stories Allen told about madness and psychiatry in "Howl" and "Kaddish" were affectively charged counterparts to the antipsychiatry activists' calls for changes in policy. On the other hand, Allen's poems were far too ambivalent to serve as the embodiment of an antipsychiatry message, compared with, for example, Ken Kesey's 1962 novel *One Flew Over the Cuckoo's Nest* and the 1972 Academy Award–winning Milos Forman film starring Jack Nicholson.

Allen surely could have thrown himself more vigorously into the antipsychiatry movement. Why did he leave it up to others to address the mental health policy issues of the day? In part because he had higher ambitions for changing consciousness and broader cultural, social, and political transformations, but also because Allen was more sympathetic to psychiatry than many imagine him to be. He told me: "Psychiatry treated me well. I have some problems with psychiatrists though. Some are simple minded."[46] As a family member of persons with serious mental illness (first Naomi and later Peter), if he was hoping for anything from psychiatry, it was more for major reform than total rejection of psychiatric approaches to mental illness.

In an interview with Barry Farrell, on January 11, 1966, while Allen was on the road in Kansas on his way to Wichita for a reading, later noted in the major poem "Wichita Vortex Sutra," Allen was asked about psychiatry. He distinguished between the "crew-cut psychiatrist" and the "real psychiatrist": "The trouble with this generation of psychiatrists is that many of them were put into medical training by the army. They had their whole formulation founded on military necessities, their medical school paid for and their internship and first practice being involved with the army."[47] These psychiatrists are too focused on "orienting the patient to suppressing his feelings and simply conform to social convention."

Regarding his hospitalization at PI, he recalled: "I was going to a doctor there . . . who was someone I could talk to." This doctor was the third psychotherapist, who made a good connection with him in the hospital and continued seeing him after his discharge.

Allen believed the limitations of PI psychiatry had mostly to do with their backing social conformity, not with a lack of understanding how to diagnose or treat patients. He was not aware that at discharge some of the psychiatrists thought him far more mentally ill than he came away believing. Nor did he realize that some of his psychiatrists may have protected him from a possible lobotomy. Although PI was an elite institution, the psychiatric treatments it offered were still saddled by the limitations of the era: an undeveloped diagnostic framework, enthusiastic promotion of lobotomies, homosexuality as a mental illness, lack of appreciation of the mental health consequences of trauma. Nonetheless, Allen thought his PI stay had helped him, and he still believed in psychiatry and hoped psychiatry could help others. He found hope in younger generations of psychiatrists and left it to others to deliver further on his hope for changes.

In the late 1980s, I felt Allen's faith in and reliance on psychiatry in our meetings. He spoke with me about his experiences getting treatment for Peter Orlovsky through the Hazelden Treatment Center. To help Peter, Allen became heavily involved in Al-Anon and other family support activities. One evening he even asked me to talk with Peter about why he should take lithium. As we walked from his apartment to First Avenue to catch a taxi heading uptown, I explained to Peter why staying on lithium could help, even though he would rather be high from his mania. "Listen to him," said Allen, in a pleading tone, as he waved down a taxi heading uptown. Allen's approach to helping Peter was the opposite of naïve. It is but one example of how throughout his life Allen remained deeply involved with a community of writers and artists, some of whom struggled with their own mental health problems, burdens he bore without bitterness.

The PI professionals may have thought it was of no special concern that the son had given consent for the mother's lobotomy. That was how consent was done in those days. It turned out that the same abysmal ethical standards that in one state hospital produced the possibility of a mother's lobotomy

Lobotomy consent form, Pilgrim State Hospital, 1947. © *Allen Ginsberg Estate; Courtesy Columbia University Libraries.*

consented for by her traumatized son also made it possible for the traumatized son to get psychiatric treatment in another state hospital, with the mother's lobotomy not even considered significant.

As I will later discuss, not adequately addressing these traumas and losses likely enabled problems in his intimate relationships to persist and eventually become potentially harmful to others. But as a poet, this was actually a gift, one that Allen received, reworked, and transformed over the next several years before it eventually blossomed in his major works, first in "Howl" and then later in "Kaddish," in strikingly different ways.

Chapter 6

Mental Muse-eries, 1950–1955

JUST OVER FIVE years elapsed between Allen's PI stay and his writing "Howl," which has been called "the poem that changed America."[1] His breakthrough poem about madness arrived suddenly and unexpectedly one afternoon while sitting at his desk in his North Beach flat. But what made this poem possible was active preparation through both life experience and creative work, much of which took place in those five years. Allen stabilized his life as an artist, further developed his poetic skills, and built an artistic project in which he was creatively reworking the experiences and perceptions associated with Naomi's mental illness and his own brush with madness and psychiatry. Yet just as he was learning to rise up through his poetic approaches to madness, his mother's condition further deteriorated, despite the lobotomy, and she was once again institutionalized at Pilgrim State.

"A poem is a small (or large) machine made out of words."[2] About the time he graduated Columbia College, Allen read William Carlos Williams's definition in the introductory statement of his 1948 publication *The Wedge*. However, Allen was so steeped in the European and lyrical traditions of poetry taught at Columbia that he had difficulty opening himself to Williams's edgy, distinctly American verse.

Back then Allen was writing visionary poems that spoke to the heavens, not constructing machines in the swamps of New Jersey. But he thought he should get to know Williams, a fellow poet from Paterson. As a still-unpublished writer, he needed poet allies other than his father, and besides, they had actually met once before.

Back in 1946, Allen had arranged to interview Paterson's most famous poet for a local weekly, the *Passaic Valley Examiner*. They met at Williams's medical office in Paterson. In the interview Allen asked: "Do you think of yourself as a doctor or as a poet?" He was surprised when Williams answered, "Doctor."[3]

When they met again in 1950, Allen recited to him from his poetry journals, but Williams was not taken by his traditional iambic pentameter verses. There was no hope in old-school stylings, he said. Allen learned how Williams drew words and inspiration from local talk he picked up from his immigrant, working-class patients. "I'll kick you in the eye," said one. "Can you head in that direction?"[4] the doctor suggested.

Allen saw Williams's writing desk, flanked by paintings by Charles Sheeler and Marsden Hartley. Later he visited the Museum of Modern Art, where he had previously gone to study Cezanne's landscapes for Meyer Schapiro's course, to look at more of their paintings.[5] Allen really liked what the modern

William Carlos Williams, 1921.

painters were doing with subject, perspective, and colors, and they further encouraged him to rethink the need for a new kind of modern verse.

After Allen wrote up the 1946 Williams interview, the editor took over and made additional changes, making Allen's complaints about Williams read as petty and unfair. But back then, Allen indeed felt critical of Williams for his "uncharitable position in regard to Paterson's attempts to spread education to the masses."

Four years later, now certain he wanted to be a poet, Allen was not too ashamed to approach Williams again. On March 2, 1950, not a week after his discharge from PI, Allen went to hear Williams give a reading at the Guggenheim Museum. Afterward he tried to greet the doctor-poet backstage, but seeing Williams being swarmed by admirers, he gave up and headed home on foot. Two days later, Allen wrote to Williams: "I envision for myself some kind of new speech—different at least from what I have been writing down—in that it has to be a clear statement of fact about misery (and not misery itself), and splendor if there is any out of the subjective wanderings through Paterson."[6] This declaration is striking for its explicit commitment to real life, suffering, and subjectivity.

Allen enclosed nine poems, including "Ode to the Setting Sun," a poem written in October 1949, when still at PI. This rhymed poem attempted to say something about being false. Despite his hope for a new speech, this poem was full of abstractions, which Williams found objectionable. Unlike Allen's poems of that period, Williams's poems sounded more like people talking. But Williams saw potential for more lively writing in the letter: Allen considered the two of them "fellow citizenly Chinamen of the same province, whose gas tanks, junkyards, fens of the alley, millways, funeral parlors, river-visions—aye! the falls itself—are images white-woven in their very beards." If only Allen could write poems as alive as some lines in his letters and journals! Williams wanted to help the ambitious young Jersey poet. About the poems, Williams wrote back the since oft-quoted phrase: "In this mode, perfection is basic, and these are not perfect."[7]

At the time Allen was still deeply involved in writing the "Shrouded Stranger" series, also started at PI, which he once had great hopes for. But after nearly two years of attempts to get those poems right, filling several entire notebooks, and still not being at all satisfied—or published—Allen needed to change up his approach.

The language of Williams's poems was not too different from what you might say to your buddy. You could put almost any words in there, then locate and rearrange the words to better concentrate intensity. Allen went through his old journals. He read each page, looking for passages with the most direct and clear prose descriptions of observations or experiences, then rearranged them on the page to imitate the open form of Williams's poems. And so he wrote:

> I attempted to concentrate
> the total sun's rays in
> each poem as through a glass,
> but such magnification
> did not set the page afire.[8]

In January 1952, Allen sent a second group of poems to Williams reflecting this new approach to writing. He didn't think there was much to these recycled prose scraps, but surprisingly, Williams wrote back: "How many of such poems as these do you own. You must have a book. I shall see that you get it. Don't throw anything away. These are it."[9]

These poems became the collection later entitled *Empty Mirror*, published in 1961. Many of the poems were adapted from the swirling prose passages Allen wrote in the uneasy days just before his admission to PI. Williams liked them so much he also wanted to include them in his epic poem "Paterson." "Wonderful! Really you shall be the center of my new poem—of which I shall tell you: the extension of Paterson. For it I shall use your 'Metaphysics' as the head."

Williams carefully went through all of Allen's poems line by line. He noted, "Better one active phrase than pages of inert talk."[10] With Williams's mentorship, Allen discovered anew how to write a poem. This is it, he wrote to Jack Kerouac and Neal Cassady:

> All you got to do is look over your notebooks (that's where I got these poems) or lay down on a couch, and think of anything that comes into your head, especially the miseries, the mis'ries, or night thoughts when you can't sleep an hour before sleeping, only get up and write it down. Then arrange in lines of 2, 3, or 4 words each, don't bother about sentences, in sections of 2, 3, or 4 lines each. We'll have a huge collected anthology of American Kicks and Mental Muse-eries.[11]

After Williams told Allen his journals were poetry, Allen's journal writing changed. Years later, looking through journals from the time, preparing them for eventual publication with his assistant's help, he wrote in the margin the very day this change took place: "Henceforth everything written has added self-consciousness."[12] This identified a potential drawback: Had it diminished the freedom of his journaling?

On March 12, 1952, Allen visited Williams in Rutherford and accompanied him to a party. Williams showed Allen a copy of *Paterson Book 4*, into which he had incorporated his letters and poems, just as he said he would. Williams also confided in Allen his own worries about his poetry. Do you really think this open form is working?

One night in 1952, Williams picked Allen up at his father's house. Louis didn't care much for Williams, perhaps because Williams had never been a part of the local poetry societies. They had a fabulous evening, driving around Paterson, stopping by the river and the falls, and dining at a local Italian restaurant. Sitting in the car before the evening's end, Allen never forgot Williams's words: "What I try to do is squeeze pictures into little lines. I have these little lines and I squeeze a picture into it."[13] In their correspondences and conversations, Williams kept at Allen to "cut down everything" and stick to "rhymeless, clean-cut work."[14]

Back in their first meeting for the newspaper interview in 1946, Allen was surprised to hear Williams say he thought of himself primarily as a doctor. Why claim doctor and not the mantle of poet if you could? Williams had certainly earned the latter title. Several years later, Allen understood better how being a doctor in the first place and a poet in the second place worked for Williams. Caring for European immigrants in New Jersey, tending to their pains and ailments, Williams encountered the world and its people and speech. It gave him a grounded position from which to see and listen and write. What was Allen's position? Did he yet have a world he could name and occupy and write from?

At age twenty-six, if he was going to succeed as an artist, he needed a way to reach out of himself and extend his experiences, language, and insights into the wider world of unfamiliar places and peoples' lives. Allen followed Williams's path out of New York City, where his mother's condition had once again recently taken a turn for the worse.

The hoped-for results of Naomi's prefrontal lobotomy did not last very long. Allen thought Naomi had lost part of her personality and still might be on the verge of losing her mind once again. Maybe they should have listened to the doctors who said she was not yet ready to leave Pilgrim State. But Naomi wanted more than anything to be out of there, and who could blame her? Now that she was out, Allen was trying to stay removed from her care as much as was possible, feeling like he had already done more than he should. But when Naomi started to get hostile toward her sister Elanor and even kicked her in the leg at her Bronx apartment, he had to act. Elanor

Form 275-p. m. n.—Sept., 1945—(Identification)

Reprint Regulated

MAY 31 1951

STATE OF NEW YORK
DEPARTMENT OF MENTAL HYGIENE

Pilgrim State Hospital
(Name of Institution)

NAME GINSBERG, Naomi   IDENT NO. *471750*   DATE OF ADM. 1951 3 5
                                                                      Year Month Day

OTHER NAMES

PSYCHIATIC CLASSIFICATION   GROUP   TYPE

SEX ~~MALE~~ FEMALE   RACE white

RESIDENCE *3556 Roclambeau Avenue, Bronx, New York,* *Bronx*
              (own)   (County)

AGE 54   DATE OF BIRTH 4/25/96
HEIGHT 5'   WEIGHT 172
EYES brown   HAIR brown
COMPLEXION light   BUILD medium
NATIVITY OF PATIENT Russia
CITIZENSHIP ~~XXXXXX~~ NATURALIZED XXX
OCCUPATION teacher
SCARS, ETC. vac. left arm

SIGNATURE AND ADDRESS OF PATIENT

PREVIOUS RESIDENCE IN A MENTAL HOSPITAL   NAME OF HOSPITAL   FROM   TO

Naomi Ginsberg, Pilgrim State Hospital, 1951. © *Allen Ginsberg Estate.*

had a heart condition, and the family was worried Naomi would give her a heart attack.

Allen called the police to have her picked up and filled out the papers required for hospital admission. On February 21, 1951, thirteen months after the lobotomy, Naomi was involuntarily admitted to Bellevue Hospital in Manhattan.

Two weeks later, Naomi was transferred from Bellevue and admitted for the second time to Pilgrim State Hospital. The admitting doctors wrote of the "outbreak of violence against family, making it impossible to live peacefully for the whole family."[15] Naomi had a "paranoid structure directed against former husband and family, held in abeyance for the last four years, reappeared with added fear that patient was being poisoned, abandoned, persecuted, etc. by own sister and family with whom she resided, and also sons." Her admission's mental diagnosis was "Dementia Praecox, Paranoid Type." Her physical diagnoses were "post-lobotomy; decompensated cardiovascular disease." They wrote: "Pt. is dull looking." She would not leave Pilgrim State Hospital alive.

The doctor's progress note from May 16, 1951, read:

The patient who still resides on Ward 24–4 has somatic complaints of a rather bizarre character stating that the blood is rushing to her right temple and makes her vomit. However, she was never noted to vomit. She states that she has pains in her mouth and constantly asks for salt to wash her mouth. She states that this is all due to the constant blood rushing to her head.

On May 17, 1951, three months later, Allen made his first visit back to Pilgrim State Hospital. It was disturbing for him to see how instead of improving, her condition had actually worsened upon hospitalization, with even more agitation and paranoia. Beginning in November 1951, Naomi had to be placed in physical restraints. When a patient is so agitated, a danger to themselves or others and unable to respond to verbal requests, then restraints are the last resort. This was still before the era of psychotropic medications sometimes called "chemical restraints," so when a patient was out of control, the staff had little to rely on other than physical restraints.[16] The nursing note from November 18 reported: "She was standing on the window sill, pushing the bed around, and walking around the room. She would not lay down."

Allen visited Naomi at Pilgrim State Hospital once again on December 2, 1951. She was still doing poorly and begged Allen to take her out of there, to do something, anything. What could he say? What could he do?

A striking figure drawn in pencil sat on the lined pages of Allen's college-ruled poetry journal from 1952, which was also filled with version after version of the "Shrouded Stranger" poems. This figure, of a skull strangely half-dead and half-alive, served as a kind of visual repository of images and ideas for many of his poetic endeavors at the time. Around the skull were spokes leading to names of many identities associated with this category of dead and living skulls. The names included: "Faust, Saxe, Poe, Shadow, Dr. Jekyll and Mr. Hyde, Bella Lugosi, Huncke, Sidney Greenstreet, Dona master Death, The Man on the Road, Dr. Habare, Satan, Bowery Bum, Madman, D. K., K., Knifethrower at Revere, Other freaks—hanged man and chained man."[17] These assorted identities were somehow related to the central image, embodying the same freakish essence.

In an earlier notebook are other drawings of heads turning into skulls accompanied by these lines: "Man who faces death or is half skull" and "He know death who know he will die." This is less a study of the dead and more a depiction of the experiences of a trauma survivor—someone who knows

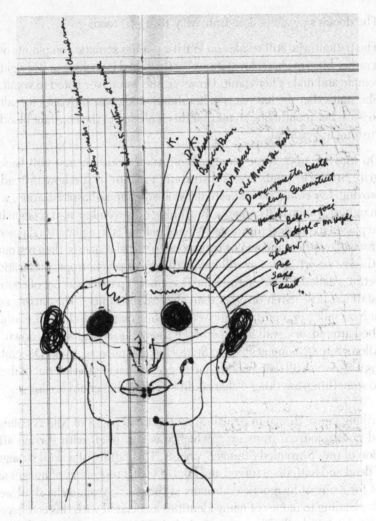

The shrouded stranger, 1952. © *Allen Ginsberg Estate; Courtesy Stanford University Libraries.*

death yet is still alive. What the trauma survivor knows, more than any living soul, is the double-sidedness of existence. Or as Allen wrote:

> He who knows he will die knows death.
> I too will die. I too know death. Madonna.[18]

All his life Allen had been aware of a double-sided existence: watching his mother go in and out of psychosis, suicidality, psychiatric hospitals, and

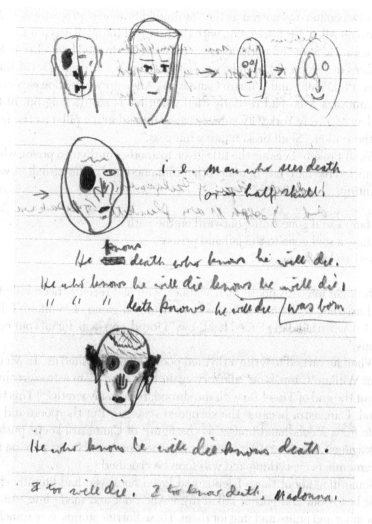

Half skull, 1949. © Allen Ginsberg Estate; Courtesy Stanford University Libraries.

debilitating treatments. Further, he was involved in her hospital admissions and treatment and then himself being admitted to a psychiatric hospital. These experiences taught him about the other side of ordinary lives. The half-living skull was a visual means of representing this involvement with the other side, including serious mental illness and confinement, which afflicted thousands and thousands of families, given the more than 13,000 patients in Pilgrim State Hospital alone.

In December 1951, even as the "Shrouded Stranger" project was losing its grip on Allen, his fascination with the image of the skull was put to some new uses. He wrote an untitled poem of twelve unrhymed lines chronicling the fates of several old friends, now jailed (Huncke) or dead (David Kammerer, Phil White, and William Cannastra). Allen drew attention especially to Cannastra, who had recently died when his head, sticking out of the window of a New York City subway car, slammed into a pillar as the train left the station. "Skull broken into whiteness."

"Skull Broken" became the title given to another unrhymed poem, which chronicled the hard fate of many other unnamed souls. The casualties were mounting.

> Many a soul gone riding outward on the path
> Many a soul gone to the jail and prison
> And asylum[19]

He brought into this poem Joan Vollmer, who had recently been killed by her husband, William Burroughs, in a drunken game of William Tell in Mexico, when a bullet pierced her brow. "I loved, you Joan, for all your crazy moons."

When he turned to write a rhymed poem, later published as "In Memoriam: William Cannastra," allegory again took over. Cannastra screamed, "I wait the end of Time! Be with me shroud, now, in my wrath."[20] This time round, Cannastra became the shrouded stranger. But the poem did not settle for a secondhand image, as the figure of Cannastra keeps pushing back against Allen's familiar allegorical preoccupations. His eyes are on fire; he remembers everything and will soon be crucified.

Something about these friends and loved ones who had literally stuck their heads out and gotten killed drew Allen out and made him want to remember and praise and sing for them. These horrific stories were somehow drawing him out of allegory and into messy existence, the tragic facts of some people's lives. He could engage those on the path to jails and asylums, in all their miseries, splendor, and "muse-eries." It was right in front of him if he wanted to claim it—a whole world of madness and madhouses. Visiting his mother at Greystone and Pilgrim State, getting admitted to PI for his own care, and standing by his many friends through their travails gave him more than enough material to work with.

This was the new direction in poetry Allen was working on as Naomi's condition worsened yet again.

Upon her admission in 1951, Naomi heard voices telling her to go home. She demanded to be let out. She also heard voices telling her to get out of bed. Because she refused to stay in bed, she was put in restraints. Naomi insisted that electricity was moving through her body. She put paper over her head to protect her or walked around the ward with clothing over her head. "You must help me. The electric voices are killing me."

She was very confused and uncooperative with the ward routine. She disturbed other patients, pushed the bed around, and stood on the window sill. She wet her head at the water fountain and stuffed her ears and nose with paper to protect herself. She wanted to be protected from the "wireless" and thought the food was poisoned. She was afraid of being electrocuted and complained of being mistreated. She said a fire was burning in her head and drank water constantly to quench the flames. She had worries about wires in her head and told the doctor to take the wires out.

On January 16, 1952, the doctor at Pilgrim State documented:

This patient has been actively disturbed over a period of several months. She is noisy, irritable and aggressive. Occasionally becomes assaultive. She is neglectful of her appearance. She hallucinates, actively, and expresses bizarre delusional trends of a paranoid nature. She is constantly harassed by voices and mental telepathy. Bad tasting substances are injected into her system. This causes her to experience "a poisonous feeling." She smells nauseating odors. In response to "night voices" which she hears, the answers come "from my own mind." The voices say something about "cerebellum." Her brain cells are lifted out when she is in bed. She knows positively that it's done. At times the voices tell her to get off the bed. They also tell her, "to break her body." She smiles in a very inappropriate fashion when she talks about these things.

A few days later: "Pt. is noisy talks loud walking up and down the hall. Put her head in toilet bowl and then puts on her dress over her head. She disturbs other patients."

In a journal entry from February 26, 1952, Allen stated: "I could write about all of these subjects and scenes of life if I wanted to": "#8 [of 50]: Madness—inside and outside madhouses."[21] This was an important realization and possibly the first time he had journaled an explicit connection to madness and madhouses as a writing topic.

Back at Pilgrim State, March 22, 1952, a nurse wrote: "Pt. is very confused. Listens to voices. Insists electricity is running through her body. Keeps her head wet all day, stuffs her nostrils and ears with paper has either her dress or paper over her head to protect her." On June 15, 1952, one month after his previous visit, Allen again visited his mother at Pilgrim State. He discovered Naomi was getting worse and worse. She spoke of the electricity, the wires, and the voices. All she wanted was to go home, but there was nothing he could do. He didn't stay too long and slept on the train home.

Two days later, he wrote a journal entry about a "stranger" project, which involved following around and then writing portraits of interesting people he'd passed by in the city. He wrote of a "woman of indeterminable age—forty or so, yet perhaps younger and aged by madness or suffering."[22] On the street "she sat there in a cramped posture; as if she had been living in hovels or homeless for years, nervous with her hands, bitten fingernails, face covered with thought and incoherent suffering."

He thought of speaking with her but did not approach her. Then he thought of something very extreme: "All I could do was take her burden & rescue her forever if I once intervened, having this suicide on my hands."

There is no indication that he ever planned to act on this disturbing impulse. It reads like a mercy killing, which may very well have also been prompted by seeing the very sad state Naomi was now in. Sometimes there is no alternative to death for releasing a loved one from extreme suffering. The impulse to rescue through a violent act could also be tied back to Allen's regret over the lobotomy—a desperate attempt to rescue Naomi from madness through cutting her brain—with disastrous results.

In his journal Allen described the woman's face: "thin, bony, elite, passively mad, anciency or nobility—intelligence beyond ideas, completely beat; shifting nervously in her seat, continually agitated by her unknown mystery." In the brief period of the stranger project, such wayward persons encountered on the street became Allen's heroines. His obligation was to chronicle their tragic luminosity. He found he could do more with one stranger on the street than he could with an imagined shrouded stranger. As a writer, the city street or the madhouse could be for him like Dr. Williams's clinic.

Allen could also concentrate the same attention he gave to strangers upon friends. A few pages later in the same journal he recorded a fantasy of Solomon, his Dadaist writer friend from PI, "half wanting to die, half wanting nuthouse, half smile on face."[23] He pictured Solomon in the nuthouse, where madness could be expressed as "the religious flowering of the imagination, the authentic genius recording his sufferings as a living deadman; uncomprehended disordered radiant humor."[24] Increasingly for Allen, the figures of actual persons who struggled with actual madness were just as compelling as the allegorical figure of the shrouded stranger.

He remembered the psychiatrists at PI telling him to back away from the visions. He had no choice but to agree with them in order to work toward discharge, but seeing Naomi the way she was at Pilgrim State, he could see himself being pulled toward idealizing madness. In another entry from June 30, 1952, he wrote about pulling himself back from his attraction to madness:

> Lucien warning me the other day not to go mad again, not to drift off into unreality or think of place where I met Carl—Madhouse. . . . I must abandon again this whole metaphysical urge that leads me further each month back to an uncreated world of bliss of my own making in my own head—bliss which I do not even remember any more, is just an idea—while the real world passes me by . . . Must stop playing with my mind, with my life. . . . What will I make happen to my life?"[25]

He visited Naomi once again on July 13, 1952. Upon returning home, he wrote nothing of this visit in his journal. This preceded by one month another turn for the worse in her condition. On August 26, 1952, her doctors wrote to the Ginsberg family stating: "Two days ago Naomi suffered seizures, which returned the following day. After she got sodium luminal intramuscularly, the severity of the seizures decreased, but she developed symptoms of left sided paralysis and was in a semi-stuporous state."[26]

A few days after the seizure, on August 31, 1952, Allen came to visit. He saw Naomi worse than ever, confused and lethargic. She was cloudy, eyes glazed, movements slowed, left side not moving at all. She didn't notice how she drooled, but he did. Naomi's condition further worsened in January 1953. Within days she became assaultive, and the nurses wrote: "Pt. of lately has been aggressive and uncooperative. Pt. continuing to complain of 'electricity' being put into her body. Very sloppy in appearance. Pulls clothes over her head. This is to protect her from electricity, she says."

The medical record documented nobody from the family visiting Naomi for almost six months. Allen and Eugene found it too painful to see her in such terrible shape.

That same month, Naomi wrote a postcard. "Dear Allen and Eugene, Please come to see me in a hurry! One son call up the other son. Tell Elanor to come see me. I'm still alive and walking around. Love, Naomi."[27] This card caught Allen's attention. On January 18, 1953, he returned to Pilgrim State Hospital to visit Naomi. Of all the visits to Naomi's hospitals over many years, this was the only visit he ever documented in any detail. He wrote:

Dear Allen &
Eugene,
Please come
to see me in
a hurry!
One can call
up the other
son.
Tell Eleanore.
to come to see
me.
I'm still
alive & walking
around.
Love Naomi

Letter, 1953. © Allen Ginsberg Estate;
Courtesy Columbia University Libraries.

Naomi at Pilgrim State today. Walked in waiting room through short hall. Small, thin, almost—flesh on her face wasted—no longer cheerful robust look—no longer fat, no longer healthy looking jokingly as I used to say as if she'd outlast us all—now suddenly her skin had shrunk all over—and the change in soul I saw—from Confidence or wrath—to pitiful batbrained hysterical fright and lack of sureness.

Her face now old old and near death it looked—something new stamped on her face—time sufferings age and strokes of sickness leaving her a hulk skull gape out of what was so rosy and sweet. Lines of age in face. I saw another Naomi than her I'm used to, one old enough to be a grandma. I could not believe so much life had passed through my hands, through her Gaze—After awhile with her telling me to get out before I was struck down or injured. I broke down, cried, and she continued weaving back and forth to the entrance and returning, sometimes asking "Why was I crying?" to get out before I was struck down. So that I came out when they led her away after a few minutes and went to the men's room and cried, sobbing saying horror "the horror of it," and groaning with grief and the reality of her death's head.[28]

For Allen, seeing her after her seizure or stroke was truly horrific and more shocking than any of the prior visits. Because he hadn't been to see her in some time, he might have been comparing her to his memory of her from earlier visits and to his natural tendency to imagine she was better than she actually was. Not only was she approaching her death, but death was a contagion that would strike him too, Naomi warned with a sense of impending doom.

What's more, Allen now had a method for writing about madness and death that he had been practicing and developing through the "Shrouded Stranger," the skulls poems, and the stranger project. He still had a ways to go in refining his approach and applying it to Naomi. But it was a start to be able to record the encounter and to incorporate what he saw in her, her foreboding warning to him, his own cataclysmic emotional response, the confrontation with death, and the tragic facts of her rapidly declining condition.

Thinking back to the drawing of the skull, it seems as if Naomi's madness-driven death mask could be at the center of the wheel. In his writings, he had been moving around the spokes of the wheel, focusing on other freaks, but was now getting a fix on her terrifying yet also inspiring central figure.

On June 18, 1953, the nurses noted: "Isn't constantly running in and out of section wetting her head. Hasn't been yelling as much about wires and electricity in her head. Pt. sits quietly most of the day now. Medication effective." At the time she was receiving Hyoscine (an anticholinergic) and Nembutal (a sedative). Unfortunately, the improvement was short-lived. Just two weeks later, the nurse's note: "Pt. noisy at night, when let out of room . . . she gets her hair and head all wet."

On July 18, 1953, Allen again visited Naomi at Pilgrim State Hospital. This time he came with Eugene, which after the disastrous previous visit, was better than going alone. Allen had to go because he knew he was about to travel and wouldn't be back for a while. Naomi wasn't getting any better.

Allen had already left the United States for Mexico when the doctors wrote in the chart that Naomi was still confined to Pilgrim State and tortured by

pain in her head . . . that is coming from the electricity in the wires that are in her head. Pt. has spit the meds out three nights. Pt. says the voices tell her not to take it. Quiet for three nights. When she is in the day hall she becomes disturbed. Quiet after going to bed the last three nights. She likes to wet her hair also she likes to wet her face.

These doctors' and nurses' notes are clinically accurate descriptions, but neither their actions nor their depictions could in any way rescue Naomi. Could the responsibility of redeeming Naomi and all the Naomis of this world be taken up by Allen through his poetry?

Ha! After years of working at it, in 1953 Allen finally found his natural voice in a poem. It came in the form of a green automobile and a rollicking drunken heroic fantasy of escape, travel, sex, and eternity. It has the feel of desire unleashed and set free. He wrote this poem in April 1953, after Kerouac's encouragement and Allen's independent studies led him to read D. T. Suzuki's *Introduction to Zen Buddhism* and to look at Chinese paintings, including Liang Kai's *Sakyamuni Coming Out of the Mountain*. He was inspired by the open forms encountered in these great works of Eastern art.

The language of "Green Automobile" is as open in structure and spirit as anything he had ever written. He is talking to himself, to Neal, to his friends, the natural way they liked to talk to one another. Just like Dr. Williams said he should, without rhyme.

The poem gives us action—driving, bounding, blasting, burning—and energetic movement through the open landscape of the American West. It captured how exhilarating it felt to be out of Paterson, New York, the East, colleges, madhouses, and market research firms. The poem presents a new hero, Neal Cassady, the sexual angel, liberated from his family, the greatest driver, leaving boys and girls swooning, and screaming into the Western sun.

The poem has a double narrative: The poet also confesses his awareness that his green automobile is imagined. Thus it says: I, poet, am giving you this gift of the imagination, this legend. He could use this new, more open style to make legend out of painful breakups and separations and, perhaps, maybe madness.

At the poem's end, the protagonist goes back to his life in New York. However, once having found this poetic voice and imagination, Allen's writing and life would never be the same.

It was time to leave the unhappy stasis of his life in New York and hit the road. A few days after the plane touched down in Merida on the Yucatan Peninsula, Allen recorded in his journal an ecstatic occurrence witnessed when, being New Year's Day, "some man in plumes and frenzied calm stood up on monuments that echoed to each other in front of a silent mob and suddenly started to yell his head off in a dancebeat scream—toward what end other than howls of joy that answered him I don't know."[29]

At Chichen Itza, Allen thought he saw Naomi's face, "young and dark haired, at a piano at a party, close up, facing me, svelte and in rapport with life."[30] Travel awakened old memories and desires. In his journal he wrote he imagined going to Europe, where he wanted to make a film of William Burroughs, Jack Kerouac, Neal Cassady, and Lucien Carr. He wanted to write a tale powerful enough to carry them all away.

He explored the ruins at Chichen Itza, Uxmal, and Palenque and in the towns watched the pilgrims come to pray at church. In writings he let his mind wander in search of the spiritual. He dreamed of the gang being reunited in a far-off city. He kept dreaming of Europe and dreamed of Naomi with a "fresh wound." He wasn't seeing visions of God, at least not yet, but he found the ancient legends and buildings compelling and did a lot of journaling.

He hooked up with some young lovers though felt ashamed about making it with boys, since he knew he was supposed to be healthy, which meant not doing so. This led to his writing up his memories of sexual encounters with all the lovers he had known who had left him.

He recorded his dreams. In one, he was living near Columbia University and went to visit his literary agent, who chided him for purchasing a book called *Remembrance Rock* on their expense account. At the time, of course, he had no literary agent. In dreams he also found "magical emotions" and an "awe of vast constructions; familiar eternal halls of buildings; sexual intensity in rapport; deathly music; grief awakenings, perfected lodgings." As repositories of images, feelings, and fantasy, dreams could be just as powerful as visions, Allen was discovering. One day he awoke with a numbness in his toe and feared he had leprosy. "What poems in a leprosarium? What imagery." Leprosariums are like madhouses, places where people whose bodies and minds are ruined are sent away.

But what really stimulated his imagination in Mexico were the Mayan ruins. "These ruins woke up in me nostalgia for the unseen old continent of ruins, marble statues, now in the last sweet days of memory before the ultimate night of war." The challenge of writing about ruins, he discovered, was to document their power, to feel the presence of the living souls who made them, and to acknowledge how they have passed as you too will pass. The ruins of ancient civilizations, in other words, resemble the skulls he wrote of and drew in his notebooks. When visiting the mummies of

Guanajuato he saw actual skulls and bodies. It had him thinking about the mortal world; he even pictured "buildings rotting under the eternal sky," as he did in his 1948 vision, but now grounded in archeological reality.

After several months in Mexico, Allen's cup was full, and he was short on money, so he got on a bus and rode through Baja to California. In his journal he wrote:

> Enter U.S. alone naked with knapsack, watch, camera, poem, beard.
> The problem is construction of an Image. An imagination real and true.
> The past image of Neal less quickens my heart than before as I approach border.
> Not yet the great image of life that justifies freedom.
> Circumnavigation of globe no end in itself. The great motivation to be discovered. Process is empty without end.[31]

Allen was searching for the perfect images, not satisfied with what he had yet generated, restless, and unsettled. He returned to the United States and entered California. He was twenty-eight and tired of who he had been; he wanted something new. "To break with that pattern entirely—Must find energy & image & act on it."

He thought back to visions. "I am at best, them, Godlike."[32] He also thought of three deaths: William Cannastra's, Joan Vollmer's, and David Kammerer's. He thought of how as a teen he had slept with his brother and had incestuous fantasies. Do these facts somehow fit together? He did not understand the connections or know what to write about. Yet he knew: "not to imagine is not to eat." He must push himself further to generate images that will settle all. "Man is as far divine as his imagination." Allen gave himself a very heavy burden.

Upon his return to the United States, Allen was thinking of writing a really big poem to chronicle his trip to Mexico, one in which he would be the hero on an archeological, ethnographic, and sexual adventure in a foreign country, exploring, excavating, wandering, dreaming, and reminiscing. A spiritual quest:

> And I in a concrete room
>   above the abandoned
> labyrinth of Palenque
>   measuring my fate,

wandering solitary in the wild
        —blinking singleminded
at a bleak idea—[33]

Although Allen came to these ruins with "my own mad mind" and an awareness that Naomi remained locked up at Pilgrim State, he was serious about studying the Mayans and their seeking eternity. The approach he describes encompasses examining the physical landscape, seeking divine contact, and risking mental collapse.

Again he dreamed of Europe and making the journey there by boat. "Europe is my own imagination." He must go and find himself in cafes, streets, churches, museums, jazz clubs, and salons. His calling was not only to Europe but to independent pilgrimage, whereby he traveled in search of traces of the divine. When he crossed the US-Mexican border by bus, Allen saw these many different parts not as opposed to one another but coming together into a satisfying whole persona:

tanned and bearded
satisfying Whitman, concerned
        with a few Traditions,
metrical, mystical, manly
. . . and certain characteristic flaws

Back in the United States, he saw industry making bombs and preparing for war, but he was not yet able to make the connection to madness at a whole other level, driving the US government's war-making activities, which would eventually take shape in his poem "America" in 1956.

Allen hitched a ride to his cousin's house in Riverside. There he slept, ate well, and visited for a few days. It felt good to be back and seeing family. He then visited Neal Cassady, now living in San Jose with Carolyn. Neal was a brakeman for the railroad but had injured his leg and was out on leave when Allen arrived. He and Carolyn kept talking with Allen about the philosophy of Edgar Cayce, much to Allen's dismay.

When Carolyn was away, Allen renewed sexual activities with Neal. Neal would drive Allen all around the Bay Area, the two of them enjoying drugs, the sun, and each other. When Carolyn found Allen in bed with Neal, she'd had enough. You come as a guest in our house to try to take Neal away and break up our marriage? You must leave! Allen felt terrible. He accepted Carolyn's offer to drive him up to San Francisco. She let him off on Broadway in North Beach and handed him twenty dollars.

Allen found a room but now had to worry about daily survival. He tried to get a job at the *San Francisco Tribune*, but they had nothing for him. He ended up back in market research with enough salary to rent his own apartment. The firm liked Allen, promoted him, and wanted him to stay on. Having a steady income agreed with Allen, but market research wasn't at all for him. If he could get his master's degree, then he could get a teaching job and have a stable academic base from which to write poetry. He enrolled in the University of California for the fall semester.

He kept up with his independent poetic and spiritual studies. Jack Kerouac was encouraging him to read Buddhism. In San Jose, he visited the library with Neal and Carolyn Cassady to read poetry. He was more and more interested in the long line, which he saw as an extension of what he had learned from Williams.

Allen flew to New York for Eugene's wedding. However, when back east he didn't make it to Pilgrim State. Maybe he was discouraged by the most recent letter he received from Naomi:

Dearest Allen, How are you? You are supposed to be in New York this month. Come to see me in a hurry! I hope you stay in the East so I could see you. The wire is on my head and the sunshine is trying to help me. It has a wire department but the wire that's outside of my head the sun doesn't touch. It is connected with the inside of me. If I were home I could be out in the sunshine. It doesn't cost anything. Drop me a line! When are you getting a regular sweetheart? With love, Naomi mother.[34]

At least Naomi had found something soothing in the sunshine.

Williams gave Allen letters of introduction he could bring to several Bay Area poets. In time Allen had lunch with Kenneth Rexroth and visited with Robert Duncan. Allen hung around Foster's Cafeteria, which was frequented by artists. There he met the painter Robert Lavigne. He had enough cash to think about buying a painting, so he asked to see some works. Lavigne took him to his studio, where he saw the painting of a nude boy with onions. Who's that? That's Peter, he's over here.

Peter Orlovsky was twenty-one years old and had been Lavigne's lover. Allen knew right away he wanted to be with Orlovsky, and with Duncan's help, they got together. Orlovsky was also a child of immigrant parents from Russia. He had four siblings who were all mentally ill and institutionalized. Orlovsky was a nurse. After they made love, Allen fell completely for Orlovsky. "His brother's in the madhouse like my mother had been, his father and mother separated just like mine, his Russian background, and then this particular visionary thing he told me about that was so beautiful."[35]

Allen then decided to start seeing a psychotherapist, Philip Hicks at Langley Porter. He told Dr. Hicks he was trying hard to be "normal" like the PI doctors told him to be. But what he really wanted to do was quit his job in market research, move in with Orlovsky, and write poetry. As Allen recalled, he wanted to "do nothing but write poetry and have leisure to spend the day outdoors and go to museums and see friends. And I'd like to keep living with someone—maybe even a man—and explore relationships that way. And cultivate my perceptions, cultivate the visionary thing in me. Just a literary and quiet city-hermit existence." Dr. Hicks said, "Well, why don't you?"[36] This was all Allen needed to hear to set him free. Free from the homophobia he had taken in and that several years earlier at PI had made him want to embrace the psychiatrists' project of ridding him of homosexuality. Free from the notions of having a conventional career that his father and professors had been expecting of him.

Before Peter Orlovsky, Allen had been with Sheila, and before her Natalie Jackson, who then hooked up with Neal. Neal asked Natalie to impersonate Carolyn to withdraw money from her bank account. Their plot failed, and they got busted. Natalie overdosed, put a knife to her throat, and killed herself.[37] Allen was horrified and felt guilty. Was there something he could have done to save her? He wrote an elegy for her. "You gave me a look so tearful/I knew it was death/or thought so/not my time yet/I ignored you."[38]

Allen felt like a failure. He still wasn't published. He hadn't written anything he was really proud of. He was getting thirty dollars a month in unemployment, but it wasn't enough to live on. He wanted to leave San Francisco for Europe, but he didn't have enough cash. At times, Orlovsky didn't seem to want him around. He hadn't seen Naomi for years and couldn't help her.

In April 1955, Eugene wrote to Allen, informing him that Carl Solomon had been admitted to Pilgrim State Hospital, where his mother remained. Allen was "heartstruck at what seemed his hopeless impasse."[39]

In June 1955, Allen wrote a poem entitled "Dream Record: June 8, 1955." He saw Joan Vollmer, who asked about Burroughs, Kerouac, Huncke, and the others. Allen asked her, "What kind of knowledge have the dead?" and "What do you remember of us?"[40]

When Allen sat at his desk in San Francisco's North Beach on August 25, 1955, he did not intend to write a poem, let alone a breakthrough work. All he wanted to do was imaginatively recall some people who had his sympathy, so he combed through his journals, as he often did before starting on a new poem, looking for jumping-off points. This time he found a line he had dropped in his journal a few months before: "I saw the best mind angel-headed hipsters damned."[41] This time he rewrote the one line about best minds with a new twist.

> I saw the best minds of my generation
> generation destroyed by madness . . .[42]

By breaking the original one-line journal entry into two distinct phrase thoughts, as he had learned from Williams, Allen put on paper a new and intensely ambivalent but ultimately liberating thought concerning madness. It said madness is destructive of our generation but also that madness may be a product of this generation's best minds or even conducive to what makes them so remarkable.

The plurality of positions concerning madness expressed in this initial line was key to unlocking the extraordinary explosion of words, ideas, and emotions that burst forth and became "Howl." This initial line called for, if not demanded, a passionate, explanatory multivoiced response to the ambivalent, powerful claim. On this day, Allen was able to deliver.

Note how he is saying "I saw," not "I was." As such he gave himself plenty of room to gather and share his knowledge and experiences based on his being a witness to madness and psychiatry. Note also how "saw" and "was" are the same word forward and backward, therein further compressing the positions of the victim and witness.

Now he had to tell what exactly he had seen. He was a witness to the best minds and the mental "muse-eries" of this generation. He was also a witness to the damage society and psychiatry had done. In one imaginative stroke, he opened up a space for telling an entirely new story about the generation coming of age in postwar America. He had been gathering and digesting these stories for years, stories that spoke to many sides of madness. He had been making his way toward adopting the voice and perspective of a witness to madness.

Once the first line appeared, it cleared a space only he could fill. By drawing from experience, literature, and imagination, he told the history that justified his initial provocative claim. Right then and there, line after line of cases came to him in the form of an elegy for the struggles of the generation he knew best.

This history came in Jack Kerouac's style of irregular long lines, almost like prose, and with the syncopated rhythm of the blues, which he had long loved, going back to one of his favorite blues artists, Ma Rainey. After the flood of images and stories he wrote to Kerouac to tell him his method had finally worked: "I realize how right you are, that was the first time I sat down to blow."[43]

In a later letter to John Hollander, Allen explained his approach to the long line:

> If you talk fast and excitedly you get weird syntax and rhythms, just like you think, or nearer to what you think. . . . The attempt here is to let us see—to transcribe the thought all at once so that its ramifications appear on the page. . . . I want to get a wild page, as wild and as clear (really clear) as the mind—no forcing the thoughts into straightjacket—sort of a search for the rhythm of the thoughts & their natural occurrence & spacings & notational paradigms.[44]

As was revealed in the famous Joan Anderson letter, Allen was also inspired by Neal Cassady's spontaneous approach to writing, which was also an inspiration to Jack Kerouac, who later wrote of "the ones who are mad to live, mad to talk, mad to be saved."[45]

The stories in the lines came from Carl Solomon but also Herbert Huncke, William Burroughs, Neal Cassady, Jack Kerouac, Naomi Ginsberg, and Allen himself. Each spoke somehow to the theme of madness and to the best minds of their generation. These stories concerning madness evoked themes that had appeared in earlier poems and writings, such as:

Madness as ecstatic visions, from the early vision poems
Madness as fearful insanity, from the late vision poems
Madness as urban ethnographic portraits, from the stranger project
Madness as rebellion, from "Siesta in Xalba"
Madness as aesthetic method, from his readings on surrealism

What was so different about the lines he wrote that August afternoon was how the rearticulation of these themes all tied into the ambivalence of the opening line and became a fully realized portrait of a generation that thought it may be brilliant but was being told by authorities and institutions it was insane. The long breadth line or strophe was perfectly suited to delivering each bolt of charged experience. Its repetition conveyed the sense of a multitude of individuals and voices comprising an entire generation.

Following literary and blues traditions, Allen used the word "who" to make a rhythm: "who bared their brains," "who passed through universities," "who were expelled." Each line sounded as insistent, outrageous, and relentless as the underlying intellectual claims that these are the best minds despite or because of madness.

Thirty years later, Allen unpacked each line in the annotated "Howl." Regarding the theme of madness, several lines stand out.

" . . . hallucinating Arkansas and Blake-light tragedy among the scholars of war." This refers to Allen's 1948 visions.

" . . . who demanded sanity trials accusing the radio of hypnotism . . . " This refers to Naomi's paranoid delusions that the doctors had during shock therapy implanted three big sticks in her back to receive radio messages from FDR.

" . . . and who were instead given the concrete void of insulin Metrazol electricity hydrotherapy psychotherapy pingpong & amnesia." This refers to Solomon's experience of treatment at Pilgrim State.

Although these lines come from his and other's life experiences, this is anything but flat factual documentation and fully engages the absurd and humorous. Allen was highly sympathetic to the persons in each of these cases and ready to celebrate their humanity and condemn whoever or whatever was responsible for their suffering or confinement.

"Howl" Part I gravitates away from the nurturing institutions of family, college, and vocation and toward the dehumanizing madhouse. Yet the ambivalence posed in the very first line carries throughout the poem in a balancing of degradation verses transcendence. Madness is at once an enactment of personal expression, an aesthetic spirit, and an isolated and depraved suicidal death. Even as the poem delivers us to the depths of Solomon's suffering, the poem never makes it easy to distinguish between the "best minds" and "madness." This ambivalence baked into the theme of madness is a key part of what engages and empowers readers who are invited to experience and reflect upon different sides of madness.

In "Howl," he wrote about lobotomy in Part I, which contains the line: "who threw potato salad at CCNY lecturers on Dadaism and subsequently presented themselves on the granite steps of the madhouse with shaven heads and harlequin speech of suicide, demanding instantaneous lobotomy." In this line, inspired by Carl Solomon, lobotomy is depicted as something a person would actually want, an absurd, comic rejection of a world gone wrong. This is not so far from the truth. According to America's leading lobotomist, Walter Freeman, for years, patients and their families did actually write to him urgently requesting lobotomies.[46]

Toward the end of Part I, which bears witness to many instances of separation, degradation, confinement, and exile, the poem leaps energetically forward by using a range of techniques that work for Ginsberg as potential artistic solutions to life's intellectual and spiritual problems. This includes

Celine's "jump cuts," Whitman's "list poems," Williams's "variable foot" technique, Cezanne's "vibrating plane," and Klee's "gaps in space." The poet is telling the reader how he does it, how he writes poems, and how we can change our worlds through creating new images.

"Howl" Part II came to Allen in another sitting several months later. It was inspired by the idea of Moloch, who he later noted was "the Canaanite fire god, whose worship was marked by parents' burning their children as propitiatory sacrifice."[47] One night while wandering downtown San Francisco high on peyote, he felt the tangible presence of Moloch in the Sir Francis Drake Hotel, an edifice not unlike Pilgrim State Hospital. In a cafeteria in front of the Drake Hotel he wrote the initial draft, where Moloch is denounced as a "nightmare . . . loveless . . . mental . . . heavy judger of men . . . crossbone soulless jail . . . vast stores of war . . . stunned governments . . . whose mind is pure Machine" and more. Through repeated revisions and experimental wordplay, he arrived at the claim, "Moloch is the name of the Mind!" The mind not only makes beauty, as in poetry, but it causes damage through ideas and plans that wound and destroy, in wars, jails, asylums, and lobotomies.

One other line from "Howl" Part II brings the lobotomy to mind: "What sphinx of cement and aluminum bashed open their skulls and ate up their brains and imagination?" This line could be referring to the monstrous destroyer behind all lobotomies, including Naomi's. However, we will never know, because in his thirtieth anniversary edition, this is one of the very few lines of "Howl" Allen chose not to annotate.

"Howl" Part III, also written several months after Part I, begins with the line "Carl Solomon! I'm with you in Rockland" and repeats it, alternating with other lines, eighteen blazing times. It maintains the ambivalence of Part I and is both an empathic declaration and cautious distancing. The empathic part says we are close enough that I share in your experience. The distancing part says we are really in different situations.

Part III catalogues the protagonist's efforts to understand what the madness taken root in his friend, Carl Solomon. Madness both murders and laughs. Its beholders are creatively expressive yet disengaged from their own bodies and minds. Madness is both deadly serious and very silly. It may lead to a lone man's isolated depravity or to a spectacular community gathering. Madness is a particular state of human existence in which an individual is at risk of absolute spiritual death but also may reach a spiritually expansive state. Madness becomes the site of a struggle to be saved from spiritual death and to attain spiritual freedom. Madness wants a fight, especially with objects of authority. Psychiatrists and psychiatric hospitals fulfill this role, imprisoning people in madhouses and torturing them with electroshock and lobotomy, engineering the despiritualization of humanity. He knew this well from witnessing his mother's fall, although she is left out of "Howl."

"Footnote to Howl," written in 1955, Allen said was "dedicated to my mother who died in the madhouse and it says I loved her anyway and that even in worst conditions life is holy."[48] It repeats "Holy" many times "Everything is holy! everybody's holy! everywhere is holy! everyday is in eternity! Everyman's an angel!" and culminates with "Holy the supernatural extra brilliant intelligent kindness of the soul!"[49]

Allen first read Part I of "Howl" at the Six Gallery in San Francisco on October 7, 1955. The other parts were left out because they were not yet finished. Not only was his reading of "Howl" the event of the evening, according to Richard Eberhart, reporting for the *New York Times*, but it instantly became an event of great literary, cultural, and political significance:

> It is a howl against everything in our mechanistic civilization which kills the spirit, assuming that the louder you shout the more likely you are to be heard. It lays bare the nerves of suffering and spiritual struggle. Its positive force and energy come from a redemptive quality of love, although it destructively catalogues evils of our time from physical deprivation to madness.[50]

"Howl" was Allen's first truly great work and has been read, translated, and celebrated around the world. Critics heaped praise, and readers sought to draw upon its revolutionary power. Allen called "Howl" an "emotional time bomb that would continue exploding in U.S. consciousness in case our military-industrial-nationalist complex solidified into a repressive police bureaucracy."[51] "Howl" turned madness into "the Beat badge of honor in a world gone insane with bombs and dictators, terror and tyranny."[52]

By 1956, Naomi had less than one year to live. In this year she would not see either of her sons. She remained on the ward at Pilgrim State, where she heard voices and desperately tried to block the wires in her head. The doctor at Pilgrim State wrote, on December 16, 1955:

> This patient is very delusional and believes she has wires in her head. She probably also reacts to auditory hallucinations. She has a habit of pulling her dress over her head in protection against wires. At times she becomes noisy and is very insistent in her demands to go home.

She is idle on the ward, is not assaultive towards others and is not interested in any sorts of activities. . . . The patient has no visitors.

Naomi wrote to Allen: "Dear Allen, Please come to see me; tell Eugene too in a hurry! Naomi."[53] She wrote again:

Dear Allen, How is my young one? I am spending my time crocheting and dreaming. I hardly ever talk. Take me out! Allen and Eugene! What sort of a lawyer is he to leave his mommy here. Allen please take me out. I'll make such lovely meals for you! With love, Naomi. Write your address legibly.[54]

She even wrote to Louis:

Dear Louis, Well did you hear from the doctors? This place is conditioned. There is a wire-less on my head for four years. It works inside with voices. It's a Jewish work. It's done something to the bone and flesh. The voices claim I do not need the wireless on my head and the mean voices. I myself never had a fight in my life. [ ] is the doctor. I told him to take the wire off. So far he hasn't done it. [ ], who was doctor before, said she doesn't want to kill me. How can you go home with a wire on your head? She doesn't come in any more. The voices, He, doesn't open the door for me. He says, go home. The girls claim its up to the doctor. Take me home. Underline it. It means serious. Take me home from this place. Its peculiar. Oblige, Naomi.[55]

She wrote to Eugene:

Dear Eugene, How are you? I am asking you most deeply to take me out of the hospital before it is too late. I underline most and deeply to impress it upon your mind. God's informers came to my bed, and God, himself, I saw in the sky. It was after Jan. 1, 1956. The sunshine showed too, a key on the side of the window for me to get out. The yellow of the sunshine also showed a key on the side of the window. I am begging you to take me out of here. I've been here over five years. I wouldn't be a burden to you. I sent a letter to Louis. Dear daughter in law. I am begging you to convince Eugene to take me out. I know you are expecting in May and I hope it will give you much joy. Take me out of here. It is most urgent. Come over to see me—once more before the little one comes. With love, Naomi Ginsberg How's Allen?[56]

On April 26, 1956, Allen wrote in his journal: "In the Times Square movie house, there's Naomi, I sit next to her, suddenly recognize her, she me, I say

'Are you Naomi' she looks at me suspiciously, I say 'It's me, Allen' & break down crying, on her shoulder, leaning over seat on her breast, weeping."[57]

Eugene's son Lyle Brooks sent me a home movie of a family visit to see Naomi at Pilgrim State Hospital that took place in late May or early June 1956. Louis and his second wife, Edith, and Eugene and his wife, Connie, are seen walking outside with Naomi. The women hold Naomi's hands, and Eugene drapes his arm over her shoulder. Naomi stares into the camera but appears unresponsive and expressionless despite the others' affection.

On June 9, 1956, Peter Orlovsky received the telegram from Allen's brother Eugene announcing Naomi's death and left Allen a note on his writing desk: "I got this at 7:30 PM and here at 10:45 PM Out to find you. Be back soon. She's in the sunshine now. Love, Peter."[58]

Eight years after the light shone for Allen in Harlem, Allen too believed that the sun shone for Naomi in her room at Pilgrim State before she passed away. The sun she wrote of in her letters had released her into a better place. The sun's light was a beacon of hope, an image to build on, if Allen ever wanted to turn the grim circumstances of Naomi's life and death into something redemptive, hopeful, or holy.

Chapter 7

Gold Blast of Light, 1956–1959

IN "HOW KADDISH HAPPENED," published initially as liner notes for the poem's recording for Atlantic Records, Allen said he started writing "Kaddish" in Paris in 1958. He then wrote most of it in a forty-hour marathon a year later in New York City. Another small section came to him while standing on a city street corner. Typing up and revising the manuscript took another year, and it was finally published in 1961.

The marathon writing session started early in the morning, with Allen poetically recording "fragmentary recollections of key scenes with my mother ending with a death-prayer imitating the rhythms of the Hebrew Kaddish."[1] Then he realized he hadn't told "the whole secret family-self tale," so he started another section roughly following a chronological narrative of Allen living with her mental illness.

The question of how "Kaddish" happened is not really answered. Perhaps we can never really understand the mystery of how poems come to be. Yet because Allen kept journaling and corresponding, we can examine evidence of his approach as he worked his way toward "Kaddish" over several years before the marathon writing session.

After Naomi's death, while Allen traveled the world, he dredged up memories and emotions of their life together and tried to find meaning and inspiration from her suffering and struggle. As always, he took guidance from literature, art, and religion. In 1957, on his first trip to Europe, at the Prado Museum in Madrid, he saw Fra Angelico's *Annunciation*, which he wrote was the greatest painting he had ever seen, prompting another vision. Looking at "Kaddish" through the prism of the *Annunciation*, suggests this one painting helped provide Allen with an artistic model both for telling Naomi's complete story in an epic poem as well as for reworking his Blake visions so as to support his emerging role as a prophet for the younger generation.

In rethinking how "Kaddish" came to be, it is possible to trace lines between the poem and Allen's decades of experiences with Naomi and her mental illness, which I have covered in earlier chapters. But we must not forget "Kaddish" is a poem, not strictly a documentary account, and should be appreciated and understood as such, especially with its remarkable imagery and language.

To Harvey Shapiro, "Kaddish" is an "exalted lament" that spreads "joy and faith" through the writing itself, despite its heavy subject.[2] "Kaddish" presents what Helen Vendler calls a "taboo-breaking openness" of his mentally ill mother, which is groundbreaking in how it offers what Tony Triglio calls a "shift away from demonization" of mental illness.[3] If "Howl" "represses signs of women in order to forge male prophetic comradeship," in "Kaddish" maternity is the main focus and source of vision.[4] Others have raised questions about whether "Kaddish" is mere "violent emotional shorthand"[5] or "gratuitous exposure" of his mother's body and sexuality.[6]

In this chapter, I first approach "Kaddish" through examining Allen's preparatory writings in the years following Naomi's death as he was discovering how to write about her madness and death. Then, I look at the poem itself with a focus on how it approaches mental illness and madness.

On June 15, 1956, within days of Naomi's death, Allen shipped out on the USNS *Sgt. Jack J. Pendleton* for a three-month sail. The USNS *Pendleton* was a former US Army ship, launched in 1944, running missions in the Pacific during and after the Korean War. The aircraft cargo ship was leaving its home port of San Francisco for a resupply run up and down the Pacific Northwest coast, eventually bound for the Arctic Circle.

For serving as a yeoman-storekeeper, Allen got paid $450 per month. If he could put away most of his salary, he would have enough cash to finance a boat crossing to Europe. Ever since his travels through Mexico in 1955, Allen dreamed of going to Europe, the continent of his ancestors and literary and artistic forbearers.

On board the USNS *Pendleton*, the work was not too demanding, and there was the benefit of down time for reading, writing, and reflection. When alone in his bunk he kept thinking about his mother's passing as well as the whirlwind of the last seven years, which had catapulted him from having visions in Harlem to the Six Gallery reading of "Howl." He brought plenty of books to read, including Shakespeare's plays, Henry Miller's *Tropic of Cancer*, Herman Melville's *Moby-Dick*, and poetry by Hart Crane, Robinson Jeffers, Walt Whitman, and the French surrealists. When not working, the other crew members saw him slip away with a pile of books and a cup of the ship's weak coffee.

As always, he brought with several pocket-sized notebooks for jotting things down during the day and several larger composition notebooks for journaling, dream recording, and composing poems. In port he could meet up with old friends, make new acquaintances, drink in seaside bars, and look for men willing to have sex with him. On ship there was the beautiful and lonely option of standing on the prow and gazing out at the endless gray sea and the "misty vast nebulous and never-to-be-knowable clouds."[7]

A few days later, when the ship put into port in Tacoma, Washington, he received an unexpected letter from Naomi at Pilgrim State Hospital, which included:

> Don't take chances with your life! I wish you get married. Do you like farming? It's as good a job as any. I hope you behave well. Don't go in for too much drink and other things that are not good for you. . . . As for myself, I still have the wire on my head. The doctors know about it. They are still cutting the flesh & bone. They are giving me teeth-ache. I do wish you were back East, so I could see you. . . . I am glad you are having your poetry published. I wish I were out of here at the time you were young; then I would be young. I'm in the prime of life now.[8]

Allen figured this final letter from deceased Naomi must have been written no more than a day or two before she passed. It was fairly coherent and even offered motherly advice. She mentioned the wire in her head, which she had been repeating ever since the 1949 lobotomy, and her grandiosity comes through. Contrary to what Allen later wrote in "Kaddish," her final letter to him did not mention the sunshine and the key in the window, her recurring vision in her later years at Pilgrim State and mentioned in many of her previous letters to Allen and Eugene.

Upon reading Naomi's letter, Allen broke down. He sobbed for Naomi and for himself, for all the troubles that had beset her, and for all that had pulled them apart from each other. He never got to say goodbye. There were no clasped hands at bedside, no final hugs in the hospital room, not even a graveside blown kiss or a final prayer. Their next-to-last meeting at Pilgrim State had been dreadful, cut short by Naomi's warning of dread and his tearful flight from the hospital ward.

Allen knew that despite her serious troubles, Naomi had given him her best. But he still did not know what kind of story to tell about who she was and what had happened to her. They had received so little helpful information from the doctors. When they need something from you, they expect you to sign and not ask a lot of questions. They don't tell you much about the diagnosis, the cause, the treatments, or whether you or your loved one will get better. This lack of information did not make it any easier for him when Naomi was alive. Nobody ever explained to him what if anything he could do for his mother, except once to lobotomize her. After Naomi passed, this lack of information meant something different, as Allen became aware there was now a big blank space for him to fill in with whatever memories he could dredge up and whatever stories he could gather.

Naomi, like most mothers, was telling him drugs are no good for you. She had never taken drugs, other than the insulin, metrazol, and tranquilizers her doctors prescribed. Even still, why put any drugs in your body, Naomi was saying. Settle down into a calm job and loving family if you want to stay healthy.

Family members of people with a serious psychiatric illness often desperately search for explanations for what caused their loved one's demise. Of course as a poet, he wasn't only thinking of explanations. On board the USNS *Pendleton*, he was also looking for the perfect language and the images for telling the great emotional, spiritual, and narrative truths of her story. Allen kept journaling and let his dreams lead the way.

On June 21, 1956, he dreamed of Naomi, and the "pressure and horror woke me up."[9] In the dream he was in familiar living quarters and ran into Naomi. To his surprise, "she had a large dull fleshy cock and a cluster of 6 genitals attached with her body." They cuddled in bed, and he could feel her cock up against his body. He recognized this place as the family house; Louis was there too. When she was in another room, he told Louis he thought Naomi was a mutant. Then he recalled an unusual image of Naomi from an earlier dream:

> The look of her face, extremely high dome hair, like a stovepipe curbed or bowler hat shape, with French black oily glistening shock of hair all over her, neatly and artificially arranged, black, as on a window dressing dummy, and black black eyes, and pallor of skin, as if a robot or mutant—the peculiar look on the face I ascribed in dream to the lobotomy.

In the dream, Louis shrugged it off, but when he went into the living room Naomi was there. He asked her, "Where did you come from? How long have you been here?" He saw Naomi using a pen to write her name on a pillow "so I would not be forgotten or feel lost."

In dreams such as this one, Allen envisioned what had become of his mother. If Naomi was a mutant, was she a mutant from the lobotomy, the schizophrenia, or both? In either case, she had been removed from normal family and social life, proclaimed socially dead, operated on, and cast into the netherworld of the madhouse. She was not only his mother but a woman who lived a horror story and who deserved to be heard and remembered.

On the very next page of the journal he kept while on the *Pendleton*, Allen wrote a twenty-six-line text entitled "Psalm III" that years later would be pruned to a tight eleven-line poem. In his "Psalm" he pledged, "To God: To illuminate all / Begin with the lowest, and illuminate all sufferers."[10] He would later cut out the clunky metaphysical lines and build off of more tangible though ugly images: "I feed on your Name like a cockroach on a crumb—this cockroach is holy." He was seeing himself not only as Naomi's protector but also as taking on a public role on behalf of all sufferers.

Losing his mother had again piqued his interest in spirituality. He brought aboard ship some religious readings including the Old Testament, the Psalms of David, Felix Timmerman's *The Perfect Joy of St. Francis*, Theodore Maynard's *Saints for Our Times*, Rene Fulop-Miller's *Saints That Moved the World*, and Clare Boothe Luce's *Saints for Now*. Although he was a nonpracticing Jew, he had developed more and more interest in how the Christian saints approached life's ultimate problems.

After reading more about the life of St. Francis, he wrote he no longer felt "the drive to truth that would flip me out on my own toward my ideal of god." Whereas before he had looked to the Catholic saints and the saintly William Blake for affirmation of his visions, he had more recently come to acknowledge he would have to learn to live with doubts. Doubts about the truth and power of his visions, doubts about Naomi's ideas and perceptions, and doubts about God and spiritual redemption. Having visions could be one of those chances that Naomi, in her final letter, was warning him not to take. Now her doubts were mixing with all his own and piling up.

In the same passages about God, Allen moved from doubts about his spiritual life to doubts about his relationship with Orlovsky. Orlovsky, who identified as straight and liked girls, could never be his ideal life partner. Next, he moved to doubts about his poems, which he thought were still "disorganized." Even "Howl," which was already being celebrated as a major breakthrough, had not achieved the kind of "perfect and lifetime fact" he aspired to write. Could he ever realize his ideals, in spirit, in love, or in poetry?

On board the USNS *Pendleton,* Allen hoped the ocean would prove to be a source of creative inspiration. Late one night, out on the deck of the ship, he spied a large, dark mysterious shape in the water, which he thought might be a whale or even, perhaps, a sign from God. He kept staring at the figure as long as he could make it out in the shadows. He dropped to his knees. "I prayed for a sign of further enlightenment—that my mind was still more confused—I didn't know what I was doing anymore—suffering acceptable if accompanied by a sign of the direction I was to go."[11] The hoped-for ecstatic vision didn't occur, and the dark shape slipped away without ever being identified. No divine force was coming to his rescue, but he still had his literary heroes.

On board the USNS *Pendleton* he read all of Walt Whitman's poems and several biographies of Whitman. He journaled: "The remarkable thing here—the clarity—the complete and open revelation in his writing and biography—of a soul. You see his insides and deepest thoughts and worries and the ground of his sense of mortality."[12] He also noticed in the biographies' photographs of Whitman "the guarded look in Whitman's eyes . . . certainly a case of sex-imposed repression and consciousness." He saw in Whitman's eyes and poems the marks of fear, lovelessness, and fear of response—or of no response—all of which Allen was determined to avoid in his life and writing. Don't be afraid to take chances. Don't be afraid to be ridiculous or insane. Don't be afraid to give and receive love.

On July 9, Allen was resting on his knees on the ship's bow under the stars, "asking for Crucifixion as St. and to feel suffering of Christ in order to feel love."[13] For St. Francis, receiving the stigmata of Christ was the ultimate demonstration of his love for Christ. Had Allen done that for Naomi, by going to PI in 1949, where he claimed for himself the mantle of madness? Even if PI was incomparable with the institutions where Naomi had been held against her will, still he knew what it was like to be in a madhouse.

On board the ship, Allen went through the "Howl" page proofs for City Lights and was having doubts about the poem. "Howl" was imperfect, Allen thought, in not talking about Naomi or reflecting the full dimensions of madness. Naomi was far worse than any of the cast of characters in "Howl." Far madder than he had ever been when he was sent to PI. "Howl" had succeeded in telling a wild but ultimately comforting story of madness. He substituted Carl Solomon, his buddy from PI, for Naomi. But what if the story in "Howl" was not the whole miserable truth? Had he allowed himself to be too swayed by the idea of madness as liberation? He still believed in a liberating madness but knew in truth it was only a part of the story. He was beginning to feel he would have to find a way to correct this shortcoming in a new poem by telling the whole story using a new tone and language.

Allen journaled of his love for Peter Orlovsky and of his failure to achieve his ideal of homosexual love. "From earliest years, 11 to 14, this has been my deepest longing, almost a mystical longing."[14] Curiously, he then switched back to religious longing. "And giving that up, replaced by a purer and more evanescent mystical longing for the Deity I saw in things once and new saw again since Harlem!" Spiritual and sexual longing were at times merged for Allen, sharing a desire for contact, ecstasy, and union. But again, Allen wondered, how could he satisfy any of his or others' desires when life's circumstances could be so bleak and disheartening?

Allen spent nights on the bow staring at the dark sea and clouds, asking himself if he was ready for death. Looking into the mist, he imagined seeing Whitman and Naomi both dying in front of him, and there was nothing at all he could do. He felt terrifyingly alone and preoccupied with death. If he could not find love or grasp faith, then death was all that awaited him.

He wrote another psalm, which begins: "real as my mother was: Lord life is fading/the sea surrounds me dark as night/I have no eloquence to offer. My confusion is blank as the sea."[15] This psalm he never published. It expressed suffering but read too much like a miserable dead end. He once thought the sea might work as a metaphor for some grand articulation about his mother, but this had not proven true so far. "Though I pray for suffering when I suffer I see nothing but suffering and no merciful release nature to it."[16]

Allen did not allow himself to succumb to despair. The writer in him and some other stores of personal strength kept working to conquer it. One of the writing strategies he had learned from Williams was to go through his small notebooks and transcribe the writings he wanted to hold on to and possibly use later. Sometimes these inspired him to write more prose or a poem.

The first line he copied was: "My mother it is a wonder she has any mind left at all—she had it blown to bits, cut and drugged, analyzed."[17] He saw that somehow, Naomi had retained a reserve of strength despite everything the hospitals and doctors had done to her brain while treating her. Maybe Naomi's strength, surprising and inspiring, was something for Allen to build on.

In another passage Allen copied down a line about Herbert Huncke, his hip junky friend from Times Square, who after the car chase and crash had been sent to Rikers. "To build a time machine of naked passion and transport you out of the world at least to eternal realms of imagination."[18] "Huncke!

Huncke! Forgive me! I did not know what I did! What I was doing!"[19] The down and out, junkies, criminals, and mental patients all needed an advocate to stand beside them to demand their just place in society and to demand they counted as persons of equal value.

Another poem, "Schumann's Kinderschomen," pictures his mother as "the withering of Naomi" and "the flower of immortality lost."[20] It does not specify what caused the withering. He bid "farewell . . . to her to myself to childhood to life itself."

Serious illness in a parent, including mental illness, often turns the generational roles upside down—the parents become the child, and the child becomes the parent. Naomi's death had shaken up that inversion, and for Allen presented an opportunity to reconnect with childhood memories he had long ago forsaken. Her passing also accentuated his sense of being haunted by death: "Death is so near."[21]

On July 27, 1956, the USNS *Pendleton* passed through the Bering Strait, the fifty-eight-mile waterway separating the easternmost point of Asia from the westernmost point of North America. Allen knew he was only miles from Russia, Naomi's home country. He badly wanted to visualize the Russian coast, but the Arctic fog was too thick. He noted small flocks of birds flying overhead, passing from one continent to another, "the worlds apart almost touching."[22] He too was straddling many worlds—the mad and the quotidian, hospitals and society, the spiritual and the prosaic, art and life.

On July 29, Allen awoke from a dream remembering the words "You have forsaken your God."[23] The very next entry Allen wrote in his journal was: "Kaddish or the Sea Poem, irregular lines each perfect,"[24] and he set his sights on writing a Kaddish while out at sea.

After using the ship's office to retype and mimeograph a final draft of "Siesta in Xalba," the long poem about his Mexican journey, Allen dismissed this poem as "unbalanced and egotistic."[25] It was supposed to build upon his experiences of the Mayan ruins in the Yucatan, but he now saw what was missing: "no outbreak of truth in it, no emotional outbreak, no decision, no discovery, just note thoughts, nostalgic lines, were a touch of pity, no crises, no drama, never comes to a point."[26] Allen knew he was not there yet.

On board the USNS *Pendleton*, Allen also wrote to friends and kept up his prodigious correspondences. To Jack Kerouac, he wrote, "I am beginning to see how important Christ is in relation to the Old Testament—he just turns it upside down, revokes the old God-spoken holy laws in person."[27] Ever since his visions, bridging the holy and the prosaic was Allen's challenge as well.

Allen wrote of "St Elizabeth of Hungary," who had founded a new religious order based upon the teachings of St. Francis of Assisi. He also wrote about "Princess Lillioukalani visiting the Malokai leper island reduced to tears."[28] This was Queen Regent Liliuokalani, who visited the famous Hawaiian island in 1881. What if not lepers but the mentally ill were his saintly focus? They too were castaways from society, rejected, dejected, and forced to live in grim sanatoria.

When Allen next wrote of "St. Peter of Long Island, St. Lucien of St. Louis, St. Neal of Denver, St. Jack of Lowell, St. Bill of Tangiers, St. Allen of Paterson,"[29] he was, without a doubt, joking. He was, however, completely committed to promoting the works of his friends and launching a literary movement with them. He was also becoming serious about becoming St. Allen for all the mad ones out there.

Allen approached this project not as a religious cleric but as an artist. On board ship, he was doing the work he had been doing for more than a dozen years: figuring out how as an artist he could address the experiences of mental illness, including the challenges of a heartbreaking loss and a family world turned upside down by Naomi's serious mental illness—challenges with many layers and moving parts. He wanted to communicate about them all. Doing so required writing a very different kind of poem than he had ever written, one with more sympathetic attitudes toward mental illness and madness.

Allen was reading widely about the Christian saints from several popular books of the day. When the Allen of 1956 looked at the saints, it was with a different focus than the Allen of 1948. Back then, he was single-mindedly focused on ecstatic visionary experiences and the question of how you make contact with God. He read religious visionary poems to see how other artists had done what he then felt he must do—write poems capable of catalyzing visions in others. As we already know, he was unable to achieve this to his satisfaction. The impact of his mother's passing had further reminded him of his and others' serious doubts about the wisdom of pursuing a visionary path.

Through his readings he was now exploring the lives of the saints in more depth. He was looking more broadly at their relationship to suffering in various forms and at their lifelong struggles to affirm their faith and to do good in the world. Allen was swimming in an ocean of suffering—grief and guilt over Naomi's death, frustration over his relationship with Peter, the loneliness of being at sea, and, finally, an incapacity to write perfect poems. Sure, he had not suffered like Naomi had suffered, but he had suffered plenty, as had his friends. If necessary, he would suffer more, like a saint, as long as he was getting somewhere. Could reading about the saints' approaches to their suffering give him a map, or at the least some signs, to follow? He hoped so.

Signs he did find, suggest his journals. The saints' lives were oriented toward the suffering of others. Even if you cannot cure them, you can stand with and for them, show them they are valued, and bear witness to their struggles. For Allen, the greatest personification of the suffering of others was no doubt his mother. He saw reflections of her struggles in some of his friends, like Carl Solomon and Herbert Huncke. The mad ones in his generation were his lepers. He also wrote about death, which had haunted him for years. The death of his mother brought to the forefront the inevitability and absolute finality of death. He had to accept death as a part of a larger plan.

The saints told him to accept God and let faith in the divine serve as a source of strength and beauty. This did not come easy to Allen, because though of Jewish origin, he did not then feel especially bound to Judaism or any particular religious tradition. Entirely on his own he had gained much knowledge about Christianity and Buddhism, but he was not one for organized religion.

The divine had to come to Allen through the senses, literally. He had to see, hear, touch, and smell the presence of God. He identified with the saints, who by some mysterious, innate virtue, had extraordinary capabilities to experience the spiritual and to share those experiences with others. All the saints he read about had experienced a miracle through which their contact with God was made plain. Allen had his 1948 visions. But for several years he had put those away upon the advice of the PI psychiatrists. Now he did not know how to get back to the visions—or if it was advisable to do so.

He felt he had to write poetry about suffering and death—and not just small sketches but epic works carrying big meanings. On the ship in July 1956 he wrote in his journal: "People are tired of listening to dead poetry— redirect them to ecstasy . . . nothing will save us, nothing will save us from the grave."[30] If all he was thinking of was death, that would lead nowhere.

He was devoted to the daily recording of his dreams, which was where he once found the sources for what Williams long ago recognized as poetry. Since then he documented each and every dream in incredible detail. In dreams, he hoped to keep his experiences and perceptions less tainted by cognition, so they could serve as sources for the new vision.

On August 2, at sea off the northern coast of Alaska, Allen wrote: "Dream, evening 7–730–8 o'clock light nite Wainwright Alaska. On which Naomi is adored as an immortal movie star of old . . . with Eugene go into movie to see Naomi as actress—a bad later film, she snake women hysterical and embarrassing bad overwrought she is 1930's acting."[31] The dream continued, and he pictured another earlier movie of hers, "as simple princess shepherd saint of flowers, a movie as Clara Bow 'The Hat' where with peculiar innocent faded film charm and nostalgia she dances and waltzes and looks girlish and lovely as a flower."[32]

He wanted to recast Naomi, but how? He saw her in two opposing female guises—snake woman and flower princess. That was a start, but it wasn't yet a story. Did a screenplay exist for telling a whole story to bring back the dead and redeem what looked to all like a most pathetic life? No, not yet.

Another journal notation announced: "Kaddish Naom/Review of life _____ aspirations sex poetry and friendship/Farewell realizing, all must die/Take life in hands—a symbolic act of _____ & purification."[33] Review her life? He had never attempted that. Never even thought there was any reason to try. Naomi had this terrible sickness, and they simply had to deal with it. But now, he thought, could he show how she and her family had tried their best to take her life into their hands, despite the circumstances? In telling her story, could he show how he was taking her and his life in his hands? Could he show how society made this tragedy possible and yet how God offered redemption for the sufferers? His thinking about Naomi was changing, and he was coming closer to realizing a story he could tell in a poem.

Allen received a letter from Louis written on August 13, 1956. On the ship he read that Louis was working on several poems about Naomi's funeral. "One of these poems, a brief 8 line lyric, called 'Burial,' has a condensation and hint of the Emily Dickinson touch. This poem has been accepted by The N.Y.Times. It should appear in a week or so."[34] Eugene had also written a poem about Naomi, which was published in the *New York Times*. Allen imagined himself to be capable of something much grander than these small sketches. But he needed much more material to work with if he was going to write anything of substance, let alone a major poem. He took the first few steps in the intimidating process of dredging up memories of childhood experiences and remembrances of Naomi. It involved making journal notes about particular times from his childhood.

the trauma—moving from _B in #7 to school #12 full of man mean dirty negroes, nasty crazy negroes, and I protested the change. I began failing at school, goofing on technique and reading books and withdrawing into dreamworld. Thereafter where was Naomi when I'd changed?[35]

This was back in the fall of 1937, when Allen was eleven years old. Louis had moved the family to a less expensive apartment, and Allen had transferred schools. The kids teased him and picked fights. To make matters worse, Naomi was hospitalized at Greystone for three years, which to any child would seem like forever. When Allen wasn't home, he was staying in Newark, with relatives from Louis's side of the family. He missed his mother terribly. Twenty years later, in his journals, he was attempting to fill in the missing pieces of their histories.

This was as far as he got when the USNS *Pendleton* arrived at San Francisco in September 1956. He had pocketed nearly two thousand dollars and even managed to print fifty-two copies of the long poem "Siesta in Xalba" on the ship's photocopier. The page proofs for "Howl" were all completed, and he was now anxiously waiting for his first book of poetry to be published. He had made good use of the time, reading, reflecting, and journaling, but he still didn't have much to show for it in terms of a new Kaddish. But at least there were signs something was on its way.

What he had earned on board the ship was enough to keep him going for the next several months. After reuniting with his friends in San Francisco, he hitchhiked to Los Angeles, where his newfound celebrity got him a reading in front of Anaïs Nin. But instead of "Howl," which everyone there expected to hear, he read the unknown and sexually provocative "Many Loves," which had been written at sea.

At the reading Allen was taunted by a drunk who wanted to know what he stood for. Allen said he stood for nakedness, spiritual nakedness, and poetic nakedness, and then he completely disrobed in front of the stunned audience. He had been witness to such behavior early in life, as Naomi had a penchant for nudism at home, but more to the point, he had recently read in one of his books on the saints about a key moment in St. Francis of Assisi's life, when in front of the authorities and his father demanding his compliance, Francis stripped naked and declared himself to be uncompromisingly on the side of the poor and Christ. Allen was learning not only how to write but what were his values and methods and how to perform in accordance with those values and methods in front of an audience. To make his point, he was not afraid to be a little bit mad.

On September 2, 1956, Richard Eberhart published "West Coast Rhythms" in the *New York Times Book Review*.[36] Although not a formal review of

"Howl," which had not yet been published, Eberhart surveyed the new poetry scene and proclaimed Allen's "Howl" "the most remarkable poem of the young group." To Eberhart, "Howl" was "profoundly Jewish" and "a howl against everything in our mechanistic civilization which kills the spirit." All of a sudden, the "Beats" were famous, and Allen was a celebrity—and with that came misunderstandings by the mainstream media.

After a wild drunken road trip to Mexico City with Gregory Corso, Peter Orlovsky, and Jack Kerouac, Allen caught a ride back to New York City, arriving in Greenwich Village in December 1956. There he made the rounds of reviewers, editors, and publishers, and worked diligently to get Kerouac's and Burroughs's books into print. He did not get much of his own writing done. Between family, friends, and networking, there were too many distractions.

In late 1956, just before returning to New York City, he wrote this haiku: "Walking to Naomi's grave/White clouds/And the sun burning over there."[37] This poem was written in anticipation of his first visit to Naomi's grave on Long Island. While at the burial grounds, he came away with an image of crows cawing, which later made its way into the short final section of "Kaddish."

Naomi Ginsberg's grave,
Beth Moses Cemetery, New York.
Courtesy Lyle Brooks.

Allen figured now he was finally ready to make good on his dream of going to Europe. There, on the continent saturated with the history and art of the Christian saints, Allen would do climactic work on the spiritual and artistic concepts he had been working on a few months back while at sea.

The money from the ship, combined with the thousand dollars Naomi left him as an inheritance, gave him a financial base for starting out. But first he wanted to stop off in Tangiers to be with William Burroughs. Burroughs's manuscript for *Naked Lunch* was a mess, and his friends would all work together as a team of editors to get it into shape. On March 19, 1957, Allen and Peter arrived in Casablanca by ship and then made it overland to Tangiers, where they were reunited with William Burroughs and Jack Kerouac.

Allen didn't get much writing or journaling done in Tangiers, as most of the effort was directed to putting Burroughs's *Naked Lunch* together. Other chroniclers of the Beats have described this effort as the setting up of an editorial office.[38] I see it as an artistic community's salvaging operation to facilitate an outsider's highly idiosyncratic expressions. Allen was putting into practice the values he was starting to articulate about helping outsiders achieve new levels of expression and consciousness.

While in Tangiers, Allen also became friendly with the writers Jane and Paul Bowles and the painter Francis Bacon. Most unfortunately, Jane Bowles had a small stroke in May, just as Paul Bowles had returned from travels to Ceylon. This made further contact impossible, disappointing Allen. With Peter and William each vying for Allen's attention, tensions were rising, as was Allen's restlessness. Once again, it was time to move on.

On June 11, 1957, Allen and Peter left Tangiers for Allen's first visit to Europe. They crossed by ferry from Tangiers to Algeciras, Spain, alongside dolphins under the crescent moon. After a few days' stopover to see the dusty, picturesque Alhambra, they reached Madrid via night train. The first day, after finding a room, Allen entered the Prado Museum on his own.

His love of painting began with his mother Naomi, who painted colorful still lifes back when she was well. During his first years at Columbia in New York City, he made many outings to the Metropolitan Museum of Art, the Guggenheim, and especially the Museum of Modern Art, with its Cézannes displayed in the basement, especially *L'Estaque*, from which he first received strange vibrations in 1948.

Coming from Paterson, New Jersey, Allen was hungry for the city and for art that spoke to the outsider's sense growing in his youthful brain and belly. After he began to travel the world, when he arrived in a new city, Allen would go straight to the museums to view their paintings.

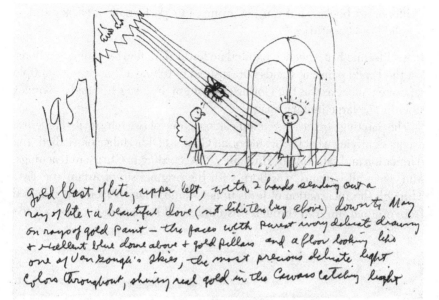

Allen's letter to Eugene Ginsberg, June 1957. © Allen Ginsberg Estate; Courtesy Columbia University Libraries.

In the Prado, Allen found Fra Angelico's *Annunciation*. Fra Angelico was born in 1400 in Vicchio, became a friar in Fiesole, and painted in Tuscany and even for the pope in the Vatican. Allen's letter to his brother Eugene reads:

One gem by Fra Angelico, a 15th century Italian painter—The Annunciationi—showing (drawing) gold blast of lite, upper left, with two bands sending out a ray of lite and a beautiful dove (not like the bug above) down to Mary on rays of gold paint—the faces with purest ivory delicate drawing and excellent blue dome above gold pillars and a floor looking like one of Van Gogh's skies, the most precious delicate light colors throughout, shining real gold in the canvas catching light from the museum window, and all the colors preserved so bright after seven centuries the picture outshines all the Rubens and Goyas and Velazquez & Breughel and Titian in the museum. . . . A guard saw me stare at it for a long space of time and nodded and said he thought it was the best piece in the museum . . . the annunciation seemed the greatest painting I ever saw first hand—I'd vaguely remember it from life, or art books—but was not aware of its perfection—delicacy and solid bright centuries.[39]

In his lifetime Fra Angelico painted no fewer than fourteen annunciations. Yet the Prado painting stands out. Instead of telling a story using multiple separate panels, as was the Gothic convention, Fra Angelico told a complex story in one large unitary image.

The painting portrays the annunciation as one of two interrelated religious events signifying what the art historian Georges Didi-Huberman called "the damnation and salvation of Humanity."[40] According to Christian teachings, Mary, like all humans, was born with the original sin of Adam and Eve. Through the Incarnation of Jesus in her womb, Mary herself was released from original sin. And through this miracle all humankind is shown it too

Annunciation, Fra Angelico, 1430–1432, Museo Prado.

may be delivered from original sin by giving itself to God's word. In Fra Angelico's painting, these two defining stories of Christian spirituality, one of sin and the other of redemption, are seamlessly integrated into one larger story about humanity and God.

Fra Angelico's *Annunciation* is what the Renaissance figure Leon Battista Alberti called an "istoria,"[41] or a fully realized and aesthetically satisfying humanistic painting. The painting is full of doubles that reflect and destabilize each other, building aesthetic interest and spiritual energy.

Spatially, we see a portico and a garden, which upon close inspection look less and less like two distinct spaces. The right frame depicts the annunciation of the Madonna, with the expulsion of Adam and Eve from Eden in the left frame. These two stories couldn't be any more different, yet in this brilliant painting, one is side by side with the other, its supposed opposite, as part of a larger network of meaning.

Mary, her back against the right edge, sits under a portico. She bows stiffly from the waist, arms crossed, with a sorrowful expression and downcast eyes. Cheeks flushed, skin pasty white like the wall behind her, draped by a golden tapestry. A heavy blue robe enwraps her body, frail and humble in a pallid rose dress. The angel Gabriel with a gold-trimmed rose robe and golden wings arrives before her under the portico and begins to kneel. As the angel does, the tips of his wings and his right foot extend beyond the portico out into the garden.

The ceiling is blue like the sky, covered by a spread of white stars. The floor is blue beside the angel, unlike beside Mary, where instead there are swirls of white, pink, and gold. One column of the portico falls between the angel and Mary, where one bird perches, and a second bird flies in the golden beam. On the far wall, between Mary and the angel, is a vestibule with a bench and a small window for looking out of, suggesting a matching space from which the viewer of the painting is looking in from.

That golden beam of light enters the portico from the garden outside, where the sun rests about the trees. The sun has within it two outstretched hands, which are releasing the golden beam. Mary and the angel each have a golden halo encircling their heads. On Mary's lap rests an open book. The angel announces to Mary that the word of God is passing into her, and in humble terror, Mary accepts God's awful gift to bear a child whom in time she will lose.

The viewer's eyes follow the straight shot of the brilliant golden ray, crossing from the sun in the upper-left corner to Mary seated under the portico on the right. The viewer looks back at Eden, thick with flowering bushes and trees, as green and dark and earthy as the portico where Mary sits is light, clean, and airy. Another angel is expelling Adam and Eve out toward the left margin of the frame.

Eve looks shiftily back at Adam and, Allen imagined, him. Her hands are clasped. She knows she has been caught giving in to temptation. Adam holds his right hand up to his eye. He knows they were wrong to sin and fears what will now happen. Three fleshy flowers off their stems lie on the ground near their bare feet. Though the sun rests in the blue sky just above their heads, the golden beam it gives off crosses over the garden to enter the portico on the other side. Will they be forgiven for enjoying the pure pleasures of each other's bodies?

In his letter to Eugene, Allen drew a sketch of a ray of light beaming at Mary, along with creatures looking more like bugs than angels. The penand-paper sketch did not include the Garden of Eden scene.

When Allen looked at the *Annunciation*, what did he see? I believe he was making connections to his own experiences with visions.

In this painting, Allen also saw Fra Angelico's brilliant "gold blast of light" coming from the sun and the outstretched hands of God, which could have brought him back to his 1948 visionary experience. This painting shows God's miracle, though without heavy-handed pronouncing, but simply with a sunbeam and a whisper. An angel's golden whisper can be more powerful than a flurry of words. If only he had understood this back in 1948.

Allen found the swirls of color on the marble floor on which the angel and Mary stood to be as beautiful and modern as Van Gogh's *Starry Night*, which he had seen many times at the Museum of Modern Art. These colors were saying something about the mystery.

By the angel the marble was blue, like the sky and like his gown, whereas by Mary, the marble was golden, from the sunlight mixing with a pale whitish pink mirroring Mary's face and hands. From Fra Angelico, Allen could have taken in an entirely new way to depict the miracle of the Incarnation. Through aesthetic creation you could represent mystical changes not through direct pronouncement—the heavy-handed and portentous phrases of which Burroughs said Allen was far too prone—but through depicting substantive changes in the physical nature of things.

While gazing at the painting, perhaps he could also have noticed how Mary now did not seem like she was bowing or submitting but was cocking her head, listening intently for the word of God. She seemed less frail, more intense and focused, listening to words only she could hear. Could Fra Angelico's painting have caused him to reimagine what had happened to him one summer day in Harlem? Maybe the sounds he heard were not just a low rumbling, as he had become used to recalling. Rather, could it have been William Blake appearing like the angel and speaking for God through his *Songs of Innocence and of Experience*? Yes, William Blake's voice passed into his ear and joined with his own bodily sounds. He was like Mary, who had accepted God's word and will. Through Allen's visions, something divine and human might be born inside of him.

This polyphonic masterpiece offered so many figures for Allen to read into. We can't know for certain, but I believe this painting helped expand his already remarkable imagination, empathy, and perspective. He might also have made the connection to scenes from his own life and his mother's. He could have seen Naomi as akin to Mary, who would give birth to a child who grew to be a very special person. He could have been like Jesus, the Jesus Ginsberg he drew ten years ago at PI, who, now infused with Blake's voice, would show all humankind how anyone could unite through God's spirit.

In the canvas he could also have seen Mary's fragility. Her eyes were heavy, almost defeated, and her arms crossed not in prayer but in a half-hearted attempt to protect herself. Her forehead and eye were exposed, her skin pale. Is it possible he could even picture the unspeakable cruelty of a surgery that used a sharp object to enter the skull and cut the white nerve tissue of the brain's cortex?

He could also have identified with Adam, who had somehow sinned with Naomi, by letting himself be persuaded by the doctor's rationale for lobotomy or, perhaps, through her paranoid delusions or by the "sexual demands" and seductions she inflicted on him as a child.

Last and most urgently, he may have wanted to be like Fra Angelico, a revolutionary artist who literally changed the world through one extraordinary work of art. Patti Smith told me that Allen would have identified with the *Annunciation* as a remarkable "announcement" portraying how one is being spoken to by a messenger from another dimension.[42] If Fra Angelico could tell the whole story of sin and redemption in one painting, so could Allen in a long poem. If he was going to be a great artist, then he had to tell the complete *istoria* of the madness in his and Naomi's life. No fragments, but a perfect whole, bringing together all these different images and stories.

Standing before the painting and seeing how remarkably Fra Angelico told a complete story, Allen might have realized that thus far his vision poems had fallen flat and that his poems about madness had leaned too far toward emphasizing its bright, liberatory aspect—the "best minds." His friend, the poet Gary Snyder, critiqued "Howl" for not overcoming dualism and for proposing that the "ordinary world of mind isn't enough," which for too many meant turning to drugs.[43] Some things he had written over the years concentrated on the darker side of madness, such as the sketches of strangers he spotted on the subway. However, these were no more than fragments. Allen knew very well there was still much from the darker side he had minimized in "Howl."

He was proud of "Howl," which, after all, brought in and defended all of his friends' madness, but he knew he could do better. He had to tell the whole story of their madness, explicitly including Naomi's, and to confess his own helplessness and sins. Could the poet learn from Fra Angelico how to announce visions, spiritual conversion, and sin and punishment without being too abstract? How do you make the holy feel human and approachable?

Just as challenging, could he fill in the left side of the drawing in his letter to Eugene, which he had left blank, and depict the consequences of sins without getting too miserable and moralistic? These were human frailties that had to be acknowledged, but sensitively. Finally, could he present conversion and sin as a part of a broader network of meanings about madness without closing off the many possible meanings this system generated? Could he do it in one great *istoria* about madness, love, God, family, suffering, and poetry? A young poet could learn a lot from a master painter like Fra Angelico. He was so glad to be in Europe: Here he could stand before great art and let it go to work on him, just as he aspired for his poems to do for others.

If only Allen could write like Fra Angelico could paint. "Infinite pictures,"[44] Allen called them. He wanted to write poems where spiritual change was brought to life through artistic representation. Poems depicting both damaging and liberating madness. Poems showing the madness that shaped all our lives, not just Naomi's and his own, but the entire human tragicomedy. Poems where the dreaded past, the confused present, and hoped-for future all came together. Poems as perfectly constructed and beautifully colored as the figures and spaces in Fra Angelico's masterpiece. Poems that could change how others saw themselves and pictured the world, just like the master painters.

It would take far more than seeing a great painting to enable the poet to write poems, let alone a great poem. But after seeing the *Annunciation* at the Prado, Allen had another artistic model to help him put it all together. More so, it built upon his long familiarity with annunciation imagery, which was all over his poems, beginning in 1948, when those visions were described with winged angels, a gleam of light, and doves chirping.

When I asked Allen about the *Annunciation*, he said those were "archaic images" and added, "The dove descending. That's from Eliot."[45] Yet we know he read far more than Eliot, right around the time of his 1948 visions, including theological manuscripts from the bookshelves of his friend's sublet. Obviously, he encountered the *Annunciation* from more than one source in his extensive literary and spiritual readings. But as we shall see, something important seemed to shift for Allen after seeing Fra Angelico's *Annunciation* in 1957. The role of this painting was again confirmed by Allen when he included his encounter with Fra Angelico's painting in a "history of visions" list he compiled in 1960.[46]

Allen also knew he needed to settle down somewhere and write all he had just taken in and learned. Paris sounded good. You could live the bohemian life in a cheap flat on a historic city street, with cheap cafes and bistros where a strong coffee or a red wine costs practically nothing.

In Paris, Allen and Peter connected with Gregory Corso and eventually found a room in a small, run-down, four-story inn. The location was 9 rue Gît-le-Cœur in the Latin Quarter, between the rue St. Andre des Arts and the Seine, with a widow innkeeper, Madame Rachou, who was known to be friendly to artists and writers. For $35 a month, three of them could squeeze into one room. The building stank, was home to rats and mice, and had hot water only three days per week. Within months, they were joined by William Burroughs and Brion Gysin. They named their new residence the Beat Hotel.

Allen awoke before the others and wrote early in the morning. He enjoyed sitting in the literary cafes of Paris, including the Café Select in Montparnasse, a famous gathering spot for writers and artists which was open twenty-four hours a day. You never knew who would walk in the door.

One day, at the Café Select, he was jotting down lines and he found a jumping-off point. "O Mother/farewell/with long black shoe."[47] The memories revolved around the word "farewell," then pivoted on the phrase "with your . . . ," and then "with your eyes . . . ," and a rhythm got worked up. Grief over her loss enveloped a surrealistic catalogue of remembrances of her body, her politics, her family, her collapse, and her death. Allen drew these lines from the French surrealist Andre Breton's poem "Free Union," which concludes:

With eyes that are purple armor and a magnetized needle
With eyes of savannahs
With eyes full of water to drink in prisons
My wife with eyes that are forests forever under the ax

My wife with eyes that are the equal of water and air and earth
and fire[48]

Allen greatly admired Breton and called "Free Union" the "singular
seminal greatest list poem of the Twentieth Century." At the cafe table,
Allen wept as he wrote, and the effect on him was to achieve a natural
rhythm around his sobs; the experience was so intense and moving that he
thought he was finally getting into the great poem about his mother. But he
could only sustain the emotion for so long before he lost the rhythm and
the words stopped coming.

Several weeks later, he wrote in his journal a title "Elegy for Mama" with
a bold underline. He began writing these declarations: "Call Peter to Come
to the Door! Open the Gate of Gold! X down from the Cross! Call Mary
out of her Iron Cloud! Call down the god out of Heaven." "Greystone risen
from New Jersey, lifted bodily the hospital up into the sky."[49] Here he was
combining Christian images of redemption (blue sky) with the name of the
state mental hospital where he once visited Naomi.

He next articulated and began responding with what must have felt like
almost unbearable honesty to a central question underlying his traumatic
grief:

> Mother, what should I have done to save you
> Should I have put out the sun?
> Should I have not called the police
> Should I have been your lover
> Should I have held your hands and walked in the park at midnight
>   for 60 years?
> I am a poet. I will put out the sun.[50]

These lines raised questions of a filial nature: If you are a son and your mother
is seriously mentally ill and making sexual demands on you, what are the
limits to what you should do for her? What kind of powers should you call
upon to help her? Should you put out the sun?

Perhaps he was talking about the sun shining brightly on Naomi's burial
day. This was the sun Louis and Eugene had told him about. It was mockingly
bright; a day of mourning should be cloudy. As a marker of his grief, he
would make it go away. Or was this line a reminder of the sun's beams, which
inspired Naomi and which she wrote about in her letters to her sons? Was
this the sun's "key" shining through the hospital window and beckoning
her? Allen had already nearly put her sun out by signing for her lobotomy.
Now, what kind of a poem can a poet write that puts out the sun?

He did not know what to do. So he wrote of not knowing what to do.

Mother after your death what can I do for you now?
Come bearing armfuls of magic roses?
Come visit your grave and stare at the winter sun?

He could write a poem telling the truth of the horrors that befell her. He would go "visit your paid piece of earth . . . your cunt in the dirt."[51] The poet would come with "death in the palm of my hand." Death defeated madness. In the dirt they could be together, "naked, singing folk songs, among the smelly tendrils and roots of trees . . . we'll all be filthy angels . . . going mad again underground." As he wrote, the poet kept reaching for memories of Elanor, Max, and Eugene, coming up with some clipped images and responding with the language of Christian redemption. His desire to tell this story was, for now at least, greater than the story being written. "Mother Mother let me begin/I'll explain in 6 languages." The problem was he only knew one.

He wrote down a verse he had penned the year before: "Walking to Naomi's grave/White Clouds/The sun burning up there."[52] This image had both the clouds and the sun, as if he knew more than one kind of weather was needed to adequately convey his experience with Naomi. Maybe he didn't have to put out the sun. Was it a question of showing what happened when the sun was out? Or in Fra Angelico's terms, what was going on in the left side of the canvas in the place where the sun was not shining?

In the next few pages, written some days or weeks later, we see him trying different ways. Under the title "Song of Naomi," a verse began with an image of Naomi's somatic delusions: "4 big sticks, 4 big sticks, 4 big sticks in my back/wires in my head the ceiling is a radio."[53] A few pages later the poet recorded his response to her death:

Now all is changed for me
As all is changed for thee, Naomi
Worry until the brain broke down
Cerebral hemorrhage
I hear the heart torn out of the world.[54]

By focusing on the medical events of a brain breaking down and a cerebral hemorrhage, his rhetoric was on the one hand pathophysiologic. But the next line took the personal and made it experiential and emotional. Who hasn't heard or felt the heart being torn out of their world? That could be the right note to strike to tell Naomi's story, turning it into a human story of anyone's pain and loss. It wasn't only about Naomi's fatal cerebral hemorrhage; it was about the ravages of mental illness, the failures of hospitals, and the loss of a parent you could not save, despite your best efforts.

This then led into some poetic philosophizing about time, desire, and death. The poet reverberated from despairing to hopeful positions:

> Would that there were a magic flash
> And Time seen thru and the grave invisible
> And its rolling wonder of unsatisfied desire
> Be revealed in the burning sun.[55]

The poet even called once again for an annunciation-like miracle:

> Would that there were a Visible God
> Come down with the Voice of st . . . . father
> And open our minds and uplift our desire."[56]

Each call for redemption he imagined, he then repudiated and thus put out the sun, or hope of the sun. And he did so with increasingly dense images of Naomi's journey into the darkness of serious mental illness and ineffective psychiatric treatment.

A few pages later we find: "My mother it is a wonder she has any mind left At all / She's had it shocked by insulin, electrocuted, blown to bits, drugged, cut, analysed—dead."[57] Maybe he had to tell all what was done to her. The poet was getting revved up for that telling but was not quite there yet. Still, he was beginning to fill in the blank spaces with stories and images that came from their lives together.

Allen's daily life was filled with frustrations. He got news from the United States of Neal Cassady being jailed for selling marijuana. Allen felt partly to blame, believing "Howl" had led to backlash by the authorities and a crackdown on drug taking. He missed Peter, who had returned to the United States to take care of his brother. He was short on cash and decided he would soon leave Paris and return to New York.

During these months, other beautiful and noteworthy poems came to Allen. Each delivered particular moments that pointed toward the major poem about his mother he still had to write.

"At Apollinaire's Grave" finds Allen and Peter visiting the grave of the famous French poet at the Pere Lachaise Cemetery. Apollinaire coined the term "surrealism" and was a part of the community of artists in Montparnasse that included Pablo Picasso, Gertrude Stein, Max Jacob, and Jean Cocteau. Allen visited the cemetery to sit and work on some poems. He brought with him a copy of "Howl" and laid it "on top of his silent Calligramme / for him to read between the lines with Xray eyes of Poet."[58] Allen employed some tricks of time in this poem. He sat in the shade by Apollinaire's tomb, observing the present moment ("an ant runs over my corduroy sleeve") while imagining himself out carousing with Guillaume's artistic Parisian gang as well as looking back over life and death with Apollinaire himself. The ability to write about the dead simultaneously in different times would be deployed again in writing "Kaddish."

"The Lion for Real" is far and away Allen's most expressive poem about his Blake visions. The protagonist finds a lion in his living room. He screams, "Lion! Lion!"[59] but can't get anyone to believe him, not the two stenographers from next door, his Reichian analyst, old boyfriend, or novelist friend. Allen was familiar with William Blake's proverbs "The wrath of the lion is the wisdom of God" and "The roaring of lions, the howling of wolves, the raging of the stormy sea, and the destructive sword, are portions of eternity too great for the eye of man."

But this lion felt real. It was not a vision that disappeared in the daylight. The lion stayed in his apartment as a living, breathing presence. The lion was starving in his apartment but "didn't eat me." The poet "Sat by his side every night averting my eyes from his hungry motheaten face/stopped eating myself he got weaker and roared at night while I had nightmares." The lion the poet describes then shifts into someone I associate with Naomi. In the poem the poet's novelist friend points out, "You said your mother was mad . . ."

Our protagonist has a dilemma. As the lion lies dying on the floor, the protagonist cries, "Eat me or die!" Eventually the lion gets up, and as it walks out the door says, "Not this time Baby—but I will be back again." This time, the lion has let him go, but the lion knows the idea of him will keep haunting the protagonist.

> Lion that eats my mind now for a decade knowing only your hunger
> Not the bliss of your satisfaction O roar of the Universe how am I
>   chosen.

The lion of this last verse roars with both the majestic power of God and the depravity of a psychotic woman. They became one and the same as the poet pledges lifelong commitment to a benevolent and threatening deity.

"To Aunt Rose" is one of Allen's most tender poems. He bids farewell to his Aunt Rose with sweet reminiscence and memories of times shared in the old neighborhood of Osborne Terrace in Newark. He recalls her "with your thin face and buck tooth smile and pain/of rheumatism—and a long black heavy shoe,"[60] and he recalls himself being cared for by her, "the time

I stood on the toilet seat naked/and you powdered my thighs with cala-mine/against the poison ivy." He recalls her welcoming Louis and celebrating his poetry book being accepted for publication. But the poem is death haunted. Louis's books are out of print. Hitler is dead. One haunting image ends the poem. "Last time I saw you was the hospital/pale skull protruding under ashen skin/blue veined unconscious girl/in an oxygen tent/the war in Spain ended long ago Aunt Rose." This image of his aunt recalls a painting from long ago of a pale young woman underneath a portico. It is also rem-iniscent of the quiet goodbye Allen and Naomi were denied.

Back in the United States, "Howl" had become the focus of an obscenity trial. The trouble began the year before, when US Customs officials seized copies of the book coming in from the printer in England. Lawrence Fer-linghetti, with help from the ACLU, mobilized legal advocates, and the US attorney dropped the case. Then on June 3, 1957, plainclothes detectives walked into City Lights Bookstore, purchased a copy of "Howl," and then arrested Shig Murao, the manager, for selling obscene literature. Allen anxiously followed these developments from abroad, concerned about the burden on Ferlinghetti and Murao, unsure what his role should be. In October 1958, Judge W. J. Clayton Horn ruled "Howl" was not obscene and of "social importance."[61]

William Burroughs arrived in Paris in January 1958, just missing Orlovsky, who had returned to New York to keep his brother Lafcadio from landing in a mental institution. During their stay, Allen, Burroughs, and Gregory Corso met Marcel Duchamp, Man Ray, Benjamin Peret, Tristan Tzara, Louis-Ferdinand Celine, and Henri Michaux. Allen then traveled to London with Gregory, where they made the rounds with journalists and writers including W. H. Auden and Dame Edith Sitwell.

All the while, Allen maintained his correspondence with his father, Louis. His letters reflected Allen's political concerns about the state of the world and evolving ideas about the problem of America's role in the world ("The U.S. has been mad as a hatter"). They were also deeply personal. Louis wrote:

> True, in the beginning, when I loved a woman who grew incurably psychotic, I was handicapped; yet in my handicap I used the hand-cuffs as bracelets by letting my spirit feed in creative poetry and also by providing the best I could for Naomi. I did more than I could, but the odds were against me. (Some day I suspect—as they are even beginning it now,—science will show that Naomi's illness was rooted

in a molecular or atomic maladjustment of her brain or nervous system.)[62]

Allen wrote back cordially about this most difficult topic:

I know some of the difficulties you must have had, having a sundered emotional relationship—I had the same myself with her. Though I find now it has not destroyed my capacity for an emotional relationship in depth—more easily with men, though now I find it slowly developing with women too. I think you are right about the biological nature of madness—have read a good deal about it recently, actually—It's one of William's specialized studies—there has been a lot of work done on it—large medical library full of learned journals summarizing current researches, that we've gone to. . . . I've had both "schizo" experiences and have also experienced mescaline, and did note the similarity. . . . In fact they were already experimenting with Mescaline in Psychiatric Institute when I was there. All quite interesting.[63]

How would all these memories, emotions, and ideas ever coalesce into the major poem he still needed to write for Naomi?

On July 23, 1958, the steamship *Liberty* entered New York Harbor. After more than a year abroad, Allen was thrilled to be reunited with Peter Orlovsky, Jack Kerouac, and Lucien Carr. Within a few weeks, Orlovsky and he found a four-bedroom apartment on the Lower East Side at 170 East Second Street for $60 per month. The apartment was only blocks away from Orchard Street, where Naomi first lived when she arrived in the United States from Russia and where her father opened an ice cream and candy shop.

A half-dozen blocks uptown, near Cooper Square, was the Five Spot Café, a hip downtown jazz bar. Allen went there night after night to hear the jazz pianist Thelonious Monk, who was in the midst of one of his several lengthy periods of residency there, which began in June 1957, when Allen was still in Paris. Allen was treated like a celebrity and let in without paying a cover charge. One night he approached Monk and gave him a copy of "Howl," and after reading it, Monk told him, "It makes sense."[64]

Like William Burroughs, Monk had been hunted by the authorities for his drug use. For seven years, he was denied a cabaret license and couldn't play in New York. With the release of the LP *Brilliant Corners* in 1957, Monk's career was finally taking off. He played a gig for six months at the

Five Spot in a band with John Coltrane on saxophone, later replaced by Johnny Griffin. Like Burroughs and Allen, as an artist Monk was somewhat of a late bloomer.

While seeing Monk at the Five Spot, Allen recalled spotting a magical-looking dwarfish man sitting at a corner table making some kind of marks on a piece of paper in response to the music. He approached the man, who turned out to be the musicologist and artist Harry Smith, and asked him what he was doing. Smith was calculating whether Thelonious Monk was hitting the piano before or after the beat—trying to notate the syncopation of Monk's piano. He was counting the variants for his animated collages. He needed the exact tempo of Monk's changes and punctuations of time in order to synchronize the collages and hand-drawn frame-by-frame abstractions with Monk's music.[65]

Allen knew he needed a new rhythmic scheme for the Kaddish he wanted to write for his mother. He was intentionally taking a distance from the sound of "Howl," which, as he described at an early reading at Reed College, was based on a be-bop saxophone phrasing: "The line length . . . you'll notice that they're all built on bop—you might think of them as a bop refrain—chorus after chorus after chorus—the ideal being, say, Lester Young in Kansas City in 1938, blowing 72 choruses of 'The Man I Love' until everyone in the hall was out of his head."[66]

"Howl" blew with the fluid, joyful, lengthy phrasings of Lester Young, a perfect cool match for the madness-as-liberation theme. Monk's reworking of be-bop, never coming quite on the beat but always aware of the beat, which Allen took in night after night at the Five Spot, gave him a new jazz model for a rhythmic scheme fitting with the disturbing and mournful themes of the Kaddish. Consider, for example, how the jazz critic Stanley Crouch, writing about the same Five Spot gigs Allen attended, described what Monk was doing, musically: "His determination [was] to sustain the power of the tradition rather than reduce it to clichés, trends, novelties, or uniformed parodies."[67]

Monk was a perfect ingredient to complete the polyrhythmic stew Allen had been cooking up for "Kaddish" for the past several years. Allen's own descriptions of "Kaddish" placed emphasis upon the rhythms of grieving, but repeated listenings to "Kaddish" show many rhythmic elements sounding off. These included:

> The chanting of the Hebrew Mourners' Kaddish, which, as one commentator noted, consists of "The rising of the 'yit,' the thud of the 'ta,'" sounds of peaks and stops, punctuated by the call and response

of the Amen. That is what makes the Mourners' Kaddish "the lullaby
of the bereaved."[68]

The pressured speech of an agitated person, which Allen recalled from
one young male patient at PI who screamed out: "All you patients on
the eighth floor, all you patients on the seventh floor, all you patients
on the sixth floor, everybody on the fifth floor, doctors, nurses, all you
attendants, you're all gonna die!"[69]

The knockout ravings of a paranoid psychotic, of which Allen's memory
was full of far too many examples from years of living with Naomi,
who feared attacks from Nazis, doctors, her mother-in-law, and her
own husband.

Waves of grief, with sobbing alternating with calm sadness and even
moments of humorous reflections, which had been washing over
Allen at cafes, docks, ships, streets, and bedrooms, across his many
years of mourning for Naomi.

The list technique of unconscious images produced by psychic automa-
tism as practiced by Andre Breton, the founder of surrealism.

The earnestness and formality of a devout's liturgical prayer.

The ecstatic joy of a mystic's unexpected spiritual contact with God.

The imaginative English poetic elegy, as in Shelley's "Adonais," which
reconstrues Keats as a victim of vicious literary critics and enthusiastically comes to his defense.

The jazzy, urbane, visionary poetics of Hart Crane's "The Bridge."

The American blues lyric tradition of Ray Charles, Robert Johnson,
Leadbelly, and Ma Rainey, which Allen had enjoyed since a child on
the phonograph and radio.

Most of "Kaddish" was written in a marathon forty-hour writing session
that took Allen by surprise in his writing room on East Second Street in New
York City in mid-November 1958. After being up all night with his friend Zev
Putterman, taking morphine and dexamphetamine to get buzzed and reading
the Mourners' Kaddish together, Allen walked home at dawn, sat himself
down at his desk, and started writing. Peter kept slipping into the room with
coffee to keep him up and hard-boiled eggs for his empty stomach.

Once Allen got himself into an emotional state and was accessing the
rhythms and images of the story, he had to get it all down. The floodgates
were open, and he needed a writing session even longer than that of "Howl"
to put down on paper his artistic reworking of all he had kept bottled up
inside. He wrote with the undaunted determination of an artist who wouldn't
let himself stop until he had the basis for a perfect poem.

As a disciplined editor, he knew it was also necessary to let the poem sit and follow it up with intensive rewriting. Over the next two years he revised "Kaddish" before arriving at the poem we know today. On October 11, 1960, he sent the "Kaddish" manuscript to Lawrence Ferlinghetti, who wanted to publish a second book of Allen's poetry to follow up the hugely successful *Howl and Other Poems.*

"Strange now to think of you, gone without corsets & eyes, while I walk on the sunny pavement of Greenwich Village."[70] This opening line, on par with that of "Howl," declares "Kaddish" as a poem of witness, reflection, death, women's mysteries, perseverance, and New York City.

"Kaddish" introduces Naomi as a Jewish girl from Russia who passed through the hovels of the Lower East Side, to Paterson, then to Manhattan skyscrapers. She received an education, got married, began a career, begot children—all as expected of a young woman of her time.

In the school of life, Naomi was also "learning to be mad," with a "nervous breakdown" coming just after "marriage" and before "operation." Both she and her son Allen, and by implication the rest of us, are "in a fix" and "accelerating toward Apocalypse." He contemplates her "suffering" and the death that, given her affliction, is all that could set her free to a good place where she could rest.

The poet calls upon several spiritual resources—the Jewish Mourners' Kaddish, the Buddhist book of answers, and Ray Charles's blues—which have helped legions of mourners with their grief.

The poet's voice is halting, with long lines broken up with dashes, giving the rhythm a start-stop quality, slowing the reader's pace and accentuating the nervousness that pervades "Kaddish"—Naomi's nervousness—which Allen, and the reader, watch over.

Allen sees Naomi as a flower, "fed to the ground—but mad, with its petals, colored, thinking Great Universe, shaken, cut in the head, leaf stript, hid in an egg crate hospital, cloth wrapped, sore." I picture the flowers in the *Annunciation*, leafy, lying on the ground, bereft of stem to hold them, colorful yet completely vulnerable. Flowers that will get cut, crated, removed from the garden, and taken away. But in Allen's hands, Naomi's life as a flower was a heroic battle: "No flower like that flower, which knew itself in the garden, and fought the/knife—lost/cut down by an idiot Snowman's icy—even in the Spring—strange ghost thought—some Death—Sharp icicle in his hand—"

When Allen read "Kaddish" in front of an audience, these lines were read with great emotional intensity. Who is the "idiot snowman?" Think prefrontal lobotomy, which was done with an ice pick. The poet changed it into an icicle. An idiot snowman, who froze all his feelings, as any lobotomist must and as Allen told me he had to do when signing consent, used the icicle to irreversibly sever living brain tissue.

This idiot snowman may be the germ seed of future cultural icons of destructive social conformity, such as the Beatles' "Nowhere Man" and Bob Dylan's "Idiot Wind." To save you, they have to cut you. To make our nation safe, we have to threaten others and let ourselves be threatened with total annihilation. This was the logic of modernity, including medicine and psychiatry, and the nuclear age. All of us who think as such are idiots, these popular artists seemed to be saying, following Allen's lead in "Kaddish."

Part II begins, "Over and over—refrain—of the Hospitals—still haven't written your history—leave it abstract—a few images." This history of Naomi's madness unfolds over thirteen dense pages, which took thirty-six minutes to recite at a rare 1985 reading at the Knitting Factory. The main voice is Allen, who speaks both as a witness and as a son, caught up in a whirlwind of his mother's paranoia, his father's worries, public mental hospitals, and his own fear and fright.

His story begins with "remembrance of electrical shocks," which is an example of undoing, as electric shocks often induce amnesia; most patients do not remember them. It continues through many episodes of Naomi being driven by psychosis as she attempts to get young Allen to understand what is wrong with her: Naomi speaks, pleading for Allen to understand how the hospital did this to her "ever since those 3 big sticks up my back—they did something to me in Hospital, they poisoned me, they want to see me dead—3 big sticks, 3 big sticks—" She pleads with young Allen to not be afraid of her. "I'm your mother."

For decades, the poet had remained silent about what Naomi's illness put her and him through, but he now recalls all those embarrassing and terrifying episodes on street corners, buses, rest homes, at home, and in bathrooms. In doing so, Allen gives us one of the first-ever family narratives of a person's serious mental illness and lobotomy, not to mention one of the most sensitive narratives of an immigrant woman.

Naomi's madness is drawn not just as hers but as a paranoid reflection on tremendously hard times—Hitler, Wall Street's collapse, the Great Depression, communism, spies and the Cold War. She took the same journey as millions of European migrants to America, and look at what happened to her. In "Kaddish," a key question underlying her story is: How much of modernity, including its conflicts, wars, weapons, refugees, and poverty, is too much for one person's mind and one family to bear? This is a question not only for migrants or for women but for all citizens of Earth in the post–World War II era.

In other words, the madness chronicled in "Kaddish" is not only an individual disease but a social diagnosis, driven by adverse social conditions and historical processes. In "How Kaddish Happened," Allen wrote he was trying to speak to "the broken consciousness of mid twentieth century suffering anguish" and "the mind-illusion mechano-universe of un-feeling time in which I saw my self my own mother and my very nation trapped desolate our worlds of consciousness homeless and at war."[71] Modernity made this madness and then through its harmful interventions made it even worse.

Psychiatric treatments made Naomi worse. Allen was dragged along with Naomi and this madness to rest homes, emergency rooms, prescription counters, mental hospitals, doctors' offices, and ambulances. Thus, "Kaddish" is also a critique of the institutions of modern psychiatry, which thought they had her correctly diagnosed and knew how to treat her but actually led her to suffer even more.

Allen has his own issues, as he was descended upon by "whole mountains of homosexuality" and a "weight on my melancholy head—" His brother Eugene was lonely, without love, studying law. His implication is her illness and suffering also caused their unhappiness and the milder form of mental illness Allen himself experienced. In "Kaddish," Allen expressed the psychiatric thinking of the day: You can be made homosexual by how poorly your parents raised you.

Naomi ran away from Louis and was living with Elanor and then in Manhattan cooking lentil soup for Allen. Allen recounted one day where she exposed herself to him; Allen thought she was trying to seduce him. If he believed it would help her, would he do it for her? Sure, why not? Shouldn't a child do anything necessary to help their desperately ill parent be well? "Kaddish" takes us to the traumatic scene of what the psychoanalyst Leonard Shengold calls "soul murder," which is "to deprive the child of his or her own identity and ability to experience joy in life."[72] But Naomi's intention was only to be well and to be free, and Allen, always looking to support her, can't hold his victimization against her.

"Kaddish" depicts how Allen and his brother and father lived with her madness and how it became their burden too. Naomi said, "Don't be afraid of me," and he told her, "Trust the Drs." The illness that could have completely severed their attachment and dashed their love actually made it stronger. Her desire and theirs, to be a loving family, to stay connected, endures in "Kaddish," which is in part a redemption story that rescues

Naomi's voice and quest for a good life and God, humanizes her struggle with madness, and invites the reader in.

She gets to the point where she could only paint "Naomiisms" at painting classes in the Bronx. These were, no doubt, "Sad paintings—but she expressed herself." She lived with her sister Elanor but one day kicked her with a long black shoe, so Allen called the police, who brought her back to the hospital. In the police car, Naomi turned to Allen, "Why did you do this?"

Then, after a two-year absence, he returned to see her again in the hospital, where he encountered Naomi after her stroke, as a freak, "a scar on her head, the lobotomy—ruin, the hand dipping downwards to death—" The implication is the lobotomy was recent, on this final prolonged hospital admission, which was what the poet either mistakenly recalled or intentionally changed. However, we know the lobotomy happened much earlier, in 1948, six months before Allen had his Blake visions.

"Kaddish" also depicts his last hospital visit, where Allen was confronted again by the horror of Naomi's demise and her failure to recognize him. "You're not Allen." This encounter is presented differently from how Allen recorded it in his journal, where it was he who didn't recognize the much-aged Naomi and Naomi who feared Allen was going to be struck down just as she had been. Whether this change was intentional or unintentional, we will never know. I note how the poem has her appear more delirious than delusional, like someone approaching death more than being driven deeper into schizophrenic psychosis. He consoles himself that she still writes letters and hymns, as does he, "work of the merciful lord of poetry."

Toward the end of Part II, "Kaddish" reimagines Naomi as a beautiful Russian-faced woman on the grass, long black hair crowned with flowers, a mandolin on her knees, "blessed daughter come to America." This idyllic image is reminiscent of a photo of Naomi with Louis, legs crossed in the grass, relaxed and smiling. And then in a surprise move Allen claims her as his muse:

O glorious muse that bore me from the womb, gave suck first mystic life & taught me talk and music, from whose pained head I first took Vision—

Tortured and beaten in the skull—What mad hallucinations of the damned that drive me out of my own skull to seek Eternity till I find Peace for Thee, O Poetry, and for all humankind call on the Origin

From the affliction of madness also come spiritual seeking and the gifts of poetry and song. But unlike "Howl," where the madness itself was liberatory and at times hilarious, the madness of "Kaddish" is heartbreaking, and the poem makes abundantly clear the tremendous costs paid, both in Naomi's life and his. Which makes Allen taking her as his muse, finding redemption, settling what was otherwise unsettled all the more remarkable.

In "Kaddish," Allen works not with one but with two narratives: Naomi's decline and his rise. He proposes a new relationship between those two story lines. Madness may be extreme suffering, but it nonetheless offers the benefit of driving searches—both his and hers—for meaning, faith, and peace. Naomi's final release and Allen's answers are found not in visions but in, "Death which is the mother of the universe!" Naomi first led the way into madness and then into death, which let her and can let the rest of us out of this life of suffering.

Not long after being notified of her death, while on board the USNS *Pendleton*, Allen received her final letter. In "Kaddish" he reported this letter had the image of the sunlight in the window, which was actually from an earlier letter to his brother. The key in the form of sunlight, which came to him in his 1948 Blake visions, was what released Allen from his doldrums and into spiritual and artistic heights. In "Kaddish," Allen changes this too. He doesn't put out the sun, as suggested in early drafts of "Kaddish." Instead he puts it in! By doing so, he offers a release from both madness and death through an image of hope that ties madness to art and spirit, including to the sun of the *Annunciation*, and of course the sun rising over all humanity every day with its gold blast of light.

The poem's next section, "Hymmnn," is a liturgy praising the Lord and the world he hath created. Of all "Kaddish" it is the most formally structured, yet in content it is anything but staid. It gives us the worlds of Newark, the madhouse, homosexuality, paranoia, and sickness. The poem's praise for the divine's endorsement of these types of social deviancy conveys a radical political vision.

What's more, Allen praises God for bringing death to us all. Should he be praising God for bringing us into the house of death? In the Jewish tradition, upon death we praise the greatness of God. But in the frightening twentieth-century world of madness and suffering, death has become a release and is thus praiseworthy. In the era of the nuclear bomb, this praise of the power of death could also refer to how all could be ushered into the house of death. He taps into and gives expression to this fundamental fear and gives holy name to the potential for total annihilation only an instant away.

Part III has the protagonist trying to make sense of Naomi's supposed last letter with its redemptive image: "The key is in the sunlight at the window in the bars the key is in the/sunlight." The key was left behind and is there for the taking. The living could take the key and go ahead and open the door, open the grave, open the universe, and open the vast sense of time. The key is afforded to the living through one's own creative responses.

Most of Part IV was written earlier in Paris in the fall of 1957. During later revisions, Allen added the lines, "Oh mother/what have I left out/O Mother/what have I forgotten" and put them at the beginning as a transition. Part IV has its own distinct rhythm, which approximates the Hebrew Mourners' Kaddish. It keeps repeating "with your eyes," which sounds like "Adonai," which means the Lord. The chant keeps going and going with nine lines of "with your . . . " and twenty-eight lines of "with your eyes of . . . ," piling on more and more details of Naomi's life and madness. It is a tally, before God, of everything Allen wants to remember and bury with Naomi, culminating in "with your eyes of shock/with your eyes of lobotomy/with your eyes of divorce/with your eyes of stroke/with your eyes alone/with your eyes/with your eyes/with your Death full of Flowers." But of course he has not buried these images but inscribed them in his elegy, which would soon become known all over the world.

Part V was written as a fugue, growing from words that came to Allen on a New York City street corner at dusk. "Caw Caw," shrieked the crows. The birds of God are announcing Allen's vision of eternity. He alternates the "Caw Caw" with "Lord Lord" until they merge in the poem's last line. He first sees and hears those crows when he goes to Long Island to visit Naomi's grave. He can also sense the presence of her body underneath the grass as he stands on top, just a few feet away. He is half the age as Naomi was when she died. Halfway through his life and before the day he will be buried like her.

This life seems so small in comparison with the vastness of the Lord's universe. Maybe the sun is not gone, though it has set on Naomi's life, like it will set someday on all our lives. Just the same, the sun will also rise another day. The sun, which like all of us eventually, belongs to eternity.

The first handwritten draft of Kaddish Parts I and II is nearly identical with the published version but does reveal some key revisions. Several personal confessions were dropped, for example: "I started a fire in the rattan waste basket she came in 1931 Bloomingdale expensive hospital—".[73] Several lines spoke about his guilt over not visiting her in Pilgrim State in her last years, including: "and why was she there? and who came to see her? three years now—not I—and I'd put her in—and no sign from me now," and "Though I had not visited, last, left her to look at the Earth alone—2 years of solitude—no one, at age nearing 60." All these lines, which were simply dropped from the final poem, may have been regarded as too much of a dead weight, by virtue of their personal confession and straight-ahead delivery.

Several other lines spoke to Allen's guilt over having had her hospitalized for the final time in Bellevue in 1951, are listed here:

> To rot another year or two or three—forever . . .
> you saw me there, my eyes, I saw your eyes, you saw me betray you
> I called the final Cops of Madness on you, Mama, and I that made
>   me do it! Mama! Mama!
> I left her to go, alone, I left for alone, to the Bellevue to go to the
>   Long Island—to the Hospital at Pilgrim State—
> I waved, and I kissed her Goodbye, "Naomi forgive me" "Goodbye,
>   allen, help me." "Goodbye."

Elements of these lines were incorporated in a more disjointed way into long lines that better maintained the rhythm, such as:

> staring at my eyes, betrayed—the final cops of madness rescuing
>   me—from your foot against the broken heart of Elanor,

and

> came in a few hours—drove off at 4 A.M. to some Bellevue in the
>   night downtown—gone to the hospital forever. I saw her led away—
> she waved, tears in her eyes.

These revisions give some insight into how "Kaddish" was made. They shift the emphasis of the poem—less about Naomi's involuntary confinement, more about her mental illness and madness.

"Kaddish" bears witness to madness and mental illness and tells a story that had not been told before. A madness like Naomi's can be a defeat worse than physical death. It is worse because if you are so psychotic as to lose consciousness, as can happen in untreated serious mental illness, then you may lose the essence of what it means to be human.

Unlike "Howl," in "Kaddish" Naomi is not a part of a flock and needs only to be understood as herself. She suffered almost entirely alone. The poem never equates Naomi's madness with Allen's. Whatever clinical condition Allen had, it was something else entirely, and he was to her son, caregiver, and witness.

"Kaddish" also says a madness like Naomi's doesn't just originate from an individual. Her suffering was also a product of her interactions with society, institutions, community, and family. So if we are going to tell a story about madness, it has to be a social story not just about one woman but about twentieth-century America. This is a story about the impossible being asked of an immigrant woman. It is a story about the failures of the people and institutions that were supposed to support and care for her. It's about a massive social letdown of all of the world's Naomis.

"Kaddish" does something "Howl" did not in giving us a woman as the central figure of the poem. Allen thus ties his "Kaddish" to the difficult life conditions of women, including immigrant women, mentally ill women, oppressed, captive, and abused women. In light of the new information about Naomi's childhood sexual abuse, sexually abused girls and women can be added to the list. Readers of "Kaddish" may have considered the possibility that Naomi was a trauma victim, and now many years later we can make explicit what the poem made implicit. Thus "Kaddish" ties Allen into another tragic realm of human experience—girls and women victimized by sexual assault from men—thus expanding the scope of his witnessing to those cursed acts that affect an estimated one of ten women globally.[74]

Naomi lost consciousness at times, but in his final rendering of her, after more than thirty years of illness and ravaging treatments, she still has some left. Even in those suffering from clinical madness or in those who have had their brains shocked, cut, drugged, and analyzed, there is the possibility of inspiring sun visions and warm farewell letters. This is consistent with a recent trend to let hallucinations and delusions go untreated.[75] Allen revised the letters in the poem so as to make the visions bigger. He needed there to be a golden light and the presence of the eternal amid an otherwise very grim story. Many years later, in the poem "White Shroud" Allen imagined a reunion with a mellowed Naomi now living on the streets of New York City.

With this came the possibility that the wisdom, insight, and joy miraculously held within madness could be transmitted through a work of art. Through "Kaddish," the poet spelled out the core components that artwork should bring: careful documentation of the facts of events; natural and physical details; remarkable language; an expression of desire, eternal seeking, and finding the keys to life; and an energetic polyrhythmic assemblage. A story of days gone by that many decades later still speaks to fearful and tragic new times.

As an innovative work of literature, "Kaddish" enabled Allen to extend his prophesying into new territory beyond the more liberatory view of madness expressed in "Howl." "Kaddish" staked out harrowing new landscapes in imagining and engaging real-world suffering, conflict, injustice, traumas, and death, in an empowering narrative of witness. This assisted Allen in becoming a poet for the terrifying contemporary era of world war, poverty, racial struggle, and nuclear weapons.

Allen wrote "Psalm IV" at some uncertain date in 1960, when he was putting the finishing touches on "Kaddish." "Psalm IV" is not a major literary work on the scale of "Kaddish," but it deserves our attention. It is the latest and final installment in his series of religious poems, which consists of "Psalm I" (1949), "Psalm II" (1949), and "Psalm III" (1956). This sacred song continues the dialogue about his spiritual life and prophetic aspirations not long after they were piqued in 1957 by viewing Fra Angelico's *Annunciation*. "Psalm IV" is also his first poem since 1949 that explicitly retells the story of his visions.

In "Psalm IV," the visions are now "secret visions" and the "face of God" an "impossible sight."[76] The "living Sun-flower" he now names comes from a book page, and the voice he hears has an "earthen measure." The visions themselves and the elements constituting them are each described in ways that loosen or undo their stability as events and objects. These are poetic equivalents of the visual displacements Fra Angelico used to treat the Annunciation in the Prado painting. The insertion of contradictory elements has the effect of destabilizing these objects and their relationships, which contributes to the sense of mystery inherent in the scene's spiritual contact.

The story of the visions is familiar, not unlike what the poet has said before in the letters and journals quoted previously. After masturbating, he is reading Blake's "Ah Sunflower" while lying on a couch in a Harlem sublet and looking out the window at the buildings across the street. The setting also echoes elements of the archetypal Annunciation. Masturbation, or ejaculation without intercourse, can be associated with incarnation, or conception without intercourse. The sunlight pours through the window while the book rests on his lap, as in the painting where Mary has an open prayer book on her lap.

A few changes grab our attention. He writes: "and heard a voice, it was Blake's," and it enters into Allen through his "secret ear." These are explicit images borrowed from the Annunciation, where the word of God was said to enter into Mary, where they do more than ordinary speech. Could seeing the *Annunciation* and reflecting on how Fra Angelico so masterfully laid the mystery down on his canvas have helped convince Allen his visions were never going to be seen as complete without including the actual voice of Blake?

The next line shifts the focus to the windows and walls on the buildings: "red walls of buildings flashed outside" and then "each brick and cornice stained with intelligence like a vast living face." Think of how Fra Angelico's marble floors did much of the work of representing the mystery of the incarnation or, in another example, his use of red blotches in his frescoes of other religious scenes. Did Allen borrow Fra Angelico's manipulations of materials into images, imagining the bricks and cornices of the city as alive and possessing intelligence?

Next, "Psalm IV" gives snippets of dialogue and interaction between a literary father and son. The return of fathers, in Allen's poetry and consciousness, after the focus in "Kaddish" on the poet's mother, is a striking development. This fourth time around, the poetic rendering of an Annunciation establishes a link with Blake, a heavenly father. Belatedly, the son thanks the father for "thy careful watching and waiting over my soul!" The father too is grateful he has not been forgotten after all these years. Allen had his mother as his mad muse but, no less importantly, his literary father William Blake to guide him. They embrace in tears, but even this soothing moment is countered by the father's "dead arms," another poetic expression of double-sidedness in the face of madness and death, packed into two simple words.

On February 5, 1959, Allen gave a poetry reading at Columbia University's McMillan Theater. It was organized by the John Dewey Society for the Study of Education and Culture and chaired by Frederick Dupee of the *Partisan Review*. He wanted a lavish homecoming reception deserved of an alumnus who had achieved literary fame.

What he got wasn't so bad—a theater jammed full with 1,400 fans, with five hundred more lined up on the streets jostling to get inside. Allen brought Peter Orlovsky and Gregory Corso, who also read their poems. That night he read "Kaddish" for only the second time.[77] When Allen realized Louis was in the audience hearing "Kaddish" for the first time, tears came to his eyes, and he worried about how Louis would respond to his version of their family history.

Allen also read "The Lion for Real," which he dedicated to Trilling. Although Lionel wasn't in the audience, his wife, Diana Trilling, also a writer and critic, was there. In the question-and-answer period, Allen criticized the Columbia English Department, saying they were stuck in the past for not embracing modern poetry.

Shortly thereafter, Diana Trilling wrote an article for the *Partisan Review* about the reading entitled "The Other Night at Columbia." Trilling recounted the history of Allen's troubles at Columbia, his expulsion, mandated psychiatric treatment, and "an encounter with the police from which he was extricated by some of his old teachers who knew he needed a hospital more than a prison." This was disconcerting because Allen had never given her permission to reveal these facts. According to her, he had publicly turned himself into a "case—a gifted and sad case, a guilt-provoking and nuisance case, but above all, a case." She elaborated: "Here was a boy on whom an outrageous unfairness had been perpetrated: his mother had fled from him into madness and now whoever crossed his path became somehow responsible, caught in the impossibility of rectifying what she had done."

To Diana Trilling, Allen was a bad boy, largely to be pitied because of how he was victimized by his mentally ill mother, whom Trilling managed to blame for her own mental illness. Clearly, she didn't understand madness, mental illness, or the poems. Wasn't this callousness and dismissal exactly what Allen was working to change through his writings? She mistakenly thought the "lion" in the "Lion for Real" was her husband Lionel. This was one example of how she thought his poems did not show evidence of "hard work." She dismissed their values: "They elaborate a new belief in the indispensability of neurosis to art, or beat the bushes for some new deviant psychoanalysis which will generalize their despair though of course without curing it."

Trilling's essay irritated Allen and became one of the first shots fired in his lifelong public feud with the New York critics. Norman Podhoretz, whom he knew from Columbia, became the most vociferous attacker of the Beats. To Podhoretz, they were "The Know-Nothing Bohemians."[78] Yet to Allen, this was more than an irritant. He genuinely wanted to have a conversation with the public about America and how it must change.

Allen entered the fray in July 1959, with an editorial published in the *San Francisco Chronicle*, then reprinted the following month in the *Village Voice*. The piece was entitled "Poetry, Violence, and the Trembling Lambs or Independence Day Manifesto." He denounced "the vast conspiracy to impose one level of mechanical consciousness on mankind" through the "systems of mass communication." But there was a "crack in the mass consciousness of America": "America is having a nervous breakdown. Poetry is the record of individual insights into the secret soul of the individual and because all individuals are one in the eyes of their creator, into the soul of the world." The poets were "ridiculed," and their writings were "mocked, misinterpreted, and suppressed by a horde of middlemen." "Poetry is hated. Whole schools of academic criticism have risen to prove that human consciousness of unconditioned spirit is a myth." Allen called upon the America of Walt Whitman and Henry David Thoreau, each supremely dedicated to an America composed of the "spiritual independence of each individual." He made clever use of the attack initiated by Diana Trilling to counterpunch with a manifesto connected to madness later adopted by the counterculture and expressing its demands for radical cultural and social change.

With "Howl" and "Kaddish" under his belt, Allen had established his reputation as a poet and set his sights beyond poetry. The 1960s had begun, and Allen made it his burden to illuminate humankind by taking action and speaking to the broad public about the twentieth century's extreme highs and lows, spoken in prophetic words and tones unlike those any politician, preacher, or journalist could muster. The vision-incarnated, madness-marked, ecstatically raving, surrealist-listing, death-haunted, saintly disciplined, jazz-intoned poet and prophet was ready to take on the universe.

Chapter 8

A Light Raying through Society, 1959–1965

AFTER COMPLETING "KADDISH for Naomi Ginsberg," Allen was more free to write and conduct activities with no particular focus on madness. Allen was interested in mysticism, how the mind works, and on changing how we think through poetry and other means. He wrote poems covering new ground and expanded into other areas, as a leader of the psychedelic movement, world traveler, and social activist. As the 1960s counterculture movement grew, he was developing a public voice protesting censorship, defending gay rights, and promoting drugs.

In 1959, on a referral from the anthropologist Gregory Bateson, Allen volunteered to take LSD-25, lysergic acid diethylamide, as part of a research study at the Mental Health Research Institute of Stanford University. He was hoping to bring back his inspiring visions. The medical laboratory where he took the LSD and the neuropsychiatric tests they put him through, however, were not conducive to a good trip. He had frightening paranoid feelings, afterward writing: "I thought I was trapped in a giant web or network of forces beyond my control that were perhaps experimenting with me or were perhaps from another planet or were from some super-government or cosmic military or science-fiction Big Brother."[1]

These paranoid feelings did not stop Allen from writing to his father how on LSD he had astounding and beautiful visual images and a "vision of that part of my consciousness which seemed to be permanent and transcendent and identical with the origin of the universe."[2] He believed LSD had the power to chemically produce mystical experiences not unlike the natural experiences he had in Harlem twelve years earlier. Amazing spiritual, aesthetic, and political changes could be accomplished with this pharmacological tool, which was currently only in the hands of a few psychiatrists who did not realize its true potential.

Unbeknownst to Allen, Dr. Paul Hoch, the lead research psychiatrist at the New York Psychiatric Institute when Allen was hospitalized there in 1949, had designed experiments with LSD for persons suffering from serious mental illness. Hoch called these chemicals "psychotomimetic," or "madness-mimicking," agents.[3] He conducted experiments on involuntary mentally ill subjects such as giving them mescaline and then seeing how it changed their condition, then further seeing how those changes could be affected by electroshock or lobotomy. Hoch's work was noticed by the Central Intelligence Agency (CIA), which hired him as a consultant. LSD was thought to be able to covertly change individual or even group behavior, which the CIA thought could have national security uses in espionage or interrogation activities.

In 1959, the Josiah Macy Jr. Foundation brought together psychiatric LSD researchers, at which Dr. Hoch spoke out against the use of LSD as a therapeutic tool. Hoch described the case of a thirty-six-year-old man diagnosed with "pseudoneurotic schizophrenia" (Allen's diagnosis at PI) who took mescaline and had visual hallucinations, fear, panic, depersonalization, and paranoia. "He expressed an ecstatic grandiose trend of having the feeling that he was God in heaven and then, however, had the feeling of being in hell."[4] After receiving a transorbital lobotomy, this man's anxiety markedly improved, reported Dr. Hoch. To the psychiatrists, this research demonstrated that people with pseudoneurotic-type schizophrenia were vulnerable to psychotic symptoms from psychotomimetic drugs—and that transorbital lobotomy could reverse these symptoms. Dr. Hoch claimed none of his patients ever asked for psychotomimetics again and thought the public should be protected from these drugs.

Allen's enthusiasm for and approach to learning about psychedelic drugs couldn't have been more different from psychiatrists like Dr. Hoch. In 1960, Allen traveled to Chile to attend a writer's conference at the University of Concepción and to search for the hallucinogenic called yage, which William Burroughs had sampled several years before. The story of the search for yage eventually was told in a published book he co-wrote with Burroughs, *The Yage Letters*, based upon their correspondence, and is also covered in Allen's *South American Journals*.

A writer friend, Peter Mattheissen, obliged by sending to Allen at his hotel a half-gallon of ayahuasca, a hallucinogen used by the Amazonians and closely related to yage. After trying it, Allen traveled to Pucallpa, Peru, to find some yage. The *curandero*, or witch doctor, named Maestro, gave him some Pucallpa ayahuasca. The brew was much stronger than the ayahuasca he had tried before, and he had terrifying visions of himself approaching death and as a "serpent self."[5] After coming down, he wrote in his journal about Naomi: "What am I that I am her product and continue to live in the world of her madness? Is that my curse, which forbids me to live or die, to give birth, but be neither man nor woman."[6] Instead of backing away from hallucinogens, Allen wanted to go deeper.

He brought back several bottles of ayahuasca to the United States, but each time he took it in New York the visions haunted by death and madness returned. Ecstatic mystical visions could not be guaranteed, at least not for him, not even with naturally occurring compounds ingested according to local native rituals. He wondered if it was because of the history of mental illness in his family. Even so, he still believed in the potential of the chemicals and wanted to experience and learn more about the power of these substances to alter consciousness.

In the fall of 1960, Allen participated in a Beat Generation symposium at the Group for Advancement of Psychiatry (GAP), a think tank for the American psychiatric establishment known to take on cutting-edge issues. GAP's Committee on Adolescence had organized the meeting in Asbury Park, New Jersey, to take a look at what was driving the disenchanted, revolting adolescents of the day. Allen's fellow Beat writer John Clellon Holmes had been invited but couldn't make it, so as a favor Allen offered to attend in his place, hoping he might connect with some of the turned-on psychiatrists.

As the first presenter, Allen told the group how things had changed for him when he'd had flashes of insight or illuminations or psychotic episodes after reading William Blake's poems while living in relative isolation in East Harlem. He then read the poem "Lion for Real," which recounted his Blake visions. The GAP event was the second time he had shared his poems with an audience of psychiatrists, after the case presentation at PI in 1949.

Though he was by then known to many of the psychiatrists for "Howl," Allen chose to read two more recent poems, which had been written while under the influence of mind-altering drugs: "Mescaline" and "Lysergic Acid." These poems offered the psychiatrists artistic documentation of the powerful changes in consciousness, emotion, and spirituality brought on by the new psychedelic drugs.

The tone of these poems was more frightening than inspiring; speaking of "the universe is a void," a death-haunted "rotting Ginsberg," and the "million eyed Spyder that hath no name spinneth of itself endlessly."[7] GAP's secretary transcribing the event actually fled the room in the middle of his presentation! Fortunately, the meeting was also being audiotaped and later transcribed. The psychiatrists in the audience appeared won over, which was later affirmed by several I met who spoke positively of the event.

The other panelists, a psychologist, an anthropologist, and a psychiatrist, offered long-winded analyses of the new bohemians as a phenomenon of adolescence. ("The beatniks are the flunk-outs from life's colleges. Fixated at adolescence, they exalt the perfectly ordinary 'cynical' disenchantment of that stage into a pretentiously permanent Weltanschauung.")[8] When it came Allen's turn to comment, he told them their attempt at age grouping is senseless. All the writers with whom he is in touch are far older than adolescents. Later he wrote to Gary Snyder, calling the psychiatrists "sociologist amateurs who were hung up with concepts of adolescent rebellion."[9]

More to the point, Allen told the psychiatrists, the writers' activities should be seen as the extension of an artistic tradition practiced in previous generations by Williams Carlos Williams and Ezra Pound. The psychiatrists may have been wrong about what drove the Beats to write, but they were right to observe how this material was having a marked impact upon youth, an insight that registered with Allen.

Allen had come to the GAP meeting with more pressing matters on his mind. It wasn't about his mother's illness or lobotomy or his own hospitalization. He was intrigued by the new chemicals and hoped to connect with psychiatrists who shared his interests. The psychiatrists of the day saw both promise and danger in the new drugs. According to Jane Kramer, the psychiatrist said Allen had achieved "a complete disintegration of the ego structure, a descent into the id, and then a re-creation and integration of the ego structure, slightly changed."[10]

He learned that psychiatric leaders and organizations were then debating about their position on the emerging psychedelic drugs. Was there a role for their use in treatment, and what kind of research was needed? Or should hallucinogens be made illegal? At GAP, he met psychiatrists experienced in the use of psychedelics, like Dr. Humphry Osmond, a British psychiatrist who had been practicing at the Saskatchewan Hospital in Weyburn. Osmond's way of talking about mental illness aligned with Allen's sympathies: "I do not accept the view that schizophrenics are to be looked upon as anything but the end process of an illness, nor do I take the view which some hold, that schizophrenic people are necessarily either antisocial or not useful."[11]

Osmond famously coined the term "psychedelic" ("psyche," mind, and "delic," manifest) to describe these chemicals. "To fall in Hell or soar Angelic/You'll need a pinch of psychedelic."[12] At the Saskatchewan Hospital, psychedelics were being used as a part of psychiatric treatment, often with psychotherapy, to treat psychiatric disorders such as alcoholism. Osmond had also been encouraging psychiatrists to try psychedelics themselves because it would give them more insight into their patients.

These new chemicals allowed willing psychiatrists to experience some of the unbelievably unpleasant and sometimes quite terrifying mental agonies of the schizophrenic patient. These experiences were strange, awesome, and among the most beautiful one could ever have. Osmond hoped the new chemicals could lead, directly or indirectly, to therapeutic breakthroughs that would end the regrettable practices of institutionalization and lobotomy. They would, he argued, not only take away the crippling symptoms but by awakening the sick person's mind to itself, even cure schizophrenia.

Osmond was also trying to use LSD to facilitate higher spiritual realization in people who were not necessarily mentally ill. In 1953, Osmond introduced the writer Aldous Huxley to mescaline. This led to Huxley's groundbreaking 1954 book, *The Doors of Perception*, a literary study of the impact of psychedelics on the mind. Huxley borrowed the title from William Blake, who wrote in *The Marriage of Heaven and Hell*: "If the doors of perception were cleansed everything would appear to man as it is, infinite. For man has closed himself up, till he sees things through narrow chinks of his cavern."[13]

After Allen read Huxley's book, he got in contact with Bateson so as to try LSD himself. Osmond remained interested in promoting the broader use of psychedelics and had recently met with Timothy Leary, a Harvard psychologist who wanted to start conducting research with psychedelics. At the 1960 GAP meeting in Asbury Park, Osmond and Allen met and talked about the creative potential of madness. Allen was very interested in this psychiatrist, who had written that "some of the most brilliant and gifted and valuable people who have ever lived have suffered from mental illness"[14] and named William Blake and Franz Kafka as examples. Osmond told Allen if he wanted to take LSD again, he should contact Timothy Leary.

Leary was a Harvard University junior faculty member in psychology who in the summer of 1960 shifted his program of research from a focus on ordinary behavioral issues to a focus on psychedelics. Leary's research on LSD was neither organized like the CIA's (forcing subjects to take LSD, then documenting their effects in disrupting behavior) nor like the clinical psychiatrists' (giving it to mentally ill persons as an augmentation to their psychiatric treatment or to clinicians so they could better understand psychoses). Leary was interested in the broader social application of psychedelics. For example, he conducted one study of maximum-security prison inmates in Concord, Massachusetts, and reported a 50 percent drop in recidivism.[15]

Leary's research was also focused on the religious nature of psychedelics. He gave acid to thirty Harvard divinity students on Good Friday to see whether or not it enhanced their having mystical visions. It did! Leary concluded: "With adequate preparation and in an environment which is supportive and religiously meaningful, subjects who have taken the psychedelic drug report mystical visions significantly more than placebo controls."[16] To both Osmond and Allen, Leary's LSD research sounded like an excellent fit with Allen's spiritual and aesthetic quest and his belief in the value of madness if given the proper social support.

A few weeks after the GAP meeting, Allen wrote to Leary, who invited Peter Orlovsky and him to come for a visit. They met at Leary's Beacon Street home in Newton, Massachusetts, where he took psilocybin with Beethoven and Wagner playing on the phonograph. This time Allen had a pleasant high, later writing, "I felt intimidated by the knowledge that I had not reached yet a perfect understanding with my creator, whoever he be, God, Christ, or Buddha, or the figure of octopus as before. Suddenly, however, realized they were all imaginary beings I was inventing to substitute for the fear of being myself—that one which I had dreamed of." "I saw a blast of light outside of the window and heard Wagner's Gotterdammerung sounding like the horns of judgment calling from the ends of the cosmos. They were calling for a Messiah. Someone to take on the responsibility of being the creative God and seize the power over the universe . . . decided I might as well be the one to do so."[17] He called Jack Kerouac at his mother's home on Long Island, proclaimed himself the King of the Universe, and told the others he wanted them to call one and all, gather everyone, and start something big here and now. They should go out into the streets of Cambridge and Boston and start the revolution that very day.

Leary and Allen believed they were on the cusp of something huge. "We're going to teach people to stop hating. . . . Start a peace and love movement." Leary had never met anyone like Allen, whom he called "secretary general of the world's poets, beatniks, anarchists, socialists, free-sex/love cultists."[18] Leary felt unchained from the academic system by Allen's "liberated Bohemian artistic mind" and responded to this calling:

We were thinking far-out history thoughts at Harvard . . . believing that it was time (after the shallow and nostalgic 1950s) for far-out

Timothy Leary and Neal Cassady, 1964. © *Allen Ginsberg Estate.*

visions, knowing that America had run out of philosophy, that a new empirical, tangible metaphysics was desperately needed; knowing in our hearts that the old mechanical myths had died at Hiroshima, that the past was over, and that politics could not fill the spiritual vacuum. . . . Politics, religion, economics, social structure, are based on shared states of consciousness. The cause of social conflict is usually neurological. The cure is biochemical.[19]

According to Leary, even the Cold War could be resolved if Kennedy and Khrushchev would drop LSD.

Leary and Allen found in each other the makings of a perfect collaborator to launch the psychedelic movement. They hatched a plan, selecting a number of hip cultural elites whom they offered the drug to. Allen would give it to Jack Kerouac, Thelonious Monk, Charles Olson, and Robert Lowell, to name a few. On January 5, 1961, Leary wrote to William Burroughs: "So at present Allen and I are roaming around New York on weekends—nirvana salesman, cosmic crusaders turning on any name we can get to volunteer."[20] If they had good trips, then they would recommend it to others, and psychedelics might catch on more broadly. After the LSD experience, nobody could possibly think the same about themselves, the world, their society, or their government. Leary and Allen targeted three groups in particular: the young, the artists, and the alienated. Allen wrote that they wanted the movement to develop "without organization, without leaders, without dogmatic doctrines and become a full-blown religious renaissance of the young."[21]

Psychiatrists and others who wanted to control the mystical experience should stay out of the way. Leary wrote to Arthur Koestler: "Psychiatric investigators (hung up as they are on their own abstractions) interpret the experience as PSYCHOTIC and think they are producing model psychosis. . . . We (mainly Allen Ginsberg and I) [want] to keep these drugs free and uncontrolled."[22] The psychedelic movement belongs to the people.

For Allen, the psychedelic movement was an extension of his belief in the liberating powers of mystical madness. They would change the world one consciousness at a time, and this could be accelerated by the new chemicals. These substances would help create individuals who regarded themselves as free of state control. Changes in individual consciousness would then lead to badly needed social, economic, and political changes ("immediate mutation of social & economic forms").[23] They must, because when conditioned reflexes are disinhibited by the new chemicals, the changes in consciousness can be so powerful. He would later write: "I think we may expect the new generation to push for an environment less rigid, mechanical, less dominated by cold war habits. A new kind of light has rayed through our society."[24]

Allen did not profess to know the mechanisms by which biochemically induced changes in consciousness led to changes in politics, nor did the best scientists of the day. However, he strongly believed the substances could be understood from the perspective of the Gnostic tradition in American and world cultures, which he had learned from William Blake, Walt Whitman, William James, and others. "Science is getting very hip,"[25] he wrote to his father. Or at least psychedelic science. With his background in visions, literary traditions, and spirituality, Allen could put psychedelics and psychedelic science in a proper perspective and, through them, change the world. That was his hope.

Given Allen's experiences with his mother's mental illness, not to speak of his own emotional struggles, he was personally aware that madness is not always pleasingly mystical and can involve paralyzing suffering. Allen was aware the psychedelic movement was going to involve casualties. He was ready to lend a helping hand to those unfortunate persons who reached out while suffering bad trips, social dysfunction, or mental illness. As the GAP psychiatrists had said in Asbury Park, this type of youth movement would always attract the neurotic adolescent fringe. Allen did his best to look after the drug casualties, as he had once looked after Naomi.[26] However, years later he thought he could have done more to protect the mentally fragile from bad outcomes. Yet this never dampened his enthusiasm for the trans- formative power of psychedelics and his recommending that everyone try them. By 1967, Allen was not just preaching about drug policy but preaching more cultural revolution: "Everybody who hears my voice, directly or indi- rectly, try the chemical LSD at least once; every man woman and child American in good health over the age of 14—that if necessary, we have a mass emotional nervous breakdown in these States once and for all; that we see bankers laughing in their revolving doors with strange staring eyes."[27]

Leary, too, recognized that to cause significant changes in behavior, as he lectured to the International Congress of Applied Psychology in August 1961, you could "have a psychotic episode . . . or expose yourself to some great trauma that shatters the gamesmanship out of you. . . . Live in a very different culture for a year where your roles and rituals and language just don't mean a thing."[28] To Leary and Allen, losing yourself to psychosis, trauma, or culture shock were all regarded as beneficial for transforming individuals and ultimately society.

Despite his enthusiasm for the psychedelic movement, in 1961 it still concerned Allen that most of his trips had been bad trips. His Blake visions hadn't returned in twelve years. Was there something wrong with how he was approaching both his natural and chemical visions? Psychiatry didn't have the answer. He decided he should consult with the world's experts in spiritual enlightenment, and this sent him traveling abroad and to the East looking for a guru.

In the fall of 1961, on their way to India, Allen and Peter Orlovsky stopped in Jerusalem. They telephoned Martin Buber and arranged to meet with the wise man with the beautiful white beard for a long conversation. Orlovsky asked him about his mystical visions, and Buber said he wasn't so interested in visions anymore. Allen told Buber he had been exploring the boundaries of human-to-nonhuman relationships on his psychedelic trips, trying to go toward death and even beyond to reach the cosmic. Buber said we inhabit a human universe and that Allen should instead focus on human relation- ships. Allen recalled being told, "Mark my word, young man, in two years you will realize that I was right."[29]

From the port of Eilat, Orlovsky and he took a boat to Mombasa, then after a several-week stopover waiting for their visas, found another boat bound for India, finally arriving in Bombay in February 1962. They took the earliest available train to Delhi and found a rest house in Old Delhi where they could stay for cheap. As planned, they met up with the poets Gary and Joan Snyder and headed for the Himalayas.

According to Deborah Baker, author of *The Blue Hand*, Allen went to India in search of a guru. His fellow poet Gary Snyder, who was practiced in Buddhist meditation, could help Allen meet spiritual guides. In Dharamsala, Allen, Snyder, and their companions got to see the Dalai Lama.

Allen told His Holiness of his psychedelic drug trips, to which the Dalai Lama replied that mental states reached through drugs are not true spiritual states. The Dalai Lama asked Allen, "If you take LSD can you see what's in that briefcase?"[30] Others in Allen's party got impatient with Allen hogging the conversations. According to Baker, it was as if Allen wanted to achieve enlightenment overnight. He was disappointed to not receive the answers he sought. Not until years later did Allen appreciate what helpful advice he received from those visits.

Allen returned to Delhi, made a tourist trip to Jaipur, then went back to Bombay. Allen visited opium dens, met with local musicians, and worked on the proofs for *Reality Sandwiches*, his third book for City Lights. He enjoyed being out of the media limelight, which was increasingly shining on the Beats back home.

When some journalists succeeded in locating him in India to ask what he was searching for, Allen told them he didn't really know. Allen was being honest about not having an agenda. He went to India as a seeker, like so many others from America and Europe who hitchhiked their way through exotic India. Allen's journey was not only for himself, however, but also for his poetry and his followers. Thus, Allen practiced in India what he had learned before— he put his private life in the public realm through writing journals, poems, and letters that would later be published. As Allen was seeking and being exposed to different concepts of the mind, body, and world, he shared his adventures, insights, and confusion with everyone in his journals.

In Bombay, Allen met a young Indian man named Asoke Fakir, whom Allen knew enough to recognize as a fake holy man. Asoke introduced Allen to *sadhus*, those Hindu men who renounce worldly possessions and wander the countryside seeking spiritual enlightenment. Asoke took Allen to the burning *ghats* by the river near the Howrah Bridge. Allen became engrossed by the death rituals at the *ghats* and was becoming more familiar with the *sadhus'* practices of meditation. He traveled with Asoke and others to the village of Tarapith for a pilgrimage festival of ganja-smoking *sadhus*. Allen bought a train ticket to Benares, known today as Varanasi and for centuries as the City of Light.

Allen arrived in Benares by train from Calcutta in December 1962; the river had flooded the city, and the air was cold and damp. Allen and Orlovsky spent the first week in a flat near the railroad station making their way by bus to the *ghats* on the Ganges's banks. The city front and *ghats* line the broad side of the gently curving wide river. Across the wide, fast, flowing waters is a sandy bank and field of grass and trees. According to Hindu beliefs, after you die, your soul crosses over to heaven on the other side of the river. The Ganges's fast current carries dirt, ash, leaves, and trash, but this doesn't stop people from bathing, washing, and even drinking the holy water.

Allen journaled, "I wanted to be a saint but suffer for what? Illusions?"[31] Here he was writing not only as a traveler but as a cultural explorer and countercultural leader who sought to build knowledge that could help show the way. Yet when he stumbled on the sacred territory of the burning *ghats* and took the wrong bus home, he humbly confessed he was human and just another seeker in a land of so many seekers, at times confused and over- whelmed. In these journals, later published as *Indian Journals*, there is no real contradiction between these two mindsets. The writer continually took personal, artistic, and intellectual risks in an unfamiliar setting and was comfortable putting his private life under the public lens, no matter what it revealed.

His first night in Benares, Allen spied the cows who inhabited Manikarnika *Ghat*, which was the main burning *ghat*. They ate the ashes or what didn't quite become ashes after the burning of the body. He spotted the ritual red round pot they handed to the lead mourner to put out the fire when the bodies finished burning. Allen associated this pot with the other clay pots he had seen used to drink milk. They made the same sound when tossed and smashed.

A few days later, he again sat with Orlovsky on a high red stone balcony overlooking Manikarnika *Ghat* and noticed a corpse in a white shroud, which in the flames became a thin black mummy. Hindus, like Jews, bury their dead in a white shroud.

He found a place to live for forty-three rupees a month with "9 great doors, three on each side North South West."[32] Orlovsky displayed his red- bellied Ganesh, and Allen hung his Blake life-mask photo. "Feel at home and happy," Allen journaled. Their flat was above an open-air market and next to one of the main *ghats*, making it one of the more frenetic places in Benares. In his journal Allen recorded the daily dramas and nighttime noises of this central gathering place and passageway. Coughing, clearing throats, dogs barking, shouts, music, cooking, and spitting. He heard "a beggar woman on the street shrieking last night at 4 AM in the darkness."[33] Then a *sadhu* took his prayer beads and shouted "Ram Ram Hare Krishna Hari Ram." The noise lasted through the night while Allen sat on the balcony writing. Back asleep, Allen dreamed of the "old traumas of Patterson."[34]

At Manikarnika G*hat*, Allen sat and smoked with the *sadhus*. A few days later he was back again with them and invited to a rest house where *sadhus* and pilgrims stayed. One *sadhu* named Shambhu Bharti Baba gave Allen some help smoking the ganja pipe. Allen snapped his photo and later put it on the cover of the published *Indian Journals*.

Allen did not consider himself a tourist. Tourists were another breed, which he spotted "floating by in rowboats."[35] Every day, Allen watched daily life in the square below his flat: "Sensing the naïveté of neighborhoods awakening, the square beginning to work, the radios are turned on, the beggars fidget in their burlap wraps, the sadhus finger their prayer beads. Pilgrims step towards the Ganges in bathing wraps carrying brass water pots. Rickshaw drivers awaken and start ringing their bells and scurrying about."[36] Allen thought of Cézanne's magical canvas and what his own eyes could see in the square: "I turn my head this way or that an inch, and the composition changes."[37] He could make a study of the beauty and complexity of street life and learn lessons for his art.

Allen in Calcutta, 1962. *Photo by Peter Orlovsky;* © *Allen Ginsberg Estate.*

Allen's response to living amid so much death was to ask if we are all walking corpses. Allen wrote of feeling closer to death than to birth. However, the feelings were less of fright and more of acceptance. They led him to ask: What am I doing with this life?

Once I thought to rebuild the world to supreme reality . . . the giant radio station of eternity would tune us into an endless program that broadcast only ourselves forever. Now I hear the reading of gongs and skull drums in Hindu temples, cries on the streets, peasant women waving sticks at hungry cows, the light bulb burning white, only so I can transcribe the weird suffering details, for whom to read, myself and my fond dying indifferent trapped fellows.[38]

Allen's notes from Benares mention smoking ganja by firelight with the *sadhus* for hours and peeing into the Ganges at night as the fires burn. A street parade coming down Desaswamedh Street causes cows and elephants to stampede in the small alleys. Can you write poetry that sounds as natural and spontaneous as life on the streets of Benares, poetry not limited by self-consciousness? After a long expedition in the heat, Allen walked back to Asi Ghat, "quiet high walled alleys and white lights that end of town."[39] He wrote in his dream, travel, and poetry journals.

Even a visit from the police could become a poem. They came around because of Allen's bad behavior at Benares Hindu University, because journalists were swarming, and because they were worried, so now Allen was worried too. Why not write a poem about it? His poems contained observations on personal experiences of living in the public eye at a time of increasing social anxiety.

Childhood memories from Paterson to Harlem came back to Allen, from the shrouded stranger by the railroad to boyfriends on Broadway. Who cared about such matters in Benares? Allen needed entirely new poems. He tried to describe the rain on Desaswamedh. His new heroes were the lepers, the beggars, the *sadhus*, and the pilgrims. Someone came too early to die into the pit yard. "Buchenwald skeletal legs and no cheek. Burn sores and festering wounds."[40] Allen and Orlovsky nursed him. They'd seen him once before. Was he an extreme *sadhu*? They called him the Kankal man. Allen and Orlovsky named the shrieking black-haired lady beggar who talked to herself like a rooster. Her husband left her there. Now she craps on the street. They called her Kali Ma.

Walking at Benares Hindu University, a German professor friend told Allen that William Carlos Williams was dead. Though he was gone, there is still life in his pages, Allen thought. "Wonder what were his last words?

Was there anything left in realms of speech after the stroke and brain thrill doom entered his thoughts."[41]

Under the spell of Benares, Allen wrote, "Death is not a single thing."[42] Benares too is many things, including death, poverty, suffering, isolation, illness, ritual, beauty, and ecstasy. Across the Ganges, in the sand on a bamboo platform sat Dehorava Baba. Allen had to see the guru who had come down from the Himalayas. When he and Orlovsky crossed the Ganges to see him, Orlovsky refused and instead goofed around in the sand. Dehorhava Baba would only see them together. Allen spoke of their troubles, and Baba said, "Oh how wounded, How wounded."[43]

By May, it was time to leave Benares. Orlovsky had taken his own room but left his Ganesh. Allen prepared for a trip to Japan, then to Vancouver and back to the United States. But first, back to the *ghats* for Allen. The Kankal man, whom Allen and Orlovsky nurtured, was retrieved by his brother from Delhi. Allen and Orlovsky contacted him after they learned how the man had been separated from his family during an episode of ethnic mob violence.

India and especially Benares changed Allen forever. It further challenged the grandiosity and naïveté he had brought to his spiritual quest. Seeing how people lived and died in Benares humbled him. It gave him a broader human framework for understanding his own life experiences, including his visions and the extreme experiences associated with his mother's mental illness, lobotomy, hospitalization, and death. It brought him closer to spiritual teachers and gave him the confidence to continue his spiritual quest in more disciplined and informed ways. He wrote journals documenting the world around him, his daily experiences, and his spiritual seeking.

In the United States, Allen could easily look down on those who did not accept or understand visions. He could think they did not have the same gift as he did. Yet he never met anyone who knew as much about visions as he did until he came to India. There he met swamis, gurus, and *sadhus* whose lives were centered on the spiritual. He was disappointed he didn't learn any great secrets about the visionary path. Instead he learned he was already on the right path. Blake was his guru. He had spent too much time inside his own head and needed to be more interested in the world and in other people.

He discovered the daily life of Indians and especially their death rites. In the United States you can hide from death and dying. Death happens in hospitals and is managed by doctors and nurses. In Benares, death happens in the open, on the street, in alleyways, and by the river, which can be both horrifying but also liberating.

The immersion in death could have potentially pulled him again away from the human and toward the nonhuman. But India did something else to Allen. It made him feel, hear, smell, and touch death as a human experience, one very much a part of this life, building on an awareness he had expressed in "Kaddish." That was a big help to the death-haunted Allen.

Allen already knew how to write about madness but less so about poverty, disease, dying, and death. Allen had long sought out the sufferer, the outsider, the stranger, from criminal to junkie to the mad. But the range of extremity he was exposed to in India far surpassed what he had seen before. In "Kaddish" he evoked death as a release from madness, but that too was an abstraction. Allen was determined not to be naïve. He had to face these heartbreaking, ugly, and cruel but inescapable facts of existence, including death. He had to describe death in prose and poetry in ways that come alive.

Allen also had the travel bug possessing so many Westerners at the time. It was not only that Allen introduced Americans and Westerners to India and these other exotic destinations. It was also that Allen, through his example and writings, showed generations how and, more importantly, why to travel. What do we hope to find when we go to a far-off place? Not only another world. We expect to be transformed, especially when our destination is a vastly different culture from our own, and even more so when we go to places of spiritual significance. Yet the possibilities for the routines of tourism to undermine the extent and depth of the journey are plentiful. It takes preparation, presence, engagement, and especially openness to allow a trip to become a journey.

Timothy Leary noted in his lecture about psychedelic drugs at an international conference in Copenhagen in 1961 that travel to a different culture is one of the most certain ways to destabilize yourself.[44] And when the place prizes different forms of consciousness, for example, in its religious rituals and spiritual life, then the potential to undermine a person's center of gravity is even more heightened. Of course, those are exactly the kinds of places Allen most wanted to go. But just going there wasn't enough. Can you let go of your preconceived notions and let yourself just experience? Allen did so, throwing himself into India and its people, not afraid to take risks. As Peter Hale said to me, "I am amazed at how many risks he took."[45]

After Allen left India and was on his way to North America, he had a moment of recognition concerning his approach to spiritual change through psychedelics and visions. The moment occurred on a train in Japan, when the advice of all the gurus he had consulted finally resonated. Srimata Krishnaji had said, "Take Blake for your guru."[46] Rinpoche had said, "If you see anything horrible, don't cling to it, if you see anything beautiful, don't cling to it." Swami Shivananda told him, "Your heart is the guru."

In the poem "The Change: Kyoto-Tokyo Express," reflecting on his experiences in India, especially the death ritual in the *ghats*, Allen renounced drugs and his quest to expand consciousness driven by his 1948 Blake visions and accepted the transitory nature of life and living in his body: "I am that I am I am the/man & the Adam of hair in/my loins This is my spirit and/physical shape I inhabit/this Universe Oh weeping/against what is my/own nature for now."[47] Later, he further explained these changes in an interview with Tom Clark in 1965: "I suddenly didn't want to be dominated by the nonhuman anymore, or even dominated by the moral obligation to enlarge my consciousness anymore. Or do anything anymore except by my heart."[48] After Allen's India stay, what Martin Buber told him in Israel had come to pass.

It was not easy for Allen to acknowledge how for the past fifteen years he had been too hung up on the Blake visions. "Now I'd have to give up this continual churning thought process of yearning back to a visionary state."[49] Instead, he was going to focus on his relationship to his body and on spiritual discipline, putting to use the Buddhist meditation and chanting he had studied in India. He was also implicitly acknowledging that visions were not only linked with his mother and her clinical madness but also to fathers, be they spiritual, literary, or biological.

When his expedition to the East came to an end and he returned to North America in the summer of 1963 to attend the Vancouver Poetry Conference, Allen seemed like a different person. He wore his hair long, had a flowing beard, preached poetry and free love, played the Indian harmonium, and chanted Hindu mantras. The poet George Bowering said Allen gave off "some kind of spiritual aura. The air shone around him."[50] Allen wanted to use poetry to help others reach the divine. Despite his optimism, to be in a position to transmit these important matters to the broader public would take more work.

After invigorating reunions with old friends in the Bay Area and protesting the Vietnam War as "black magic," by November 1963 Allen settled back in New York with Peter Orlovsky in an East Village apartment. He spent precious time with Louis and Edith Ginsberg in Paterson and with his brother Eugene and his family in Long Island. Allen and the photographer Robert Frank tried to write a screenplay for "Kaddish" and even managed to complete a script, but they failed to attract the necessary funding to make the film. Allen met the songwriter Bob Dylan for the first time, in a friend's apartment, enthralling both and initiating a long friendship. Allen and other Beat writers were a big inspiration to Dylan, and Allen was moved by Dylan's poetic sensibility and social consciousness.

Allen became involved in political advocacy in New York City, defending the bohemian art scene, which was being harassed with the application of laws restricting public gatherings in coffeehouses. The battle against censorship was very familiar to Allen from the initial "Howl" trial and other subsequent attacks. Allen led a petition against the arrest of Lenny Bruce, under the banner of the Committee on Poetry, an organization Allen formed to protect artists, and wrote an essay entitled "Back to the Wall," which expressed his concerns: "The individual soul is under attack and for that reason a "beat" generation existed and will continue to exist under whatever name."[51] In January 1965, Allen testified at another trial regarding the obscenity of Burroughs's *Naked Lunch*, where his defense included reading the Burroughs quote from one of his poems: "Don't hide the madness."[52]

Allen was invited by the Cuban government to attend a writer's conference in Havana, and he planned to go from there to Czechoslovakia and the Soviet Union. While he was making the rounds with writers and editors in Havana, Allen learned about the persecution of homosexuals and opponents of the revolution. To his hosts, Allen made challenging statements condemning such persecution, suggesting that the opponents be allowed to use marijuana and the homosexuals be allowed to live in their bodies as they pleased. Allen found himself openly confronting Cuban officials until one night he was unexpectedly summoned from his hotel room, taken to the airport, and put on a plane to Czechoslovakia.

Compared with Cuba, Allen had less trouble in Prague. He met writers, gave readings, and was able to meet and bed male partners, as homosexuality was legal. From Prague, Allen flew to Moscow, where he met with some of Naomi's relatives, who had decided to return from New Jersey to the Soviet Union. Allen met with Russian writers, including especially Yevgeny Yevtushenko, who had little tolerance for Allen's talk about homosexuality, drugs, or Russian dissidents. Allen's complaints about the lack of freedoms regarding sexuality and drugs seemed like "juvenile problems" compared with the challenges of daily survival and censorship in the Soviet Union.

Allen returned back through Prague and was asked by the Czech poet Josef Skvorecky to accept the honor of being elected the Kral Majales, or King for May Day, in Skvorecky's place. Allen accepted and was given a cardboard crown, improvised throne, and festive parade. Then a few days later, Allen was attacked on the street by a man, most likely sent by government agents, who shouted "Fairy," hit him, and took one of his notebooks.

The following day two plainclothes policemen took Allen to a police station, where he was told he was no longer welcome. He would be flying to London the next day. Allen believed that he was right to speak his mind and to be himself and came away feeling more, not less, empowered to be outspoken and willing to challenge authorities that utilize "the police bureaucracy brainwash tactic—feeling exactly like Time-Mag-type putdowns—to make people feel that, because you're vaguely shameful, they have the right to SMASH YOUR TEETH OUT."[53]

From Prague, Allen ended up in London, where once again he met up with Bob Dylan, who invited him to attend his shows at the Royal Albert Hall. Dylan even invited Allen to join him and the Beatles, where he famously asked John Lennon, "Have you ever read William Blake, young man?" Lennon responded, "Never heard of the man."[54] In May, Allen was filmed wearing a Talmudic-looking shawl and carrying a cane in the background of Dylan's "Subterranean Homesick Blues" music video directed by D. A. Pennebaker. In June, Allen participated in the blockbuster International Poetry Reading at the Royal Albert Hall, where he read two poems, including "The Change," and chanted mantras. As impressive as it was, Allen knew he couldn't reach as many people as Dylan and other rock-and-roll revolutionaries who were writing protest songs that could "shake the walls of the city" and usher in a new social order based upon peace, not more war.[55]

As the countercultural movement of the 1960s was gathering momentum, Allen was becoming a major public figure beyond that of a poet, and some started referring to him as a prophet or poet-prophet. At Harvard University in November 1964, he was introduced as "the bardic prophet of an entire generation,"[56] and such introductions would be repeated at readings all over the United States and Europe for the next thirty plus years.

To explain who he was and how he got there, we hear Allen referencing the story of his 1948 Blake visions, but now with one key difference—he mentions hearing William Blake's voice. In 1960, in a piece for the *Writer's Digest*, he wrote, ". . . I heard his voice."[57] At the GAP meeting, in the fall of 1960, he tells the psychiatrists, "while reading, when I heard Blake's voice, or had an auditory hallucination of Blake's voice, reading to me a poem called 'The Sunflower.'"[58] An unpublished 1961 poem speaks of "That day I heard Blake's voice/I say I heard Blake's voice."[59] In a 1961 prose piece published in a small press, Allen complains of his critics' assaults on his claim to knowing poetic tradition: "Must I be attacked and condemned by these people, I who have heard Blake's own ancient voice recite me the 'Sunflower' a decade ago in Harlem?"[60] In 1965, upon receiving a

Guggenheim Fellowship in poetry, he wrote a short essay on the "Poet's Voice," stating he heard Blake's voice: "deep, earthen, tender, suffused with the feeling of ancient days" and recognized it as the "sound of prophecy."[61]

The first known poetic notations of Blake's voice came a few years earlier. In July 1958, in "Back on Times Square, Dreaming of Times Square," Allen writes: "and dreamed of Blake's voice talking—"[62] In "Ignu" from November 1958, Allen writes: "he hears Blake's disembodied Voice recite the Sunflower in a room in Harlem."[63] These lines suggest Allen may have dreamed and imagined a voice before incorporating it as a lived experience. Many contemporary readers believe Allen heard the voice initially, but nothing he wrote suggests it was so.

One noteworthy anomaly from many years earlier (1951) can be found in John Clellon Holmes's *Go*, which was one of the first Beat novels. Allen is depicted as the fictional character David Stovsky, who says he heard the voice of William Blake ("he became aware of a voice that seemed to be reading along with him" and "He was serenely content to hear the echoes of that deep, gentle voice in his intelligence").[64] Holmes said he based this depiction on Allen's letters to him, but those letters describe the visions without ever mentioning hearing Blake's voice. This raises fascinating, unanswerable questions: If Allen did not tell Holmes he heard Blake's voice, did Holmes create it and Allen much later appropriate it from Holmes's fictionalization?

In an era of potentially explosive street demonstrations, Allen was looked upon as a leader of nonviolent tactics. In November 1965, the Free Speech Movement at the University of California–Berkeley feared the Hell's Angels would violently attack their antiwar demonstration. They invited Allen to advise them, and Allen's remarks were published on November 19, 1965, in the *Berkeley Barb* with the title: "Demonstration or Spectacle as Example, as Communication or How to Make a March/Spectacle."[65] The idea was not to give into the Angels' "negative psychology" and the "war psychology" and to "go over, the habit-image reaction of fear/violence." How so? "Use our imagination. A spectacle can be made" using masses of flowers, American flags, crosses or Jewish stars, bongs, tambourines, and balloons. If there is "heavy anxiety, confusion, or struggle," then the marchers could sit down, do calisthenics, and recite together "The Lord's Prayer," "Three Blind Mice," "OM," the "Star-Spangled Banner," or "Mary Had a Little Lamb."

To Allen, the US government and law enforcement were in the grips of paranoia, so he drew upon what he learned from calming Naomi, his own time in the psychiatric hospital, Buddhism, and poetry. In the face of fear and threat, each person should remain calm and together create a playful spectacle. Allen's flower-power strategy is built on personal change: If I can first change my own mind, then I can change one other mind, then another, and so on, then we can join together and change the world. This "flower power" concept was later expanded into guerilla theater and deployed at protests across the country, culminating in the 1967 March on the Pentagon, and more generally to flower children and the hippie counterculture movement centered in Haight-Ashbury in 1967, the Summer of Love.

The poet Tom Clark met Allen in a bar in Bristol after hearing him read. The two hitchhiked to Glastonbury and visited King Arthur's tomb and the Abbey. They met up two weeks later in Cambridge, and Clark interviewed Allen for four hours over several sittings. The interview was published in the spring 1966 issue of the *Paris Review* and went on to become one of the most quoted texts on Allen Ginsberg.

Allen spoke explicitly and at length about the 1948 Blake visions. This time he said he was reading Blake's "Ah, Sun-flower" when

> suddenly, simultaneously with understanding it, heard a very deep earthen grave voice in the room, which I immediately assumed, I didn't think twice, was Blake's voice; it wasn't any voice that I knew, though I had previously had a conception of a voice of rock, in a poem, some image like that—or maybe that came after this experience.
>
> And my eye on the page, simultaneously the auditory hallucination, or whatever terminology here used, the apparitional voice, in the room, woke me further deep in my understanding of the poem, because the voice was so completely tender and beautifully . . . ancient. Like the voice of the Ancient of Days. But the peculiar quality of the voice was something unforgettable because it was like God had a human voice, with all the infinite tenderness and anciency and mortal gravity of a living Creator speaking to his son.[66]

By 1965 when he gave the *Paris Review* interview and his countercultural star was rising, Allen's narrative downplayed the psychiatric terminology that had held him back and instead reveled in his connection to artistic repositories of visionary experiences. Telling the long and tortured story of the impact of his mother's mental illness would not do. No hallucinations, hospitalization, or schizophrenia. Instead, the primary narrative Allen offered of his personal evolution was a mystical vision in which William

Blake reached out and helped him discover his own visionary power. His mother was his muse, as he revealed in "Kaddish," but he was also now the disciple of William Blake. Allen spoke of Blake's voice with the tone, language, and details of one who was announcing the truth and who walked with Blake daily. Allen shared his conviction of William Blake's ancestry and of himself as his modern-day heir and invited all to awaken and discover their own spiritual and creative potential.

Allen's tale of making contact with the divine was just as clear and convincing as the extraordinary Fra Angelico canvas of the *Annunciation*, which likely helped shape it, along with Holmes's *Go*. Compared with the Clark interview, the retellings from the early 1960s, which also mention the voice, read like dress rehearsals. As Patti Smith told me, "What it all comes down to is the truth of him hearing it."[67]

The Clark interview in the *Paris Review* was widely read, regarded as fact, and relied upon by many critics and biographers to tell the story of Allen. In accepting Allen's 1965 retelling, which centers on Blake's voice, many wrote as if they wanted more to believe and less to understand the role of narrative truth in Allen's life and art.[68] This then inscribed into nearly all literary criticism and biography on Allen Ginsberg a mythologized history of how he became a poet through his 1948 visions. It also minimized the seventeen years of uncertainty, struggle, seeking, artistic work, resilience, and achievement since the 1948 visions, not to mention his troubled earlier life history with Naomi.

By the time I met Allen in 1987, he had long been living within the myths he and others had spun. They were true enough for him and for his readers, critics, and biographers. He acknowledged that he misremembered when the lobotomy took place and had only partial knowledge about Naomi's illness and treatment. He wanted me to fill in those gaps and tell Naomi's story, and his "that's extreme" comment drew my focus to the possible connection between the lobotomy and his visions. Even still, he was yet adhering to the Clark interview as the best description of the vision.

Allen's post-India change, his pivot away from his obsession with changing consciousness, didn't last very long. After taking some distance from drugs and visions, at Big Sur in 1965 Allen took LSD again and wrote to his father, "All the young people out here are experimenting with it—by all I mean a huge number, maybe 10% of college kids, and those are the ones interested in poetry or politics or art. It'll have an effect."[69] The phenomenon of adolescent rebellion mentioned by the psychiatrists at GAP was now becoming reality.

Human Be-In, Allen and other poets on stage, 1967. © *Lisa Law*.

Allen fully intended to be at the center of the new fervor and to be the leader of these youth. A youth psychedelic revolution is what Leary and he had dreamed of since 1960 and what the GAP psychiatrists noted with caution and concern. At a social level, hearing the voice of William Blake gave Allen the legitimacy he needed to be a poet and prophet for the revolution. At a personal level, making contact with Blake was a key resilient experience that he had salvaged from his and Naomi's madness and cultivated through years of devotion to visionary poetics and careful reworking. It all came together.

Allen carried himself so convincingly, few considered the connections between the Blake visions and the difficulties of living with Naomi's and his own madness and all the painstaking work he had done to make the salvaging possible. Most importantly, they believed that Allen now walked with Blake, a truth that was dramatically enacted many times after, such as before thousands in the iconic images from the Gathering of the Tribes for the Human Be-In of 1967 in San Francisco's Golden Gate Park. Allen danced, chanted, and read before more than twenty thousand people. At the closing, Allen chanted "Om Sri Maitreya" with finger cymbals. Allen later explained what that day was all about: "People are lonesome. I'm lonesome. It's strange to be in a body. So, what I'm doing—what we're all doing—on a day like today is saying, 'Touch me, sleep with me, talk to me.'"[70] Allen's way of talking about individual and social change has an innocence that is at the same time touching, empowering, naïve, and provocative. He called for universal love, like the Beatles, but with more sex and more longing, which many embraced, but it also hinted at language and behavior that was not so different from other rock stars of that era and that decades later would get Allen into trouble.

Chapter 9

White and Black Shrouds, 1987

LONG AFTER NAOMI'S demise and his writing of the major poems about madness that brought him fame, Allen kept close with people who had their own issues with madness and mental illness. Allen did not shut them up, shut them away, or pretend they did not exist. He always showed them great sympathy. Bob Rosenthal recalled that when Allen went through the fan mail he was sent, he always responded to anyone who appeared unstable or mentally ill.

"Allen," he wrote, "has special skill in deciphering the most confused and anguished letters. To Allen mental pain is a means of expressing love. The pain in these convoluted letters excites him by bringing him back to a primal love."[1] By primal love, Rosenthal meant Allen's filial attachment with Naomi.

Allen got a lot of messages from people who were despairing, suffering, hallucinating, anxious, or called mad. He got phone calls from people on bad trips and from ward payphones in psychiatric hospitals, and he provided any help he could, especially simply by listening. His telephone number, 212-677-7876, was easy to remember. Despite his celebrity and the incessant phone calls, Allen never had it changed or unlisted.

It wasn't just strangers in his life who reached out to him, knowing that he would be there for them. Allen's life partner, Peter Orlovsky, had serious drug and alcohol problems, most devastatingly with injecting methedrine, but also smoking crack, snorting cocaine, smoking crystal meth, and drinking alcohol. By the 1980s, it got to where every month Orlovsky would spend his entire government check to binge on drugs. Orlovsky himself was all too familiar with mental health problems from his brother, Julius, who was diagnosed with schizophrenia; this relationship was the subject of a 1969 film directed by Robert Frank, *Me and My Brother*.[2] In this film, Peter Orlovsky gets his catatonic brother discharged from Bellevue Hospital and then must rely on Orlovsky and Allen to survive day to day.

Over the years as Orlovsky's addictions grew worse, Allen sought help from psychiatrists and hospitals, desperate for answers. He brought Orlovsky to Hazelden and himself attended Al-Anon meetings. In 1987, Allen himself started seeing a psychiatrist to help manage Orlovsky and the toll on him, which he wrote about in his poem "Personals Ad": "going to lady psychiatrist who says Make time in your life/for someone you can call darling, honey, who holds you dear/can get excited & lay his head on your heart in peace."[3] In May 1987, Allen invited R. D. Laing to lecture at Naropa and then solicited his counsel concerning Orlovsky's increasingly wild and dangerous behavior. Nothing could put the brakes on Orlovsky's spiraling madness.

Allen also remained committed to and supportive of several other associates who happened to have mental health problems, including Gregory Corso, Herbert Huncke, Harry Smith, and Carl Solomon. He wasn't put off by their extreme behavior and got them professional help when they needed it. People struggling with mental health and addiction can descend into poverty, debt, and homelessness. Allen gave them money. He found out about their debts and settled them.

He handled the money through the Committee on Poetry, a small non-profit organization he formed in 1966. Allen didn't want his taxes to go to the Vietnam War budget, so he put his modest earned income into the committee, where it could "sustain artists and their projects in times of stress . . . help unlucky poets and painters avoid confinement in jails and madhouses or ease their return to freedom; and otherwise aid in spiritual emergencies."[4]

In 1968, the Committee on Poetry served as a vehicle for advocacy. They wrote a letter in support of LeRoi Jones (aka Amiri Baraka), who had been imprisoned following the Newark riot: "LeRoi Jones is not only a black man, a Newark man, a revolutionary, he is a conspicuous American artist imprisoned for his poetry during a crisis of Authoritarianism in these States."[5]

The Committee on Poetry purchased and supported the East Hill Farm in upstate New York to serve as "a haven for comrades in distress."[6] First among them was Orlovsky, especially as his addiction and psychosis grew more and more problematic. Allen wanted to make use of every resource to help Orlovsky, so when the committee got this farm, he could send Orlovsky upstate to try to keep him away from easy access to drugs in New

York City. For Orlovsky's sake, others at the farm were strictly forbidden from using drugs. Being on a farm also harkened back to the early-twentieth-century practice of exposing hospitalized mentally persons to farming and gardening.[7] To Allen, anything was better for Orlovsky than prolonged hospitalization.

Carl Solomon, who dubbed himself the "professional lunatic-saint" and whom Allen called an "advanced CCNY Dadaist intellectual," had a special place in Allen's life.[8] As Allen explained, at the time of writing "Howl," he could not have imagined this poem would circulate beyond small poetry circles. Thus, he did not intend to launch the actual persona of Carl Solomon "in the world with my stereotype—a poetic metaphor—as a large part of his social identity."[9]

This notoriety was a heavy burden for Solomon and their relationship, which lasted until Solomon's death in 1993. In December 1957, Solomon wrote to thank Allen "for the sentiments expressed in 'Howl.'"[10] Then in July 1959, Solomon reversed his position: "I disapprove of 'Howl' and every-thing that was contained therein." And a few months later: "All rights reserved is on a page of the book. Does this mean I can't use my name anymore?"[11] At times, Solomon was pissed that he had been used as a char-acter in his friend's poem, that he and his madness had been publicly appropriated by Allen, even if unintentionally.

The burden placed on Solomon was not lost on Allen, who in 1963 recorded the following dream notes: "I was all wrong to conspire with *Time* to create this Beatnik myself and to throw out into world a howl of Carl Solomon which fixed him in my idea of him a name a madness a hospital a mass public image surrounding him confusing him furthermore."

As the Beats became a cultural phenomenon, Solomon rode that wave as a writer himself. But, unlike many of the other Beats, his books, *Mishaps, Perhaps* (1966) and *More Mishaps* (1968), were published without Allen's interventions. They included short prose pieces and several poems where Solomon spoke for the one who has gone insane but doesn't want to acknowl-edge it, partly because "you desire to turn things around and make the ugly beautiful."[12] In "The Abyss (A story of philosophy and mental illness)," he is a self-effacing survivor of madness: "I suppose I am lost though temporarily at least found, and talking to you. And it is not so terrible to be lost . . . "[13] Solomon's "Report from the Asylum: Afterthoughts of a Shock Patient" has him pushing back against the poeticization of mental illness: "For the ailing intellect, there has been great danger in the poeticizing of the coma-void."[14] Yet he remained aware and bothered that his most famous and important role was being mad in someone else's poem.

Carl Solomon and Allen, 1991. © *Allen Ginsberg Estate.*

None of this was lost on Allen. He stayed loyal to Solomon throughout his life. For Allen's course on the "Literary History of the Beat Generation" at Brooklyn College on March 23, 1987, I was there when Allen introduced Solomon as a guest faculty member. His thankful, laudatory, and apologetic tones echo his "Reintroduction to Carl Solomon" from the thirtieth anniversary edition of "Howl." Allen wrote he was wrong about claiming Solomon was madder than he was: "His lifelong virtues of endurance, familial fidelity, and ultimate balance make my appeal seem hysterical, myself overwrought."[15] This is an extraordinary act of revision concerning one of the most important poems of the twentieth century. Allen walked back his own judgment about best minds as applied to Solomon and himself, to show respect, appreciation, and loyalty to Solomon. That day at Brooklyn College, Solomon was irritated, and Allen gave him the space to express that. Solomon told the class he felt trapped by Allen and the other Beats. He was attacked by Kerouac for being the "fake madman." The Beats had accepted a specific construction of a "mad artist" that did not accept "madness in all its forms," including what he himself had lived through.

After Solomon's "second sickness," in 1954, he too was hospitalized at Pilgrim State. From there Solomon wrote to Allen, who was traveling, that he even saw Naomi at a dance. Solomon became paranoid and hostile toward

Allen. Regarding Allen and his literary gang Solomon said, "I thought that they had all rejected me because I was madder than they were. I thought that they were neurotics and I was a psychotic, an outsider."[16] Who gets to own madness? Solomon was challenging Allen's mental illness, his appropriation of his own experiences, and Allen's claim to madness. In the world Allen's "Howl" had ushered in anyone and everyone can be mad. Then what happens to those who are actually living with psychosis? Who speaks for them?

After Solomon does his reading, the class is on break. I go up and introduce myself to Solomon. After a few minutes, he says, "Do you think you can come by and visit me?"[17]

Several days later, I take the #6 subway to the Pelham Bay Park station. I wait to meet Solomon in front of the candy store across the street from where he lives. When I don't see him I start to worry, not just because I've never been to this part of the Bronx but because I have no idea what I'm doing here. Ten minutes later, he appears, dressed all in black except for white sweat socks, not exactly cool, but comfortable.

"I called Bob Rosenthal, who told me that you are a psychiatrist," he says.

Not really, I explain; I'm just a medical student.

Nevertheless, Solomon has made up his mind that he is now talking to a psychiatrist, and while walking to his building begins to talk to me like I most want to know about his medications. "I have been on tranquilizers continuously for the past twenty-five years. Nowadays I'm on a minute dose of 50 mg of Mellaril. I had been on Thorazine, and much more sizeable doses, in crazier days."

We climb to the third floor, where he lives in his mother's apartment. She is in a nursing home, and he is caring for his senile uncle. There is a hospital bed in the living room for the uncle, who naps in a wheelchair in front of the window. In Solomon's room are two single beds and dressers with piles of books on top, including Allen's *Collected Poems, Howl and Other Poems, The Beat Vision*, Saul Bellow, Garrison Keillor, and *The Poet's Craft*. He has a typewriter and a stack of his own pages. "This is what I'm working on now. I have some people interested in a new book."

"I'm a lonely guy." Solomon has come a long way from the days of Pilgrim State, and he does not want to go back. He fears if he tries to articulate what he was feeling back then, he may inadvertently bring on the sickness once again. How different he is from Allen, who holds onto all memories and feelings and enthusiastically speaks of past events, including his visions. Solomon has seen too much, and paid too high a cost, to play those games anymore. "Now my jokes are very bad. I've exhausted my humor and can't work my brain to that extent because I have to be responsible for my own functioning." As a writer, he still collects anecdotes and has an eye for the absurd. He is now, as he says, "a messenger boy with weak nerves."

Another time I come down from New Haven and we meet for coffee in Manhattan. We end up talking about *The Plague*'s Dr. Rieux, who was horrified by the suffering before him and refused to accept it as divine intervention. Solomon is impressed to find a psychiatrist who has read Camus.

On another visit, when we sit at a busy luncheonette counter in Midtown, he seems taken aback when I ask him about madness within earshot of all the working people eating their sandwiches in their suits and ties. Unlike Allen, Solomon still has to go to work among those people tomorrow and felt embarrassed. It hadn't crossed my mind. I wished I could offer Carl the fellowship or security that would enable him to open up more, but it does not seem possible.

Allen must have felt something similar. When Allen inscribed for Solomon a copy of his *Collected Poems*, he wrote: "With thanks for his advice, sympathy, critiques, invitations, despairs, happinesses & friendships for 3 and a half Decades now."

In 1968, Jane Kramer wrote about Allen's attention upon the "freak-outs, flip-outs, and drop-outs who were arriving daily," adding: "Ginsberg had an incredible concern for these casualties."[18] Allen didn't forget about Naomi, Carl Solomon, or where his education on madness came from. He acknowledged the mental illness and other daily hardships that helped make them who they were and still afflicted them. Allen knew the lofty projects of writing poems of madness and changing society could not be separated from support, companionship, and love for those in need and from building a welcoming and supportive community with and for them. He wanted everyone to show the same generosity to those of us who experienced madness and mental illness. Even today, his dream remains ambitious, very far from being realized, yet no less empowering or necessary.

Allen's "White Shroud,"[19] from 1986, is his own poetic epilogue to "Kaddish." The "bittersweet magical" poem, and its darker companion, "Black Shroud," are the centerpieces of this collection and do further work on "Kaddish," extending, though by no means resolving, Allen's ambivalent relationship with his mother, Naomi, his muse. They revisit the narrative of Allen transforming madness into revolutionary poetry more directly and explicitly than any other of his writings.

"White Shroud," a fantasy reunification with his long-lost mother, begins with the poet being summoned from sleep in a dream. Allen discovers his mother is an old woman with chronic mental illness living on the streets of New York City. They will live together out on the street. The poem is washed over by the sun's rays, reminiscent of "Kaddish," which begins on the sunny pavement of New York City, as well as the sunshine in the window of Naomi's hospital room at Pilgrim State.

"Black Shroud" begins with Allen in China, vomiting in his hotel room, awash in regrets. He dreams of his mother in 1937 vomiting and defecating on the bathroom floor and then confesses to having sliced off her head with an ax, but telling nobody. Next the poem flashes to a family gathering many years later, where his cousin the lawyer tells Allen how as an author he will get special protection from a team of lawyers. The protagonist poet regrets not only the murder and his silence but also the confession, none of which he can undo.

In these two poems, Naomi is two very different persons.

In "White Shroud," she is a poor shopping bag lady living on the street, white haired, sharp-eyed, with bad teeth. She speaks: "I'm living alone, you all abandoned me, I'm a great woman." She is calm enough for Allen to imagine he can live with her. The decades have mellowed her, as is sometimes the case with persons with schizophrenia who survive into middle and later adulthood.[20]

In "Black Shroud," Naomi is a writhing, screaming mess who in a flash becomes a headless corpse. The reader identifies not with her but with the poet protagonist, who confesses his guilt, and with the cousin who receives his confession. Neither poem says the word "lobotomy."

"White Shroud" imagines Naomi returned from the hospital back to the street, without any indication of a lobotomy. "Black Shroud" recasts an imagined lobotomy as axe murder. "White Shroud" depicts Naomi's return to life. Allen no longer wishes to be a great poet but only to see his mother content and reunited with him in comfort and peace. "White Shroud" ends with an image of domestic bliss. As Allen has finished writing his poem, Peter Orlovsky, who twenty-four years before fed him eggs and tea as he wrote "Kaddish" in their Lower East Side flat, is awake at dawn watching the weather news on TV when Allen gets up from his writing desk.

If "White Shroud" is linear, hopeful, and domestic, "Black Shroud" mixes up time and place and is murderous. The poem begins in a hotel in Kunming in 1984, where the poet is traveling and lecturing. Kunming is a modern capital city in Yunnan Province, a place of more than 2,400 years of history. In his dream he goes back to 1937, where he imagines the beheading. This image is a screen memory in that it falsely recalls, exaggerates, and masks the lobotomy.[21] Then he flashes forward to the 1980s, where he is at a family wedding and sees his cousin. But the dream itself is reported from a later point in time where he is confessing to what he had earlier done wrong. In contrast, "White Shroud" is written entirely in the present tense.

In "Black Shroud," he confesses to the murder of Naomi. But given how she begged to be killed, maybe it can be forgiven as a mercy killing. He does not confess to putting her in the hospital and signing for the lobotomy or for his infrequent hospital visits or missing her funeral. He also does not confess to holding the special privilege of being an artist and remaining silent about his self-perceived wrongdoings.

These two poems explore the complications of an artistic project and a life built on madness and its artistic transformation. Trauma, loss, regret, guilt, rage, and sadness do not disappear. Writing poems and becoming a countercultural leader were not a therapy that rid this poet of pains, much less chaos, confusion, contradiction, behavioral problems, or regrets. But this was never his intent in writing "Howl" and "Kaddish," "White Shroud" and "Black Shroud," or any other poems.

Allen wrote poems of vision, confession, prophecy, elegy, and protest, all of which were aimed at a liberation of consciousness. Strikingly, "White Shroud" and "Black Shroud" reveal the life events and creation myths that, for forty years and counting, were fundamental to his poetry and public role. Mental illness, suicide attempts, hospitalizations, lobotomy, visitations, and burial. Remembering, writing, memorializing, reworking, and poeticizing.

Shrouds are the cloths Jews and people of other faiths use to dress the body for burial. With the two shroud poems, Allen put to rest his telling the story of his mother and her madness and simultaneously opened up new possibilities. The two sides of the tale woven together in "Kaddish" are teased apart and left standing in two striking companion poems: one of regret over shortcomings and sins; the other of joy over renewals and redemption.

In leaving not only one long "Kaddish" but two distinct and intertwined shroud tales from thirty-six years later, Allen returns to the interaction between hardship and hope and how these are not simply resolved but will go on and on. What's more, sins and redemption, shortcomings and renewals, trauma and resilience, poetry and prophecy, coexist, become entangled. What seems finalized today can be reworked (though not necessarily resolved) tomorrow and then reworked again the next day or years or decades later. Allen did the work of poetically unpacking these highly difficult experiences so that we might better know the complicated ways that people come to know who they are in this hard world.

Though rooted in tremendously difficult personal and social hardships, Allen's poetic madness is full of longing and dangers yet stubbornly hopeful. He discovered aesthetic ways of working with life's traumas and losses, convincing us we can too, which is something he tried to live as well. If we are willing to take risks, change our consciousness and remake ourselves, then we may be able to brighten up a world short on spirit and empathy, both in poetry and in praxis.

Yet the white and black shrouds Allen leaves us with also reflect a tendency toward dualism. Gary Snyder noted this years ago, in response to "Howl," and felt it may have bound Allen in relation to madness and mental illness. Dualism can hide pain, but it can't resolve it. When Allen spoke with me about his mother, I sensed the intense emotional pain he carried decades after her death. He found ways to lessen the dualism, especially through his Buddhist practice. Yet the burdens of living in a world where madness and sanity are considered opposites, and where the sorrows and renewals of traumatic loss uncomfortably coexist, remained heavy for Allen.

EPILOGUE

IN HER INTRODUCTION to a collection of poems by William Blake, Patti Smith writes that art has one eye and science another.[1] Nowhere has this dichotomy been so charged, complicated, and polarized as in literature and psychiatry. Today's psychiatry is not the same as it was in the 1940s and 1950s, but still the two eyes see madness differently. We are often at the mercy of monocular understandings, when opening both eyes would offer much more.

Allen, whose approach to madness in his poems and writings could be so moving and thought provoking, was committed to looking at madness through both artistic and scientific lenses. He was a man of literature, but he also witnessed, suffered under, learned from, and respected psychiatry. By looking through both lenses, he was trying to fundamentally change our way of seeing madness. He was even excited to mentor a young psychiatrist who was also committed to looking through both eyes, and he gave me access to his most personal and private papers. This Epilogue reflects further on Allen's perspective on madness and why it matters today.

Allen's poetry came from his passion for art and words, his insatiable curiosity for understanding the human experience, and a childhood and early adulthood shaped by his mother's serious mental illness. His poetry reflected and considered a psychiatric profession limited in scientific knowledge, therapeutic methods, and ethical practices. He was informed by the biological

237

and psychoanalytic formulations of mental illness but was constantly looking for new narratives and ideas in the everyday genius of people living through hardships and suffering. The person and poet he became was a living testimony that going through too much, such as a person with mental illness or their family member, could make somebody engaged, compassionate, wise, funny, and compelling instead of just wounded, scarred, and symptomatic.

In his poems, letters, interviews, and lectures, he invited readers and listeners not to fear but to accept and fully engage with the madness in themselves and others. Allen's creed: "Don't hide the madness."[2] He fought against how we hide from ourselves and others and the cruel ways we hide those we don't want around.

To Allen, madness is not limited to illness, dysfunction, derangement, or any other one thing, as both earlier and current psychiatrists have often claimed. Madness can also be deviancy, ecstasy, visions, inspiration, genius, creativity, and spirituality. Madness can be a condition of individuals, but it is also part of family and social life. Madness can afflict leaders, organizations, cultures, governments, and whole societies. Madness comes in all these various forms and possibilities which is an essential part of life that must be acknowledged and engaged.

Allen, like William Blake and other great artists, knew that madness should not be romanticized. Madness may bring devastating suffering and hardship. It can also provide valued knowledge or freedom from constraints on what we are allowed to see. Madness can redeem when it disrupts the existing order, with new perceptions, strong passions, bold ideas, striking imagery, and intense energy. Madness, if handled with care and respected and heard with compassion and support for its miseries, may lead to spiritual, political, and social breakthroughs. Allen knew that to reject madness is to reject our full human potential.

In coming to terms with madness, Allen changed the culture and emboldened a new generation of thought leaders, including R. D. Laing and the antipsychiatrists, who in turn helped shape psychiatry and the treatment of mental illness. Yet Allen did not make all his concerns about changing psychiatry explicit, because psychiatry was just one part of his highly ambitious social advocacy goals and activities. He tied his work to spirituality, to LSD, to fighting censorship and protesting the Vietnam War and nuclear weapons, to changing American society, to protecting the environment, and to being in dialogue with many of the world's greatest artists. He did not want to be bound by the circumstances of his personal or family history of mental illness. He was a poet and thought leader who aimed to speak beyond poetry and, of course, far beyond the psychiatric practices of his day, to the suffering, cultural norms and values, social practices, and political systems limiting human possibilities.

Allen constructively utilized his experiences with his mother's mental illness and lobotomy and his own mental health struggles to develop a highly original poetics of madness. His poems evolved from and incorporated multiple positions or voices, including those of ecstatic visions, fearful insanity, urban ethnography, social rebellion, aesthetic methods, witnessing, and the elegy. He offered many-sided explorations of madness as well as consciousness for a public wanting a way out of conformity while trying to make sense of the world going up in flames.

Despite Allen's literary achievements, he was only human and had his flaws. As far as I know, based on my direct experiences and what I learned from others, Allen was not mean or vindictive, but at times made choices that hurt others. In earlier chapters, I shared that he did not visit Naomi very often at Pilgrim State and didn't attend her funeral. As a leader of the psychedelic movement, he was not as vigilant as he could have been about the risks for mental health casualties, especially among adolescents.

We also need to examine a controversy that came to public attention when Allen was in his sixties, when he joined the North American Man Boy Love Association (NAMBLA), an organization that supports pedophiles, and revealed that he slept with teenage boys. Allen believed in "consensual intergenerational affairs" and told Andrea Dworkin he had had many affairs with boys who were sixteen, seventeen, or eighteen, some of whom were close to or possibly below the age of consent, and certainly much younger than himself.[3] Bob Rosenthal noted that Allen often spoke of his affection for "boys" but that he never saw Allen with a prepubescent boy and trusted Allen around his own young sons. Allen later confessed to Rosenthal that his position on NAMBLA was "completely indefensible."[4]

So what was he doing? Allen leaned into this controversial organization in part because defending those who are indefensible was consistent with his solidarity with those in the grips of madness, a belief that everyone needs to be heard and that there is value in what is not valued. Allen's art and advocacy championed the transgressive and even called them the "best minds." This approach is not without risks, and in this instance Allen and his affiliates are the ones we must be concerned about. Just because Allen was brilliant and famous, we should not gloss over or downplay this behavior.

We cannot say Allen did not know what NAMBLA stood for and what its members did. Allen was willfully naïve about whom he was affiliating with and how they served as cover for abuses against children. He had a blind spot when it comes to advocating adult sexual activity with children. This is no excuse for his harmful choices, but may help us to explain what was driving these choices.

As discussed in Chapters 2 and 5, Allen and Naomi's psychosexual history is complicated. Naomi, who was a victim of child sexual trauma, was known for nudism and sexually provocative behavior with Allen ("making sexual demands"), something that could very well have been his own trauma of childhood sexual abuse. As a child, Allen exposed himself to strangers and rubbed up against his father in bed for sexual stimulation. Though most victims of sexual abuse do not become perpetrators in any way, some do in various ways, which introduces the possibility that Allen was himself traumatizing adolescents through sexual exposure.[5] According to Bob Rosenthal, Allen had a complete lack of empathy for children. He didn't seem to acknowledge them as children, which Bob relates to Allen never having a real childhood, because he had to grow up fast to care for his mother—a not uncommon situation for children of the seriously mentally ill.

Allen was part of a celebrity culture along with musicians and artists who were openly having sex with young groupies. He was committed to freedom and sexual liberation, but this could be used to justify potentially damaging and illegal behaviors associated with having sex with much younger people. Allen has said his relationships with boys were precisely the opposite of coercive or traumatizing. Allen felt that he was giving a gift of experience and intimacy to consenting teens, as has been done by other men throughout history.[6] Some narratives shared publicly by some of his young lovers support Allen's perspective, but it is possible that this was not always the case, especially given the way that powerful abusers can silence those who did not "welcome" the abuse. Bob Rosenthal has shared that not all of Allen's encounters turned out well. Over the years, several adolescents and young men approached Rosenthal distressed about Allen propositioning them.

Allen's actions do not fit the pattern of pedophilia. However, calling them ephebophilia (sexual attraction to mid-to-late adolescents) should not mean simply agreeing with Allen and others that this behavior is acceptable. Allen liked to have sex with teenage boys and whether or not it is legal, it is not acceptable. I believed that when I heard him talking about it in the 1980s, and it is my opinion now that I am aware of the lasting psychological damage such sexual contact can cause among teenage boys and girls. I see it as a major blind spot that can be traced back to the burden of having a mother with serious mental illness at a time when psychiatry had little to offer.

Whether Allen's actions could have been a felony is a matter of state laws that specify age of consent, minimum age, and age differential.[7]

Allen acknowledging his position on NAMBLA as indefensible takes it to another level. There was an element of Allen punishing himself in the public eye, willing to take on indefensible positions and to accept the consequences. We can only speculate on what drives self-punishment. There was something about Allen that compelled him to align himself with those society deems unacceptable, such as junkies and criminals like Herbert Huncke. Could Allen be paying a self-inflicted price for other acts he experienced as indefensible—the lobotomy and sending Naomi back to Pilgrim State—for which he felt enormously guilty? Or for not being able to make her well or get her out of the hospital? Importantly, Allen brought the NAMBLA controversy upon himself in the years following his publicly revealing, in 1989, that he had signed consent for his mother's lobotomy. The NAMBLA controversy served as a distraction from a sin he believed he committed and perceived as even worse.

For the public, the NAMBLA controversy expressed something highly transgressive about how in his sixties Allen, a master poet, seasoned activist, and celebrity, saw himself and wanted to be seen by others. Some have taken steps to cancel Allen, but that is no solution. Let's acknowledge his ugly and potentially harmful actions and communications and remember he was human. Though Allen was able to write poems of madness, powerful enough to liberate many, tragically he never managed to heal the traumas and losses associated with his mother's mental illness which he experienced earlier in his own life.

As a young man, Allen came to believe in visions and in connecting with dimensions that most people cannot see. He grabbed hold of the madness in and around himself and turned it into powerful poems and cultural explosions. How so? First, through being exposed to actual mental illness and madness in his mother and then through the many other people with mental health problems in his life he befriended and looked after. Second, by being committed to independent literary and spiritual studies, looking to artistic models of transformation to recast traumatic life experiences and deviant experiences, developing his writing day by day over many years, and sustaining a sympathetic network of fellow writers, mentors, and mentees. Third, by getting psychiatric treatment and support to help redirect his efforts in less dangerous and more productive ways and by developing powerful stories about madness that could fuse personal and social experiences.

When faced with disappointing, painful, and unspeakable experiences, Allen found ways to respond in literature. Beginning in childhood, to reflect on the juxtaposition of madness and sanity in his life, he started to keep a journal. He turned to literature and art, to learn how others have transformed lives and worlds marked by woe into something more. He poured himself into reading, journaling, corresponding, and creative writing. He could not right the world around him, but he could write a more perfect world in a text. He worked closely within a small group of writers who were equally committed to experimenting with mystical experiences. When disappointments and losses came knocking, he pushed himself toward new poetic discoveries, especially the poetic long line. He kept the boundary between art and life open, taking life as a subject and inspiration for works of art and giving us poetry writ from some of life's most difficult and painful experiences. He was always doing the work of an artist, looking for that blast of light.

His poems and other writings tell evocative stories about innumerable madnesses, and these stories tell many different tales. In "Howl," madness is liberation, whereas in "Kaddish," madness is more injurious, both to those afflicted by mental illness and to their loved ones. Yet despite the suffering madness imposes, precisely because it always comes in multiples, allowing several different connections, madness creates possibilities in its survivors and witnesses for new meaning, identities, and outcomes. Allen opened these doors.

Allen's ongoing work on expanding consciousness, especially through drugs and poetry, aimed at inspiring and elevating others' minds. The changes he sought to bring about are not equivalent to psychiatric treatments of mental illness. However, his methods of experimenting upon himself, writing under the influence, learning to control his own breath, and dream journaling are potentially valuable alternative approaches for consciousness- and thinking-focused research, and they merit further reflection and investigation. Allen's radical acceptance of madness as a basic human capacity, which includes the potential for good, invites us to change how we understand madness and mental illness and is itself another powerful way of expanding consciousness for the benefit of humankind.

When I visited Allen at his apartment on East Twelfth Street in the late 1980s, you first had to ring the bell, and then Allen, Bob, or someone else leaned out the window and dropped the key in a sock down to the street. For years, I actually dreamed of standing on the street and looking up into the sky waiting for that key in the sock to drop that would let me go upstairs. I hoped contact with him would help me become a different kind of person and psychiatrist. I believe it did, but Allen and I had to work at it. Allen was incredibly open and generous to me, encouraging me to tell the complete story of his experiences with madness and psychiatry, even though these experiences were deeply personal and painful for him.

He asked what I was learning about psychiatry at Columbia and then later at Yale. One day after a dinner in the East Village, he looked at me and announced, "I want to make you into my kind of psychiatrist." I smiled and nodded, "Sure, Allen, that sounds fine to me, but just what does it mean?" I came to learn it means being accepting, nonjudgmental, and supportive toward those with mental illness. It also means listening to accounts of hardship, trauma, or suffering not just as reflecting individual experiences but also as manifesting social, cultural, historical, spiritual, and political dimensions. His mentoring involved listening to my stories about working with psychiatric patients and the dilemmas I was having trying to reconcile very different experiences and views of madness. It also involved listening to his stories about his mother, Peter Orlovsky, Carl Solomon, William Burroughs, Jack Kerouac, Herbert Huncke, and other friends and sharing ideas and quotations from poetry and literature.

Back then, the lessons Allen taught me about psychiatry did not strike me as being as radical as his poetry, the choices he made in his life, or the books he encouraged me to read. But over time I grew to appreciate how he was sharing powerful and transformative ways of seeing illness, hardship, outsiders, art, drugs, and love, ways of seeing that were clearly different from what I was hearing from my professors and reading in professional journals.

Once when we were talking about diagnoses, I read to him from Hoch and Polatin's articles and the *Diagnostic and Statistical Manual*. This prompted him to say, "I have no objections to such approaches when applied evenly and accurately to the whole population. But this is often not the case. Rich and poor get treated differently. Like when I was sent to the 'bughouse' instead of jail like Huncke."[8] The other big problem with psychiatry he focused on is that they "adjust you to reality rather than in relation with it," like his big-eared psychiatrist at PI.

Once he asked to see my copy of *The Varieties of Religious Experience* and quickly pointed out the most important passages, especially the ones on conversion experiences. I was amazed that after all these years he still knew the book so well. As I was studying psychiatry during medical school and then in my residency at Yale, I also got to visit Allen in the East Village and learn to see madness through the lenses of spirituality, poetics, and protest. Allen urged me not to forget William James's teaching that some of those who are considered ill may be the most likely candidates for mystical experiences and conversions. He worried that too often the potential inherent in madness is overlooked by psychiatrists. He had higher hopes for me. "I think you'll become more like R. D. Laing." On my way home from meeting with him, I stopped by the Strand bookstore to pick up a copy of Laing's *The Divided Self* and started reading it on the subway back to Washington Heights.

I attended Allen's readings and sat in on his class at Brooklyn College on the "Literary History of the Beat Generation." He was a serious teacher and created a classroom structure that intentionally allowed room for deviance. His "Ground Rules" read: "Classroom discussions will sidetrack and loop around chronology. Visiting poets loop around chronology; classroom talk will deviate accordingly."[9] Allen's lectures integrated talk of poetics with politics, sexuality, and hallucinogens. At those classes he introduced me to Carl Solomon, Robert Creeley, Herbert Huncke, Gregory Corso, Ted Joans, and William Burroughs. At lunch, Burroughs was especially amused to see Allen's young psychiatry student in tow. Burroughs was smirking at me, so I smirked back at him, wondering what could possibly be on his mind. I didn't dare ask.

I do what Allen instructs his students to do: Devour all the readings, and speak with him about them. They include Huncke's *The Evening Sun Turned Crimson*, Burroughs's *The Yage Letters*, and Solomon's *Mishaps, Perhaps and More Mishaps*. I am especially taken by Solomon's weary absurdist reflections on madness. Solomon wrote: "I was Lautréamont a long time ago and now a psychiatrically disabled ex-ice-cream salesman whose life history can be figured out by nobody."[10] Compared with Allen, Solomon suffered more from his own mental illness and from ECT treatments, yet he still managed to pursue his intellectual and literary passions.

What are the implications of *Best Minds* for scholarship on Allen Ginsberg and the Beats? Regarding Allen, this book has revealed several significant new findings: One, Naomi's lobotomy came in 1948, several years earlier than Allen recalled, and six months before his visions. Two, Allen's reporting that in 1948 he heard William Blake's voice came at least ten years later than he or others have previously conveyed. Three, Allen experienced multiple traumas and losses in relation to Naomi's serious mental illness. Four, Allen's suffering and mental health problems were genuine, and his hospitalization was of some help to him. These findings are important because they modify the widely understood narrative of Allen, which has been shaped as much by myth as fact. I hope that future scholars and writers will incorporate and examine these findings into their works on Allen Ginsberg.

Regarding implications for scholarship on the Beats, others may be in a better position to answer this question, but I will offer three takeaways. One, madness is more than mental illness and pathology. Let's approach these phenomena with complexity, from multiple levels, perspectives, and disciplinary lenses. Two, having visions or mystical experiences are not just momentary events but also products of language, which can change their meaning and significance over time. Three, because the very concept of "Beat," as explained by John Clellon Holmes, overlaps with the concepts of trauma, moral injury, and resilience, and given that several Beat writers had such life experiences, we need to learn more about the relationship of the Beats to trauma.[11] What about Jack Kerouac, William Burroughs, Gregory Corso, and Diane Di Prima, for starters? How might the ethos of the Beats—a weary, open, questioning, and believing response to a world of hurt—teach something valuable about responding creatively to traumas?

For more than twenty-five years since Allen's death, I have kept a conversation going with him about the many issues we discussed. Learning from Allen was part of the reason I chose to become a psychiatrist. Yet Allen never explicitly told me what I should or should not do as a psychiatrist. There is probably a little bit of Allen in many things I do, and sometimes a lot.

Allen never said or implied I should reject psychiatry. I believe Allen expected me to extend his words and teachings further into psychiatry. And so, I keep asking, what can young psychiatrists and other health professionals learn from Allen? Allen's poems humanize madness; challenge psychiatry's power over the lives and treatment of persons with madness; redefine how we can be more humane in families, communities, and societies; offer alternative paths to personal meaning and change; and see literature and art as offering keys to understanding human experience.

Allen's poems portray a psychiatry that did not understand his generation and labeled them as mad. The psychiatry in the 1940s and 1950s often did not understand or did not care to change how it had become caught up in large societal processes of implementing social control. With lobotomy and other injurious treatments such as metrazol shock therapy, psychiatry had become even more dangerous than mental illness itself. This form of psychiatry made Naomi and Carl Solomon far worse and did not value Allen's visions. This psychiatry left its destructive mark on many hundreds of thousands of people with mental illness involuntarily held in public psychiatric hospitals in the decades before deinstitutionalization began in 1955. Amazingly, enough of these stories have still not been heard, and psychiatry has still not reckoned with all the damage it did. This should change.

On the brighter side, Allen's poems also bear witness to how people with mental illness and their family members have stories to tell, can make meaning, and can find hope. In his poetry, Allen recorded scores of missing voices. His stories document the heartbreak of serious mental illness but also the possibilities for new perspectives and social value, ecstasy, humor, illumination, and rebellion. Allen also wanted to bring his homespun ideas of positive psychiatry, cross-cultural psychology, and psychedelic therapy to help individuals in pain and a society under tremendous duress.

When Allen attended the GAP meeting in Asbury Park in 1960, he did not speak with the psychiatrists about how psychiatry had treated him or Naomi but instead about his mystical and psychedelic experiences. He advised understanding those experiences from the vantage point of literature. Although it is sadly too late for Allen to attend any more psychiatric conferences or training programs, I envision creating new encounters between Allen's poems and other writings and today's students in psychiatry, which would raise issues of urgency for the present and future. Let's not create a new antipsychiatry to battle mainstream psychiatry, but instead let's get psychiatry, literature, history, anthropology, religion, and philosophy engaging more seriously with one another. We can also strengthen emerging hybrid fields of inquiry, such as narrative medicine, madness studies, hearing voices, and disability studies.

I picture gathering young psychiatrists together in their training programs and asking them to read Allen's major poems on madness: "Howl" and "Kaddish." These poems would expand upon their individual- and diagnostic-focused approaches to mental illness and invite family, social, literary, and spiritual perspectives on madness and healing. I would have them first read each poem to themselves, then do a group oral reading, followed by a group discussion.

I would start with "Howl," because it is such an extraordinary "liberating document" and offers a "comforting madness,"[12] and then move on to "Kaddish," the elegy for Naomi, which describes a damaging madness and offers new ways to approach prayer and mourning. I would invite them to reflect on how the poems feel, what they are each about, and how the long line works differently in each. Then I would focus the discussions on what each poem is saying about madness, mental illness, psychiatry, lobotomy, and death. Along the way I would make the following points, which I learned from Allen directly and from turning to his works over many years.

Allen was critical of psychiatrists who didn't listen to and engage with their patients so as to understand how they were experiencing their madness and mental illness. I would ask the young psychiatrists to consider how

"Howl" and "Kaddish" might change how they listen to and interact with patients, especially when patients and their families have values, worldviews, or insights different from theirs.

Allen was a caregiver for his mother, Naomi, but was not given any support by her psychiatrists or much from his own. What do "Howl" and "Kaddish" have to say about the experience of family caregivers? I would ask students to think about the experiences and perspectives of family members and what they want and need from psychiatry to help their loved one and themselves.

Allen didn't want psychiatrists to blindly follow authority or rush to perform irreversible procedures like the lobotomy. From the poems, what did you learn about lobotomy and psychiatry? I would share historical facts about lobotomy and the early uses of electroconvulsive therapy, which is rarely discussed among psychiatrists. I would ask them to think about the tragic history of the lobotomy and what psychiatrists should do with these institutional memories. Can we prevent anything like that from happening ever again?

Allen's poems draw attention to the social, political, and historical context of madness and especially to injustices, oppression, and traumatic life experiences in their patients' lives. How do "Howl" and "Kaddish" make the case for mental illness as a social diagnosis? If psychiatrists were thinking from this perspective, how would it change the ways we relate to people with mental illness?

Allen believed madness could be redeemed through artistic witness. This requires deep engagement with the suffering individual, dedication to both literary tradition and imaginative innovations, and support from family and friends. Allen personally supported struggling artists and countless seekers, students, and madman saints who ended up on his stoop, in his classroom, at readings or rallies. I want us to discuss how we help communities and society be more tolerant and supportive of people with mental illness.

Allen was able to look at people suffering from madness both through the lenses of psychopathology and those of spirituality and literature. What do the poems tell us about looking through these different lenses? How might psychiatrists open themselves up to other healing practices and perspectives derived from religion and art, including meditation, journaling, poetry therapy, and art therapy?

Allen was way ahead of mainstream psychiatry regarding the use of LSD and other psychedelics for treating mental illness, such as PTSD and depression. I would like young psychiatrists to think about how psychiatry can approach the use of hallucinogens as a therapeutic tool, which in recent years has become a topic of considerable public and scientific interest.[13] His explorations of expanding consciousness through poetry, journaling, and meditation also have not been adequately appreciated or studied and should be examined in relation to innovations in the neuroscience study of consciousness and literature.[14]

These are some of the many points I learned from Allen and have used throughout my life while working as a psychiatrist.

In October 1987, Allen journaled about a dream in which he had asked some financial experts to find a way to be better off, and they told him he should go to medical school.

> I was surprised a little shocked at that, then was very moved and almost cried when I realized the implication, that I was so experienced in suffering and in the grief of madness that I should go into that grief like a doctor and obtain credentials and become a great mental physician—But how at my age?—It meant I could begin a new life, drop all my old attachments and obligations, get an apartment uptown near Columbia, and be supported while I spend half a decade studying new fields and emerge professional capable of keeping mankind in an accurate and penetrant way—reform the whole system of mental health, hospitals, addiction, alcoholism, dependencies, aids, psychic illness and poverty of body and mind.[15]

He could dream it but not himself do it. But he could channel the power of dreams into his mentoring and teaching, through which he multiplied himself through all the young people he taught and influenced.

It was not until many years later that I read this dream, which had come during the years we were in contact and I was living in Washington Heights and then New Haven, working at becoming a psychiatrist. Allen imagined another life for himself, putting to work all that suffering in a completely different way for him, not unlike what I was pursuing those very years. This sheds some light on what he saw in me and how he responded to getting to know me as a young psychiatrist.

One thing for sure: Allen contained multitudes. Somewhere within him there was a psychiatrist and psychiatric reformer waiting to be born. I believe there are many ways to become Allen Ginsberg's kind of psychiatrist. It could be to reform mental health hospitals. It could be to change the way we relate to addicts and alcoholics. It could be to promote the use of psychedelics as therapy. It could be about peace psychology, violence prevention, or working with refugees and immigrants. I became my own version of Allen

Ginsberg's kind of psychiatrist, but there are many more possible versions yet to be realized.

Allen had a "genius for attentiveness and generosity,"[16] became a counter-cultural leader, sold millions of books, and impacted generations of readers. His legacy and broad cultural impact live on. His works on madness are especially meaningful for those of us involved with trauma and mental illness, either in our personal or professional lives.

To learn from Allen is to accept that "The bum's as holy as the seraphim! the madman is holy as you my soul are holy!"[17] To walk with Allen is to believe the madness within us and around us is essential and should be handled with reverence and care.

ACKNOWLEDGMENTS

DURING THE MORE than several decades I have spent writing this book, many colleagues and friends have engaged with this project and offered their wise counsel. I cannot possibly name them all. I am especially indebted to my extraordinary mentors who read draft after draft and believed in this project: David Forrest, Daniel Levinson, Jerrold Maxmen, and Ivan Pavkovic. My good friend Schuyler Henderson was a close and enthusiastic reader who always pushed me to go further. Along the way, I got valuable assistance from Aliriza Arënlieu, Dan Becker, Mark Caro, Andrei Codrescu, Marshall Edelson, Donald Faulkner, Suzanne Feetham, Laura Frankel, Sander Gilman, Laura Hamady, David Kopacz, Tvrtko Kulenovic, Bart Lazar, Burton Lerner, Ira Levine, Robert Jay Lifton, W. J. T. Mitchell, Nancy Olson, Syd Phillips, Chloe Polutnik Smith, Tamara Razi, Mort Reiser, Jack Saul, Carl Solomon, Andrew Stone, John Strauss, David Rothman, Chuck Wasserburg, and Bob Welch. Patti Smith shared her remarkable insights on Allen, William Blake, and visions.

This book could not have been written without studying the writings of others on Allen Ginsberg and the Beats. I want to acknowledge the works of Deborah Baker, Peter Conners, Lewis Hyde, Jane Kramer, Barry Miles, Bill Morgan, Ted Morgan, Paul Portuges, Bob Rosenthal, Jason Schinder, Michael Schumacher, Tony Triglio, Gordon Wills, and, of course, William Burroughs, Neal Cassady, John Clellon Holmes, Herbert Huncke, Jack Kerouac, Carl Solomon, and Anne Waldman. All of their works greatly informed my research and writing. I want especially to thank Michael

Schumacher for keeping me grounded in the existing scholarship on Allen and the Beats.

Thank you to the Columbia University and Stanford University Libraries and their helpful staff for being the keepers of the Allen Ginsberg Papers, which were invaluable for my research. I also want to thank the New York State Psychiatric Institute and Pilgrim State Psychiatric Institute for providing me with Allen and Naomi Ginsberg's medical records, with Allen Ginsberg's consent.

At Fordham University Press, I want to thank Director Fred Nachbaur and Managing Editor Eric Newman for their steady guidance, Angela Moody for her wonderful cover design, Rob Fellman for precision copyediting, and two anonymous peer reviewers for their expert advice and support. It has been such a pleasure to work with a publisher who completely gets it.

I have been fortunate to learn and work in academic psychiatry departments that support multidisciplinary inquiry into the experiences of mental illness: Columbia University, Yale University, and the University of Illinois at Chicago. I especially want to thank Herb Pardes, Boris Astrachan, and Joe Flaherty for their leadership.

I am grateful for the support, encouragement, and wisdom of the Allen Ginsberg Estate, including its executor Bob Rosenthal, whom I first met twenty years ago, when he was Allen's secretary, as well as archivist Peter Hale. From the first time I met Allen, Bob has been there for me, lending his experience and wisdom. Peter has been a constant source of help, including with permissions necessary for this book. I am also indebted to Lyle Brooks and Paula Litsky for their assistance as representatives of the Ginsberg family.

I am grateful to the Group for the Advancement of Psychiatry for inviting me to deliver a keynote lecture reflecting on Allen's remarkable visit there more than fifty years earlier. *Critical Inquiry* and the *American Journal of Psychiatry* published my earlier writings on Allen Ginsberg.

This project was only possible because Allen Ginsberg read my letter, called me back, met with me, opened his archives, gave me consent, sat for interviews, acted as a mentor, and encouraged me to pursue this inquiry without trying to control it. I am indebted to the trust and faith he placed in me years ago.

My family has not only endured hours and hours of writing but also supported me on my journey, provided a sounding board, and shared our lives in houses full of books. Everlasting gratitude to my parents, David and Esther; brothers Andy and Ken; in-laws Rhoda and Jerry; sister-in-law Barbara; daughters Daniella and Kate; and especially Laura, my beloved wife, who has been there all the way.

NOTES

Prologue

1. New York State Psychiatric Institute, medical record of Allen Ginsberg, 1949–1950. All subsequent quotations from this medical record are noted in the text.

2. Allen Ginsberg, *Collected Poems, 1947–1997* (New York: HarperCollins, 2006), 48.

3. Assen Jablensky, "The Diagnostic Concept of Schizophrenia: Its History, Evolution, and Future Prospects," *Dialogues in Clinical Neuroscience* 12, no. 3 (2010): 271–87.

4. D. L. Rosenhan, "On Being Sane in Insane Places," *Science* 179, no. 4070 (1973): 250–58.

5. Ginsberg, *Collected Poems*, 134.

6. Jerry Aronson, dir., *The Life and Times of Allen Ginsberg*, 1994.

7. Richard Eberhart, Allen Ginsberg, and Jerome Kaplan, *To Eberhart from Ginsberg: A Letter about "Howl," 1956: An Explanation by Allen Ginsberg of His Publication "Howl" and Richard Eberhart's New York Times Article "West Coast Rhythms," Together with Comments by Both Poets and Relief Etchings by Jerome Kaplan* (Lincoln, MA: Penmaen, 1976).

8. Tony Triglio, *Allen Ginsberg's Buddhist Poetics* (Springfield: University of Illinois Press, 2007).

9. Institute of Contemporary Arts, Allen Ginsberg, and R. D. Laing, *Allen Ginsberg with R. D. Laing* (London: ICA Video; Northbrook, IL: Roland Collection, 1986).

10. Ginsberg, *Collected Poems*, 142.

1. Death and Madness, 1997–1998

1. Bob Rosenthal, *Straight around Allen: On the Business of Being Allen Ginsberg* (St. Andrews: Beatdom, 2018), 163.

2. Allen Ginsberg, *Collected Poems, 1947–1997* (New York: HarperCollins, 2006), 967.

3. Louis Ginsberg to Allen Ginsberg, June 11, 1956, Allen Ginsberg Papers, Department of Special Collections, Stanford University Libraries, Stanford, CA.

4. Allen Ginsberg, *Family Business: Selected Letters between a Father and Son*, ed. Michael Schumacher (New York: Bloomsbury, 2002), 51.

5. Eugene Brooks to Allen Ginsberg, June 9, 1956, Allen Ginsberg Papers, Stanford.

6. Barry Miles, *Ginsberg: A Biography* (New York: Simon and Schuster, 1989), 206.

7. Bill Morgan, *I Celebrate Myself: The Somewhat Private Life of Allen Ginsberg* (New York: Penguin, 2007), 219.

8. Ginsberg, *Collected Poems*, 217–35. Subsequent poem quotations come from this same reference.

9. Naomi Ginsberg to Allen Ginsberg, Allen Ginsberg Papers, Special Collections, Columbia University Libraries, New York, NY.

10. Michael McClure, *Scratching the Beat Surface* (Berkeley, CA: North Point, 1982), 15.

11. Richard Eberhart, Allen Ginsberg, and Jerome Kaplan, *To Eberhart from Ginsberg: A Letter about "Howl," 1956: An Explanation by Allen Ginsberg of His Publication "Howl" and Richard Eberhart's New York Times Article "West Coast Rhythms," Together with Comments by Both Poets and Relief Etchings by Jerome Kaplan* (Lincoln, MA: Penmaen, 1976).

12. Allen Ginsberg, *Mid-Fifties: 1954–1958*, ed. Gordon Bell (New York: Harper Collins, 1995), 260.

13. Louis Ginsberg to Allen Ginsberg, June 20, 1956, Allen Ginsberg Papers, Stanford.

14. Naomi Ginsberg to Eugene Ginsberg, 1956, Allen Ginsberg Papers, Columbia.

15. Allen Ginsberg to Eugene Ginsberg, 1956, Allen Ginsberg Papers, Stanford.

16. Allen Ginsberg, *Howl: Original Draft Facsimile, Transcript & Variant Versions, Fully Annotated by Author, with Contemporaneous Correspondence, Account of First Public Reading, Legal Skirmishes, Precursor Texts & Bibliography*, ed. Barry Miles (New York: Harper Perennial, 1995), 156.

17. Naomi Ginsberg to Allen Ginsberg, postmarked June 11, 1956, Allen Ginsberg Papers, Columbia.

18. Louis Ginsberg to Allen Ginsberg, July 29, 1956, Allen Ginsberg Papers, Columbia.

19. Jack Kerouac and Allen Ginsberg, *The Letters*, ed. Bill Morgan and David Stanford (New York: Viking, 2010), 368.

2. An Unspeakable Act, 1986–1987

1. Jack Kerouac, "Belief & Technique for Modern Prose: List of Essentials," from a 1958 letter to Donald Allen, published in *Heaven & Other Poems* (Bolinas, CA: Grey Fox, 1983).

2. Judith L. Herman, *Trauma and Recovery* (New York: Basic Books, 1997), 1.

3. Stevan Weine to Allen Ginsberg, April 27, 1986.

4. Stevan Weine, "Allen Ginsberg's Kind of Psychiatrist," *American Journal of Psychiatry* 171 (2014): 23–24.

5. I am partial to a Foucault book I discussed with Allen: Stephen W. Sears, Pierre Rivière, and Blandine Kriegel, I. Pierre Rivière, *Having Slaughtered My Mother, My Sister, and My Brother . . . : A Case of Parricide in the Nineteenth Century*, ed. Michel Foucault (New York: Pantheon, 1975).

6. Allen Ginsberg, *Howl: Original Draft Facsimile, Transcript & Variant Versions, Fully Annotated by Author, with Contemporaneous Correspondence, Account of First*

Public Reading, Legal Skirmishes, Precursor Texts & Bibliography, ed. Barry Miles (New York: Harper Perennial, 1995), 111.

7. Michael Schumacher, *Dharma Lion: A Biography of Allen Ginsberg* (Minneapolis: University of Minnesota Press, 2016); Bill Morgan, *I Celebrate Myself: The Somewhat Private Life of Allen Ginsberg* (London: Penguin, 2007).

8. Barry Miles, *Ginsberg: A Biography* (New York: Simon and Schuster, 1989), 95.

9. David V. Forrest, "E. E. Cummings and the Thoughts That Lie Too Deep for Tears: Of Defenses in Poetry," *Psychiatry* 43, no. 1 (1980): 13–42.

10. Allen Ginsberg, interview by Stevan Weine, October 1986.

11. Ginsberg, interview by Weine.

12. Ginsberg, interview by Weine.

13. Jenell Freeman-Johnson, *American Lobotomy: A Rhetorical History* (Ann Arbor: University of Michigan Press, 2015), 29.

14. Andrea Tone and Mary Koziol, "(F)ailing Women in Psychiatry: Lessons from a Painful Past," *Canadian Medical Association Journal* 190, no. 20 (2018): E624–E625.

15. Larry O. Gostin and Paul Bridges, "Ethical Considerations of Psychosurgery: The Unhappy Legacy of the Pre-Frontal Lobotomy [with Commentary]," *Journal of Medical Ethics* 6, no. 3 (1980): 149–56.

16. Mical Raz, *The Lobotomy Letters: The Making of American Psychosurgery* (Rochester, NY: University of Rochester Press, 2013), 11–25.

17. Bonita Weddle, *Mental Health in New York State, 1945–1998: A Historical Overview* (New York State Archives, 1998), 8.

18. Richard Noll, *The Encyclopedia of Schizophrenia and Other Psychotic Disorders* (New York: Facts on File, 2009), 171. See also Ashley Robin and Duncan Macdonald, *Lessons of Leucotomy* (London: Kimpton, 1975).

19. Harry W. Allison and Sarah G. Allison, "Personality Changes Following Transorbital Lobotomy," *Journal of Abnormal Psychology* 49, no. 2 (1954): 219–23.

20. "Lobotomy Disappointment," *Newsweek*, December 12, 1949, 51.

21. Ginsberg, interview by Weine.

22. H. J. Worthing, H. Brill, and H. Wigderson, "350 Cases of Prefrontal Lobotomy," *Psychiatric Quarterly* 23 (1949): 624.

23. G. J. Diefenbach et al., "Portrayal of Lobotomy in the Popular Press: 1935–1960," *Journal of the History of Neuroscience* 8, no. 1 (1999): 60–69.

24. F. López-Muñoz et al., "History of the Discovery and Clinical Introduction of Chlorpromazine," *Annals of Clinical Psychiatry* 17, no. 3 (2005): 113–35.

25. Ginsberg, interview by Weine.

26. Ginsberg, interview by Weine.

27. Pilgrim State Hospital, medical records of Naomi Ginsberg, 1947 to 1949, 1951 to 1956. All subsequent quotations from this medical record are noted in the text.

28. Allen Ginsberg, *The Book of Martyrdom and Artifice: First Journals and Poems, 1937–1952* (Cambridge, MA: Da Capo, 2006), 15.

29. Pauline Boss, *Ambiguous Loss: Learning to Live with Unresolved Grief* (Cambridge, MA: Harvard University Press, 2009); Rosa De Stefano et al., "Complicated Grief: A Systematic Review of the Last 20 Years," *International Journal of Social Psychiatry* 67, no. 5 (2021): 492–99.

30. For readings on trauma, see Herman, *Trauma and Recovery*; Bessel A. Van der Kolk, *The Body Keeps the Score: Brain, Mind, and Body in the Healing of Trauma*

(London: Penguin, 2018); and Nadine Burke Harris, *The Deepest Well: Healing the Long-Term Effects of Childhood Trauma and Adversity* (New York: HMH, 2018).

31. Allen Ginsberg, *Collected Poems, 1947–1997* (New York: HarperCollins, 2006), 138.

32. Raz, *Lobotomy Letters*, 69–100.

33. Ginsberg, *Collected Poems*, 217–35. Subsequent poem quotations come from this same reference.

34. Allen Ginsberg, *Allen Ginsberg Reads Kaddish* (Atlantic Recording Corp., Atlantic Verbum Series 4001, 1966), 9.

35. O. Sjoqvist, "Diagnóstico dos hematomas intracerebrais consecutivos à lobotomia frontal [Diagnosis of intracerebral hematomas following frontal lobotomy]," *Jornal do Médico* (Oporto) 12, no. 302 (1948): 469.

36. Allen Ginsberg, interview by Tom Vitale, PBS, 1990, https://allenginsberg.org/2011/10/tom-vitale-interview-asv-18/.

37. Allen Ginsberg, interview by Terry Gross, *Fresh Air: Writers Speak*, 1994, https://www.youtube.com/watch?v=fMANtDcx3Bs&t=192s.

3. Refrain of the Hospitals and the New Vision, 1943–1948

1. Allen Ginsberg, *Collected Poems, 1947–1997* (New York: HarperCollins, 2006), 220.

2. Pilgrim State Hospital, medical records of Naomi Ginsberg, 1947 to 1949, 1951 to 1956. All subsequent quotations from this medical record are noted in the text.

3. R. Sommer, R. Dewar, and H. Osmond, "Is There a Schizophrenic Language?," *Archives of General Psychiatry* 3, no. 6 (1960): 665–73; D. V. Forrest, "Poiesis and the Language of Schizophrenia," *Psychiatry* 28, no. 1 (1965): 1–18.

4. Allen Ginsberg, *The Book of Martyrdom and Artifice: First Journals and Poems, 1937–1952* (Cambridge, MA: Da Capo, 2006), 187.

5. Pilgrim Psychiatric Center, History, Office of Mental Health, New York State, https://omh.ny.gov/omhweb/facilities/pgpc/#History.

6. Information on Naomi's life history was drawn from the Allen Ginsberg biographies by Barry Miles, Michael Schumacher, and Bill Morgan. Barry Miles, *Ginsberg: A Biography* (New York: Simon and Schuster, 1989); Michael Schumacher, *Dharma Lion: A Biography of Allen Ginsberg* (Minneapolis: University of Minnesota Press, 2016); Bill Morgan, *I Celebrate Myself: The Somewhat Private Life of Allen Ginsberg* (London: Penguin, 2007).

7. Bloomingdale Hospital, abstract of case history, 1931.

8. Leonard Shengold, *Soul Murder: The Effects of Childhood Abuse and Deprivation* (New York: Fawcett Columbine, 1991); Laura Davis and Ellen Bass, *The Courage to Heal: A Guide for Women Survivors of Child Sexual Abuse*, 3rd rev. and exp. ed. (London: HarperCollins, 1994).

9. J. M. Sheffield et al., "Childhood Sexual Abuse Increases Risk of Auditory Hallucinations in Psychotic Disorders," *Comprehensive Psychiatry* 54, no. 7 (2013): 1098–1104.

10. T. Friedman and N. N. Tin, "Childhood Sexual Abuse and the Development of Schizophrenia," *Postgraduate Medical Journal* 83, no. 982 (2007): 507–8.

11. David DiLillo, "Interpersonal Functioning among Women Reporting a History of Childhood Sexual Abuse: Empirical Findings and Methodological Issues," faculty publication, Department of Psychology, University of Nebraska–Lincoln, 2001, 146.

12. Kenneth Kendler, "The Dappled Nature of Causes of Psychiatric Illness: Replacing the Organic-Functional/Hardware-Software Dichotomy with Empirically Based Pluralism," *Molecular Psychiatry* 17, no. 4 (2012): 377–88.

13. Maurice Isserman, "When New York City Was the Capital of American Communism," *New York Times*, October 20, 2017.

14. Alexandra Minna Stern, Martin S. Cetron, and Howard Markel, "The 1918–1919 Influenza Pandemic in the United States: Lessons Learned and Challenges Exposed," *Public Health Reports* 125, no. 3 suppl. (2010): 6–8.

15. Margo Nash, "Memories of Woody Guthrie," *New York Times*, February 9, 2003, 11.

16. Allen Ginsberg interview, BBC Face to Face Interview, 1994 (ASV #21), https://allenginsberg.org/2011/11/bbc-face-to-face-interview-1994-asv21/.

17. Ginsberg, *The Book of Martyrdom and Artifice*, 5–6.

18. F. E. James, "Insulin Treatment in Psychiatry," *History of Psychiatry* 3, no. 10 (1992): 221–35; L. Meduna, "The Use of Metrazol in the Treatment of Patients with Mental Diseases," *Convulsive Therapy* 6, no. 4 (1990): 287–98.

19. E. Kraepelin, *Dementia Praecox and Paraphrenia* [1919].

20. American Psychiatric Association, *Diagnostic and Statistical Manual of Mental Disorders: DSM-5* (Arlington, VA: APA, 2013).

21. Katherine Karlsgoft, Daqiang Sun, and Tyrone D. Cannon, "Structural and Functional Brain Abnormalities in Schizophrenia," *Current Directions in Psychological Science* 19, no. 4 (2010): 226–31.

22. L. Halle, and J. F. Ross, "Neurological Complications of Insulin Shock Therapy with Electroencephalographic Studies: Case Studies," *AMA Archives of Neuropsychology* 65, no. 6 (1951): 703–12; C. F. Read, "Consequences of Metrazol Shock Therapy," *American Journal of Insanity* 97, no. 3 (1940): 667–76.

23. Ginsberg, *The Book of Martyrdom and Artifice*, 5.

24. New York State Psychiatric Institute, medical record of Allen Ginsberg, 1949–1950.

25. Arthur Rimbaud, *Complete Works* (London: HarperCollins, 2008), 116.

26. Ginsberg, *The Book of Martyrdom and Artifice*, 30.

27. Ginsberg, *The Book of Martyrdom and Artifice*, 31.

28. Ginsberg, *The Book of Martyrdom and Artifice*, 38.

29. Ginsberg, *The Book of Martyrdom and Artifice*, 50.

30. Ginsberg, *The Book of Martyrdom and Artifice*, 69.

31. Ginsberg, *The Book of Martyrdom and Artifice*, 79.

32. Ginsberg, *The Book of Martyrdom and Artifice*, 121.

33. Schumacher, *Dharma Lion*, 52.

34. Ginsberg, *The Book of Martyrdom and Artifice*, 123.

35. Ginsberg, *The Book of Martyrdom and Artifice*, 143.

36. Ginsberg, *The Book of Martyrdom and Artifice*, 134.

37. Ginsberg, *The Book of Martyrdom and Artifice*, 166.

38. Bill Morgan, *The Typewriter Is Holy: The Complete, Uncensored History of the Beat Generation* (London: Free Press, 2010), 41.

39. Allen Ginsberg, letter to William Burroughs, 1947, Allen Ginsberg Papers, Department of Special Collections, Stanford University Libraries, Stanford, CA.

40. Ginsberg, *The Book of Martyrdom and Artifice*, 172.

41. Ginsberg, *The Book of Martyrdom and Artifice*, 180.

42. Arthur Rimbaud, *The Drunken Boat* (London: Two Rivers, 1999), 93.

43. Naomi Ginsberg to Allen Ginsberg, July 1947, Allen Ginsberg Papers, Special Collections, Columbia University Libraries, New York, NY.

44. Naomi Ginsberg to Allen Ginsberg, 1947, Allen Ginsberg Papers, Columbia.

45. Naomi Ginsberg to Allen Ginsberg, 1947, Allen Ginsberg Papers, Columbia.

46. Naomi Ginsberg to Allen Ginsberg, 1947, Allen Ginsberg Papers, Columbia.

47. Harry Worthing to Allen Ginsberg, November 1947, Allen Ginsberg Papers, Columbia.

48. H. J. Worthing, H. Brill, and H. Wigderson, "350 Cases of Prefrontal Lobotomy," *Psychiatric Quarterly* 23 (1949): 617–56.

49. Robert Burton, *The Anatomy of Melancholy* (London: Dent, 1932).

50. Paul Hoch, "Theoretical Aspects of Frontal Lobotomy and Similar Brain Operations," *American Journal of Psychiatry* 106, no. 6 (1949): 448–53.

51. Jenell Freeman-Johnson, *American Lobotomy: A Rhetorical History* (Ann Arbor: University of Michigan Press, 2015).

52. "Lobotomy: The Brain Op Described as 'Easier Than Curing a Toothache,'" BBC, January 30, 2021, https://www.bbc.com/news/stories-55854145.

53. Naomi Ginsberg to Allen Ginsberg, February or March, 1948, Allen Ginsberg Papers, Columbia.

54. Naomi Ginsberg to Allen Ginsberg, April 21, 1948, Allen Ginsberg Papers, Columbia.

55. Ginsberg, *The Book of Martyrdom and Artifice*, 260.

56. Ginsberg, *The Book of Martyrdom and Artifice*, 205, 310, 361, 365.

4. The Actuality of Prophecy, 1948–1949

1. Lewis Hyde, *The Gift: Creativity and the Artist in the Modern World* (London: Knopf, 2009), 194.

2. Barry Gifford, ed., *As Ever: The Collected Letters of Allen Ginsberg and Neal Cassady* (Berkeley, CA: Creative Arts Books, 1977), 44.

3. Allen Ginsberg, *The Book of Martyrdom and Artifice: First Journals and Poems, 1937–1952* (Cambridge, MA: Da Capo, 2006), 255.

4. Jack Kerouac and Allen Ginsberg, *The Letters*, ed. Bill Morgan and David Stanford (New York: Viking, 2010), 39. "Ardenesque" refers to the Forest of Arden.

5. Gifford, *As Ever*, 52.

6. Ginsberg, *The Book of Martyrdom and Artifice*, 256.

7. John of the Cross and Kieran Kavanaugh, *Collected Works of St. John of the Cross* (Washington, DC: Institute of Carmelite Studies, 1973).

8. William James, *The Varieties of Religious Experience: A Study in Human Nature* (London: Collier, 1961), 120.

9. Marc Eliot Stein, "Kaddish," *Literary Kicks*, https://www.litkicks.com/Poems/Kaddish.html.

10. Allen Ginsberg, unpublished draft, 1987.

11. Ginsberg, *The Book of Martyrdom and Artifice*, 297.

12. Allen Ginsberg, *Collected Poems, 1947–1997* (New York: HarperCollins, 2006), 14.

13. Lionel Trilling, *Life in Culture: Selected Letters of Lionel Trilling* (New York: Farrar, Straus and Giroux, 2018), 170.

14. Mark van Doren to Allen Ginsberg, December 24, 1948, Allen Ginsberg Papers, Department of Special Collections, Stanford University Libraries, Stanford, CA.

15. Oliver C. G. Harris, *The Letters of William S. Burroughs: 1945–1959* (London: Viking, 1993), 45.

16. Naomi Ginsberg to Allen Ginsberg, March 1949, Allen Ginsberg Papers, Special Collections, Columbia University Libraries, New York, NY.

17. Naomi Ginsberg to Allen Ginsberg, March 1949, Allen Ginsberg Papers, Columbia.

18. Ginsberg, *Collected Poems*, 26.

19. Ginsberg, *Collected Poems*, 50–51.

20. John Clellon Holmes, *Go* (New York: Ace, c. 1952).

21. James, *The Varieties of Religious Experience*, 23.

22. James, *The Varieties of Religious Experience*, 23.

23. Ginsberg, *The Book of Martyrdom and Artifice*, 49.

24. John of the Cross and Kieran Kavanaugh, *Collected Works of St. John of the Cross*.

25. Gifford, *As Ever*, 58.

26. John Clellon Holmes to Allen Ginsberg, June 14, 1949, Allen Ginsberg Papers, Columbia.

27. Allen Ginsberg, *The Letters of Allen Ginsberg* (Ukraine: Hachette, 2008), 42–51.

28. Kerouac and Ginsberg, *Letters*, 106.

29. Ginsberg, *The Book of Martyrdom and Artifice*, 264–78. Subsequent journal quotations are from the same source.

30. Ginsberg, *The Book of Martyrdom and Artifice*, 279–80.

31. R. W. B. Lewis, *The American Adam: Innocence, Tragedy, and Tradition in the Nineteenth Century* (Chicago: University of Chicago Press, 1955), 89.

32. Ginsberg, *The Book of Martyrdom and Artifice*, 276–313. Subsequent journal quotations are from the same source. Several quotations are drawn from passages from the same journal that were unpublished and are included in the Allen Ginsberg Papers, Columbia.

33. Ginsberg, *Collected Poems*, 13.

34. Jacques Barzun to Allen Ginsberg, June 1, 1949, Allen Ginsberg Papers, Columbia. See also https://allenginsberg.org/2011/02/faulty-memory-syndrome-a-note-on-an-interview-with-jacques-barzun/.

35. Ginsberg, *The Book of Martyrdom and Artifice*, 314–18. Subsequent journal quotes are from the same source.

5. The Psychiatric Institute, 1949–1950

1. Allen Ginsberg, interview by Stevan Weine, October 1986.

2. Jane Kramer, *Allen Ginsberg in America* (New York: Random House, 1969), 41.

3. Ginsberg, interview by Weine.

4. "Report of the Director of the Psychiatric Institute," Annual Report of the Psychiatric Institute, 1950, 6–7.

5. Bruce Shlain and Martin A. Lee, *Acid Dreams: The Complete Social History of LSD: The CIA, the Sixties, and Beyond* (New York: Grove, 1992). We will discuss this further in Chapter 8.

6. Paul Hoch and Philip Polatin, "Pseudoneurotic Forms of Schizophrenia." *Psychiatry Quarterly* 23, no. 2 (1949): 248–76.

7. Paul Hoch et al. "The Psychosurgical Treatment of Pseudoneurotic Schizophrenia." *American Journal of Psychiatry* 111, no. 9 (1955): 653–58.

8. Allen Ginsberg, *The Book of Martyrdom and Artifice: First Journals and Poems, 1937–1952* (Cambridge, MA: Da Capo, 2006), 316.

9. Jack Kerouac and Allen Ginsberg, *The Letters*, ed. Bill Morgan and David Stanford (New York: Viking, 2010), 80.

10. Ginsberg, *The Book of Martyrdom and Artifice*, 488.

11. Allen Ginsberg, *Collected Poems, 1947–1997* (New York: HarperCollins, 2006), 50–51.

12. New York State Psychiatric Institute.

13. For a highly personal and thoughtful meditation on grandiosity see: W. J. T. Mitchell, *Mental Traveler: A Father, a Son, and a Journey through Schizophrenia* (Chicago: University of Chicago Press, 2020).

14. Ginsberg, *The Book of Martyrdom and Artifice*, 321.

15. Carl Solomon, *Mishaps, Perhaps* (San Francisco: City Lights, 1966).

16. Kerouac and Ginsberg, *Letters*, 93.

17. Ginsberg, journal, July 4, 1949, Allen Ginsberg Papers, Department of Special Collections, Stanford University Libraries, Stanford, CA.

18. Jack Drescher, "Out of DSM: Depathologizing Homosexuality," *Behavioral Science* 5, no. 4 (2015): 565–75.

19. Ginsberg, *The Book of Martyrdom and Artifice*, 322.

20. Ginsberg, *The Book of Martyrdom and Artifice*, 322–24.

21. N. Kellogg, "Sexual Behaviors in Children: Evaluation and Management," *American Family Physician* 82, no. 10 (2010): 1233–38.

22. K. Lalor and R. McElvaney, "Child Sexual Abuse, Links to Later Sexual Exploitation/High-Risk Sexual Behavior, and Prevention/Treatment Programs," *Trauma, Violence, & Abuse* 11, no. 4 (October 2010): 159–77.

23. Ginsberg, *The Book of Martyrdom and Artifice*, 324–25.

24. Ginsberg, *The Book of Martyrdom and Artifice*, 325.

25. Carl Solomon, *Emergency Messages: An Autobiographical Miscellany* (New York: Paragon House, 1989), 178–81.

26. Solomon, *Emergency Messages*, 112.

27. Kramer, *Allen Ginsberg in America*, 54–55.

28. Ginsberg, *The Book of Martyrdom and Artifice*, 325–26.

29. Ginsberg, *The Book of Martyrdom and Artifice*, 326.

30. Otto Fenichel, *Outline of Psychoanalysis* (New York: Taylor & Francis, 1934).

31. Kramer, *Allen Ginsberg in America*, 41.

32. Ginsberg, interview by Weine.

33. Kay Jamison, *An Unquiet Mind* (New York: Vintage, 1996).

34. Michael Schumacher, *Dharma Lion: A Biography of Allen Ginsberg* (Minneapolis: University of Minnesota Press, 2016), 114.

35. P. H. Hoch et al., "The Course and Outcome of Pseudoneurotic Schizophrenia," *American Journal of Psychiatry* 119 (1962): 106–15.

36. Other relevant concepts include moral injury, described by Jonathan Shay, and developmental trauma. J. Shay, "Moral Injury," *Psychoanalytic Psychology* 31, no. 2 (2014): 182–91; B. A. van der Kolk, "The Developmental Impact of Childhood Trauma," in *Understanding Trauma: Integrating Biological, Clinical, and Cultural Perspectives*, ed. L. J. Kirmayer et al. (Cambridge: Cambridge University Press, 2007), 224–41.

37. Louis Sass, *The Paradoxes of Delusion: Wittgenstein, Schreber, and the Schizophrenic Mind* (Ithaca, NY: Cornell University Press, 1995).

38. W. R. McFarlane et al., "Family Psychoeducation and Schizophrenia: A Review of the Literature," *Journal of Marital and Family Therapy* 29, no. 2 (2003): 223–45.

39. A. Källquist and M. Salzmann-Erikson, "Experiences of Having a Parent with Serious Mental Illness: An Interpretive Meta-Synthesis of Qualitative Literature," *Journal of Child and Family Studies* 28 (2019): 2056–68; H. S. Herbert et al., "Growing Up with a Parent Having Schizophrenia: Experiences and Resilience in the Offsprings," *Indian Journal of Psychological Medicine* 35, no. 2 (2013): 148–53; S. Hussain, "The Impacts of Parental Schizophrenia on the Psychosocial Well-Being of Offspring: A Systematic Review," in *Quality of Life: Biopsychosocial Perspectives*, ed. F. Irtelli et al. (London: IntechOpen, 2020).

40. Bob Rosenthal and Peter Hale, personal communication.

41. Carl Solomon to Allen Ginsberg, n.d., Allen Ginsberg Papers, Stanford.

42. Ginsberg, *Collected Poems*, 48.

43. Ginsberg, *Collected Poems*, 50–51.

44. Sean O'Hagan, "Kingsley Hall: R. D. Laing's Experiment in Antipsychiatry," *Guardian*, September 1, 2012.

45. Institute of Contemporary Arts, Allen Ginsberg, and R. D. Laing, *Allen Ginsberg with R. D. Laing* (London: ICA Video; Northbrook, IL: Roland Collection, 1986).

46. Ginsberg, interview by Weine.

47. Allen Ginsberg, interview with Barry Farrell, transcription, Allen Ginsberg Papers, Stanford.

6. Mental Muse-eries, 1950–1955

1. Jason Shinder, *The Poem That Changed America: "Howl" Fifty Years Later* (New York: Farrar, Straus and Giroux, 2006), xiii.

2. William Carlos Williams, "Author's Introduction (The Wedge)," from *Selected Essays of William Carlos Williams* (New York: New Directions, 1954).

3. Allen Ginsberg, *Recollections of Encounters with W. C. Williams*, typed transcription of tape #11, Allen Ginsberg Papers, Department of Special Collections, Stanford University Libraries, Stanford, CA.

4. Ginsberg, *Recollections of Encounters with W. C. Williams*.

5. For more on Ginsberg and Cezanne: "Cosmic Vibrations in Cezanne," https://allenginsberg.org/2012/10/cosmic-vibrations-in-cezanne/; Paul Portuges, "Allen Ginsberg's Paul Cezanne and the Pater Omnipotens Aeterna Deus," *Contemporary Literature* 21, no. 3 (Summer 1980): 435–49.

6. Ginsberg to Williams, March 4, 1950, Allen Ginsberg Papers, Stanford.

7. Ginsberg, *Recollections of Encounters with W. C. Williams*.

8. Allen Ginsberg, *Collected Poems, 1947–1997* (New York: HarperCollins, 2006), 41.

9. Williams to Ginsberg, February 27, 1952, Allen Ginsberg Papers, Stanford.

10. Ginsberg, *Recollections of Encounters with W. C. Williams*.

11. Ginsberg to Kerouac and Cassady, February 1952, Allen Ginsberg Papers, Stanford.

12. Ginsberg, journal, February 1952, Allen Ginsberg Papers, Stanford.

13. Ginsberg, *Recollections of Encounters with W. C. Williams*.

14. W. C. Williams to Allen Ginsberg, May 4, 1952, Allen Ginsberg Papers, Stanford.

15. Pilgrim State Hospital.

16. For a recent discussion, see Glenn Currier, "The Controversy over 'Chemical Restraint' in Acute Care Psychiatry," *Journal of Psychiatric Practice* 9, no. 1 (2003): 59–70.

17. Ginsberg, journal, 1949, Allen Ginsberg Papers, Stanford. These terms also connect the shrouded stranger with Kerouac's version of the same, in his novel *Dr. Sax: Faust, Part Three*, first written in 1952.

18. Ginsberg, journal, 1949, Allen Ginsberg Papers, Stanford.

19. Allen Ginsberg, *The Book of Martyrdom and Artifice: First Journals and Poems, 1937–1952* (Cambridge, MA: Da Capo, 2006), 503–4.

20. Ginsberg, *Martyrdom and Artifice*, 504.

21. Ginsberg, *Martyrdom and Artifice*, 352–53.

22. Allen Ginsberg, *Mid-Fifties: 1954–1958*, ed. Gordon Bell (New York: Harper Collins, 1995), 19–21.

23. Ginsberg, *Mid-Fifties*, 23.

24. Ginsberg, *Mid-Fifties*, 23.

25. Ginsberg, *Mid-Fifties*, 25.

26. Pilgrim State Hospital.

27. Naomi Ginsberg to Allen Ginsberg, January 5, 1953, Allen Ginsberg Papers, Columbia.

28. Ginsberg, journal, 1953, Allen Ginsberg Papers, Stanford. Partially quoted in Barry Miles, *Ginsberg: A Biography* (New York: Simon and Schuster, 1989), 150.

29. Ginsberg, *Mid-Fifties*, 31.

30. Ginsberg, *Mid-Fifties*, 33.

31. Ginsberg, *Mid-Fifties*, 72.

32. Ginsberg, *Mid-Fifties*, 73.

33. Ginsberg, *Collected Poems*, 105–18.

34. Naomi Ginsberg to Allen Ginsberg, June 21, 1956, Allen Ginsberg Papers, Columbia.

35. Allen Ginsberg, interviewed by Jane Kramer, "Paterfamilias—I, Allen Ginsberg's Work to Preserve the Universe," *New Yorker*, August 17, 1968.

36. James Breslin, "The Origins of 'Howl' and 'Kaddish,'" in *On the Poetry of Allen Ginsberg*, ed. Lewis Hyde (Ann Arbor: University of Michigan Press, 1984), 405.

37. Other accounts say she jumped off a roof to her death. James Campbell, "Allen Ginsberg: Howl at the Movies," *Guardian*, February 11, 2011.

38. Allen Ginsberg, unpublished poem, cited in Miles, *Ginsberg*, 201.

39. Allen Ginsberg, "Reintroduction" to *Howl: Original Draft Facsimile, Transcript & Variant Versions, Fully Annotated by Author, with Contemporary Correspondence, Account of First Public Reading, Legal Skirmishes, Precursor Texts & Bibliography*, ed. Barry Miles (New York: Harper Perennial, 1995), 111.

40. Ginsberg, *Collected Poems*, 132.

41. Ginsberg, *Mid-Fifties*, 159.

42. Ginsberg, *Howl: Original*, 13.

43. Ginsberg, *Howl: Original*, 149.

44. Jane Kramer, *Allen Ginsberg in America* (New York: Random House, 1969), 173.

45. Jack Kerouac, *On the Road* (London: Penguin, 2003), 5.

46. Jenell Freeman-Johnson, *American Lobotomy: A Rhetorical History* (Ann Arbor: University of Michigan Press, 2015), 29.

47. Ginsberg, *Howl: Original*, 139.

48. Allen Ginsberg, letter to John Hollander, September 7, 1958, in *Howl: Original*, 163.

49. Ginsberg, *Collected Poems*, 142.

50. Richard Eberhart, "West Coast Rhythms," *New York Times Book Review*, September 2, 1956.

51. Ginsberg, *Howl: Original*, xii.

52. Jonah Raskin, *American Scream: Allen Ginsberg's "Howl" and the Making of the Beat Generation* (Berkeley: University of California Press, 2004), 81.

53. Naomi Ginsberg to Allen Ginsberg, 1955, Allen Ginsberg Papers, Columbia.

54. Naomi Ginsberg to Allen Ginsberg, 1955, Allen Ginsberg Papers, Columbia.

55. Naomi Ginsberg to Louis Ginsberg, 1955, Allen Ginsberg Papers, Columbia.

56. Naomi Ginsberg to Allen Ginsberg, 1956, Allen Ginsberg Papers, Columbia.

57. Ginsberg, *Mid-Fifties*, 96.

58. Peter Orlovsky to Allen Ginsberg, June 9, 1956, Allen Ginsberg Papers, Columbia.

7. Gold Blast of Light, 1956–1959

1. Allen Ginsberg, "How Kaddish Happened," in *Deliberate Prose, 1952–1995* (New York: Harper Perennial, 2001), 233.

2. Harvey Shapiro, "Exalted Lament, Rev. of Kaddish and Other Poems 1958–1960, by Allen Ginsberg," in *On the Poetry of Allen Ginsberg*, ed. Lewis Hyde (Ann Arbor: University of Michigan Press, 1984), 86–91.

3. Tony Triglio, "'Strange Prophecies Anew': Rethinking the Politics of Matter and Spirit in Ginsberg's Kaddish," *American Literature* 71, no. 4 (1999): 773–95; Loni Reynolds, "'The Mad Ones' and the 'Geeks': Cognitive and Physical Disability in the Writing of Jack Kerouac and Allen Ginsberg," *Journal of Literary & Cultural Disability Studies* 9, no. 2 (2015): 153ff.; Helen Vendler, *Soul Says: On Recent Poetry* (Cambridge. MA: Belknap, 1995).

4. Triglio, "'Strange Prophecies Anew,'" 151.

5. A. Alvarez, "Review of Kaddish and Other Poems," *London Observer*, May 14, 1961, in *On the Poetry of Allen Ginsberg*, ed. Lewis Hyde (Ann Arbor: University of Michigan Press, 1984), 93.

6. Marjorie Perloff, "A Lion in Our Living Room: Reading Allen Ginsberg in the Eighties," in *Poetic License: Essays on Modernist and Postmodernist Lyric* (Evanston, IL: Northwestern, 1990), 199–230.

7. Ginsberg, journal, June 20, 1956, Allen Ginsberg Papers, Department of Special Collections, Stanford University Libraries, Stanford, CA.

8. Allen Ginsberg, *Family Business: Selected Letters between a Father and Son*, ed. Michael Schumacher (New York: Bloomsbury, 2002), 50.

9. Allen Ginsberg, *Mid-Fifties: 1954–1958*, ed. Gordon Bell (New York: Harper Collins, 1995), 268–69.

10. Ginsberg, *Mid-Fifties*, 269.

11. Ginsberg, *Mid-Fifties*, 272.

12. Ginsberg, *Mid-Fifties*, 273.

13. Ginsberg, *Mid-Fifties*, 275.

14. Ginsberg, journal, Allen Ginsberg Papers, Stanford.

15. Ginsberg, journal, Allen Ginsberg Papers, Stanford.

16. Ginsberg, journal, Allen Ginsberg Papers, Stanford.

17. Ginsberg, journal, Allen Ginsberg Papers, Stanford.

18. Ginsberg, journal, Allen Ginsberg Papers, Stanford.

19. Ginsberg, *Mid-Fifties*, 265.

20. Ginsberg, *Mid-Fifties*, 243.

21. Ginsberg, journal, Allen Ginsberg Papers, Stanford.

22. Ginsberg, *Mid-Fifties*, 287.

23. Ginsberg, *Mid-Fifties*, 293.

24. Ginsberg, journal, Allen Ginsberg Papers, Stanford.

25. Ginsberg, journal, Allen Ginsberg Papers, Stanford.

26. Ginsberg, journal, Allen Ginsberg Papers, Stanford.

27. Ginsberg to Kerouac, August 12, 1956, Allen Ginsberg Papers, Stanford. See also Barry Miles, *Ginsberg: A Biography* (New York: Simon and Schuster, 1989), 210.

28. Ginsberg, journal, Allen Ginsberg Papers, Stanford.

29. Ginsberg, journal, Allen Ginsberg Papers, Stanford.

30. Ginsberg, *Mid-Fifties*, 277.

31. Ginsberg, journal, Allen Ginsberg Papers, Stanford.

32. Ginsberg, journal, Allen Ginsberg Papers, Stanford.

33. Ginsberg, journal, Allen Ginsberg Papers, Stanford.

34. Ginsberg, *Family Business*, 55.

35. Ginsberg, *Mid-Fifties*, 287.

36. Richard Eberhart, "West Coast Rhythms," *New York Times Book Review*, September 2, 1956.

37. Ginsberg, journal, Allen Ginsberg Papers, Stanford.

38. Barry Miles, *William S. Burroughs: A Life* (London: Orion, 2014), 351.

39. Allen Ginsberg to Eugene Ginsberg, June 1957, Allen Ginsberg Papers, Stanford.

40. Georges Didi-Huberman, *Fra Angelico: Dissemblance and Figuration* (Chicago: University of Chicago Press, 1995).

41. Leon Battista Alberti and Rocco Sinisgalli, *On Painting: A New Translation and Critical Edition* (Cambridge: Cambridge University Press, 2011).

42. Patti Smith, personal communication.

43. Triglio, "'Strange Prophecies Anew,'" 149.

44. Jack Kerouac and Allen Ginsberg, *The Letters*, ed. Bill Morgan and David Stanford (New York: Viking, 2010), 243.

45. Ginsberg, interview by Weine.

46. Ginsberg, "History of Visions," Allen Ginsberg Papers, Stanford.

47. Ginsberg, *Mid-Fifties*, 390.

48. André Breton, Jean Pierre Cauvin, and Mary Ann Caws, *Poems of André Breton: A Bilingual Anthology* (Boston: Black Widow, 2006).

49. Ginsberg, *Mid-Fifties*, 393.

50. Ginsberg, *Mid-Fifties*, 395.

51. Ginsberg, *Mid-Fifties*, 395.

52. Allen Ginsberg, journal, Allen Ginsberg Papers, Stanford.

53. Ginsberg, *Mid-Fifties*, 397.

54. Ginsberg, *Mid-Fifties*, 397.

55. Ginsberg, journal, Allen Ginsberg Papers, Stanford.

56. Ginsberg, journal, Allen Ginsberg Papers, Stanford.

57. Ginsberg, journal, Allen Ginsberg Papers, Stanford.

58. Allen Ginsberg, *Collected Poems, 1947–1997* (New York: HarperCollins, 2006), 188.

59. Ginsberg, *Collected Poems*, 182–83.

60. Ginsberg, *Collected Poems*, 192–93.

61. Bill Morgan, *Howl on Trial: The Battle for Free Expression* (La Vergne: City Lights, 2021).

62. Ginsberg, *Family Business*, 99.

63. Allen to Louis Ginsberg, 1958, Allen Ginsberg Papers, Stanford.

64. Bill Morgan, *I Celebrate Myself: The Somewhat Private Life of Allen Ginsberg* (London: Penguin, 2007), 278.

65. Allen Ginsberg interview by Paola Igliori, https://allenginsberg.org/2010/03/paola -igliori-interviews-allen-ginsberg-on-harry-smith/; Bill Breeze, *American Magus: Harry Smith, a Modern Alchemist* (New York: Inanout, 1996).

66. John Sutter, "When the Beats Came Back," *Reed Magazine*, December 1, 2008. See also Allen Ginsberg, *At Reed College: The First Recorded Reading of Howl & Other Poems* (Omnivore Records, April 2, 2021).

67. Stanley Crouch, *Considering Genius: Writings on Jazz* (New York: Basic Civitas Books, 2006), 87.

68. "Kaddish: A Mourner's Prayer," Death and Mourning in Judaism, Mazor Guides, http://www.mazornet.com/deathandmourning/reformkaddish.html.

69. Morgan, *I Celebrate Myself*, 116.

70. Ginsberg, *Collected Poems*, 217.

71. Ginsberg, "How Kaddish Happened," 235.

72. Leonard Shengold, *Soul Murder: The Effects of Childhood Abuse and Deprivation* (New York: Fawcett Columbine, 1991).

73. Allen Ginsberg, "Kaddish," New York University.

74. David Finkelhor, "The International Epidemiology of Child Sexual Abuse," *Child Abuse & Neglect* 18, no. 5 (1994): 409–17.

75. Caroline Mazel-Carlton, "Doctors Gave Her Antipsychotics. She Decided to Live with Her Voices," *New York Times*, May 17, 2022.

76. Ginsberg, *Collected Poems*, 246.

77. The first time was in Chicago a few weeks earlier, at a fundraiser for the magazine *Big Table* organized by Irving Rosenthal and covered by *Time*, https://media.sas.upenn .edu/pennsound/authors/Ginsberg/Chicago-1959/Ginsberg-Allen_10_Kaddish-part-1_Big -Table-Chicago-Reading_1959.mp3.

78. Norman Podhoretz, "The Know Nothing Bohemians," *Partisan Review*, Spring 1958, 305–19.

8. A Light Raying through Society, 1959–1965

1. Martin A. Lee and Bruce Shlain, *Acid Dreams: The CIA, LSD, and the Sixties Rebellion* (New York: Grove, 1985), 59.

2. Allen Ginsberg, *Family Business: Selected Letters between a Father and Son*, ed. Michael Schumacher (New York: Bloomsbury, 2002), 121.

3. P. H. Hoch, J. P. Cattell, and H. H. Pennes, "Effects of Mescaline and Lysergic Acid (d-LSD-25)," *American Journal of Psychiatry* 108, no. 8 (1952): 579–84.

4. Lee and Shlain, *Acid Dreams*, 69–70. See also Mike Jay, *Mescaline: A Global History of the First Psychedelic* (New Haven, CT: Yale University Press, 2019).

5. William Burroughs and Allen Ginsberg, *The Yage Letters* (San Francisco: City Lights, 2001).

6. Burroughs and Ginsberg, *The Yage Letters*, 62.

7. Allen Ginsberg, *Collected Poems, 1947–1997* (New York: HarperCollins, 2006), 239.

8. Weston L. Barre, letter to Edward J. Hornick, February 21, 1961.

9. Allen Ginsberg and Gary Snyder, *The Selected Letters of Allen Ginsberg and Gary Snyder, 1956–1991* (Berkeley: Catapult, 2008), 33.

10. Jane Kramer, *Allen Ginsberg in America* (New York: Random House, 1969), 186.

11. Humphry Osmond, "Research on Schizophrenia," in *Neuropharmacology. Transactions of the 2nd Conference, May 25–27, 1955, Princeton, NJ*, ed. H. A. Abramson (New York: Josiah Macy Jr. Foundation, 1956), 183.

12. *Psychedelic Prophets: The Letters of Aldous Huxley and Humphry Osmond* (London: McGill-Queen's University Press, 2018), 266.

13. William Blake and Geoffrey Keynes, *The Marriage of Heaven and Hell* (Oxford: Oxford University Press, 1975).

14. Osmond, "Research on Schizophrenia," 183.

15. Timothy Leary, "The Effects of Consciousness-Expanding Drugs on Prisoner Rehabilitation," *Psychedelic Review* 10 (1969): 29–45. See also R. Doblin, "Dr. Leary's Concord Prison Experiment: A 34-Year Follow-up Study," *Journal of Psychoactive Drugs* 30 (1988): 419–26.

16. Walter Norman Pahnke, "Drugs and Mysticism: An Analysis of the Relationship between Psychedelic Drugs and the Mystical Consciousness," thesis presented to the Committee on Higher Degrees in History and Philosophy of Religion, Harvard University, June 1963. See also R. Doblin, "Pahnke's 'Good Friday Experiment': A Long-Term Follow-up and Methodological Critique," *Journal of Transpersonal Psychology* 23, no. 1 (1991): 1–25.

17. Barry Miles, *Ginsberg: A Biography* (New York: Simon and Schuster, 1989), 276–77.

18. Peter Conners, *White Hand Society: The Psychedelic Partnership of Timothy Leary and Allen Ginsberg* (San Francisco: City Lights, 2010), 64.

19. Lee and Shlain, *Acid Dreams*, 79.

20. Conners, *White Hand Society*, 103.

21. Timothy Leary, *High Priest* (United States: Ronin, 1995), 133.

22. Timothy Leary to Arthur Koestler, 1961, Leary Project, http://www.leary.ru/english/letters/index.php, January 4, 1961.

23. Allen Ginsberg, "Remarks on Leary's Politics of Ecstasy," *Village Voice* 14, no. 9 (December 12, 1968).

24. "The Narcotic Rehabilitation Act of 1966: Hearings Before a Special Subcommittee . . . 89–2, Pursuant to S. Res. 199," 89th Cong., 492.

25. Ginsberg, *Family Business*, 122.

26. Kramer, *Allen Ginsberg in America*, xv.

27. Allen Ginsberg, "Public Solitude," address delivered at Arlington Street Church, Boston, November 12, 1966, repr. Allen Ginsberg, *Deliberate Prose, 1952–1995* (New York: Harper Perennial, 2001).

28. Timothy Leary, "How to Change Behavior," in *Clinical Psychology: Proceedings of the XIV International Congress of Applied Psychology, 1961*, vol. 4, ed. G. S. Nielsen (Copenhagen: Munksgaard, 1962).

29. Allen Ginsberg, "The Art of Poetry No. 8, Interview by Tom Clark," *Paris Review* 37 (Spring 1966).

30. Deborah Baker, *A Blue Hand: The Beats in India* (New York: Penguin, 2008), 126.

31. Allen Ginsberg, *Indian Journals: March 1962–May 1963* (New York: Grove, 1996), 11.

32. Ginsberg, *Indian Journals*, 126.

33. Ginsberg, *Indian Journals*, 128.

34. Ginsberg, *Indian Journals*, 128.

35. Ginsberg, *Indian Journals*, 128.

36. Ginsberg, unpublished draft of *Indian Journals*, Allen Ginsberg Papers, Department of Special Collections, Stanford University Libraries, Stanford, CA.

37. Ginsberg, *Indian Journals*, 133.

38. Ginsberg, *Indian Journals*, 136.

39. Ginsberg, *Indian Journals*, 147.

40. Ginsberg, *Indian Journals*, 180.

41. Ginsberg, *Indian Journals*, 189.

42. Ginsberg, *Indian Journals*, 199.

43. Ginsberg, *Indian Journals*, 3.

44. Leary, "How to Change Behavior."

45. Peter Hale, personal communication.

46. Allen Ginsberg with Alison Colbert, "A Talk with Allen Ginsberg," *Partisan Review* 3 (1971): 292. See also Baker, *Blue Hand*, 208.

47. Ginsberg, *Collected Poems*, 335–36.

48. Ginsberg, "The Art of Poetry No. 8, Interview by Tom Clark."

49. Ginsberg, "The Art of Poetry No. 8, Interview by Tom Clark."

50. Tom Hawthorn, "Remembering Ginsberg and the Summer of Poetry," *Globe and Mail*, January 4, 2011.

51. Allen Ginsberg, "Back to the Wall," *Times Literary Supplement*, August 6, 1964.

52. Ginsberg, *Collected Poems*, 122.

53. Ginsberg, Letter to Corso, qtd. in Michael Schumacher, *Dharma Lion: A Biography of Allen Ginsberg* (Minneapolis: University of Minnesota Press, 2016), 444.

54. Marianne Faithfull and David Dalton, *Faithfull: An Autobiography* (New York: Cooper Square, 2000), 55.

55. Allen Ginsberg, "When the Mode of the Music Changes, the Walls of the City Shake," in *Poetics of the New American Poetry*, ed. D. Allen and W. Tallman (New York: Grove, 1973), 41.

56. Michael Blumenthal, "Allen Ginsberg, Millionaire?," *New York Times*, October 29, 1994.

57. Allen Ginsberg, "What Way I Write," *Writer's Digest*, October 1960.

58. Allen Ginsberg, panel presentation at the Group for Advancement of Psychiatry, Asbury Park, New Jersey, 1960.

59. Paul Portuges, *The Visionary Poetics of Allen Ginsberg* (Santa Barbara, CA: Ross-Erickson, 1978), 7.

60. Allen Ginsberg, "When the Mode of the Music Changes," 41.

61. Allen Ginsberg, "Poet's Voice," July 11, 1965, repr. Allen Ginsberg, *Deliberate Prose, 1952–1995* (New York: Harper Perennial, 2001), 257–58.

62. Ginsberg, *Collected Poems*, 196.

63. Ginsberg, *Collected Poems*, 211–13.

64. John Clellon Holmes, *Go* (New York: Penguin, 2006), 85–86.

65. Allen Ginsberg, "Demonstration or Spectacle as Example, as Communication or How to Make a March/Spectacle," in *The Portable Sixties Reader* (New York: Penguin, 2003).

66. Ginsberg, "The Art of Poetry No. 8, Interview by Tom Clark."

67. Patti Smith, personal communication.

68. Portuges, *The Visionary Poetics of Allen Ginsberg*.

69. Ginsberg, *Family Business*, 239.

70. Gene Anthony, *The Summer of Love: Haight-Ashbury at Its Highest* (San Francisco: Last Gasp of San Francisco, 1980), 123.

9. White and Black Shrouds, 1987

1. Bob Rosenthal, *Straight around Allen: On the Business of Being Allen Ginsberg* (St. Andrews: Beatdom, 2018), 10.

2. Robert Frank, *Me and My Brother* (Göttingen: Steidl, 2007).

3. Allen Ginsberg, *Collected Poems, 1947–1997* (New York: HarperCollins, 2006), 970.

4. See the Committee on Poetry's website: https://committeeonpoetry.org.

5. Committee on Poetry, *New York Review of Books*, April 25, 1968. See https://www.nybooks.com/articles/1968/04/25/leroi-jones/.

6. Gordon Ball, *East Hill Farm: Seasons with Allen Ginsberg* (Berkeley, CA: Counterpoint, 2011), 14.

7. David J. Rothman, *The Discovery of the Asylum: Social Order and Disorder in the New Republic* (Boston: Little, Brown, 1971).

8. Carl Solomon, *More Mishaps* (San Francisco: Beach Books, Texts & Documents, 1968), 51–52; Allen Ginsberg, lecture at Brooklyn College.

9. Allen Ginsberg, *Howl: Original Draft Facsimile, Transcript & Variant Versions, Fully Annotated by Author, with Contemporaneous Correspondence, Account of First Public Reading, Legal Skirmishes, Precursor Texts & Bibliography*, ed. Barry Miles (New York: Harper Perennial, 1995), 111.

10. Carl Solomon to Allen Ginsberg, December 29, 1957, Allen Ginsberg Papers, Department of Special Collections, Stanford University Libraries, Stanford, CA.

11. Carl Solomon to Allen Ginsberg, September 22, 1959, Allen Ginsberg Papers, Stanford.

12. Carl Solomon, *Mishaps, Perhaps* (San Francisco: City Lights, 1966), 9.

13. Carl Solomon, *Emergency Messages: An Autobiographical Miscellany* (New York: Paragon House, 1989), 96.

14. Solomon, *Mishaps*, 45.

15. Ginsberg, *Howl: Original Draft Facsimile*, 111.

16. Carl Solomon, lecture at Brooklyn College, 1987.

17. Carl Solomon, personal communication.

18. Jane Kramer, *Allen Ginsberg in America* (New York: Random House, 1969), xv.

19. Ginsberg, *Collected Poems*, 889–92.

20. D. V. Jeste and J. E. Maglione, "Treating Older Adults with Schizophrenia: Challenges and Opportunities," *Schizophrenia Bulletin* 39, no. 5 (2013): 966–68.

21. Sigmund Freud introduced this concept in 1899 in an article entitled "Screen Memories," in *The Standard Edition of the Complete Psychological Works of Sigmund Freud*, ed. James Strachey et al. (London: Hogarth, 1955), 3:303–22.

Epilogue

1. William Blake, *Poems*, intro. Patti Smith (New York: Random House, 2010).

2. Allen Ginsberg, *Collected Poems, 1947–1997* (New York: HarperCollins, 2006), 122.

3. Allen's affiliation was not a secret. He spoke at their conference, allowed himself to be seen in a 1994 film about them, and wrote an essay explaining his position as a matter of protecting civil liberties. Allen wrote: "NAMBLA's a forum for reform of those laws on youthful sexuality which members deem oppressive, a discussion society not a sex club. I joined NAMBLA in defense of free speech." Allen Ginsberg, *Deliberate Prose, 1952–1995* (New York: Harper Perennial, 2001), 170–72. Many didn't agree and instead saw Allen as endorsing sex with children. It didn't help that he referred to his teenage partners as "boys." Allen's stated beliefs were not inconsistent with NAMBLA doctrine. Andrea Dworkin, *Heartbreak* (London: Continuum, 2007). In 1988, Mark Ewert met Allen and became a sexual partner of both Allen and William Burroughs. In his 40s, Ewert fondly recalled: "That's why I call these guys my boyfriends, because I feel like I really was there with them, body and soul, and they were there with me." Luke Malone, "The Teenage Boyfriend of the Beat Generation", *Vocativ*, March 28, 2014, https://www.vocativ.com/culture/art-culture/teenage-boyfriend-beat-generation/.

4. Bob Rosenthal, *Straight around Allen: On the Business of Being Allen Ginsberg* (St. Andrews: Beatdom, 2018), 127

5. M. Glasser et al., "Cycle of Child Sexual Abuse: Links between Being a Victim and Becoming a Perpetrator," *British Journal of Psychiatry* 179, no. 6 (2018): 482–94; M. Plummer and A. Cossins, "The Cycle of Abuse: When Victims Become Offenders," *Trauma, Violence, & Abuse* 19, no. 3 (2018): 286–304.

6. Ephebophilia is the sexual attraction to mid-to-late adolescents, ages fifteen to nineteen. It is considered different from pedophilia (which is focused on prepubescent youth) and is not considered a psychiatric disorder. J. Bering, "Pedophiles, Hebephiles and Ephebophiles, Oh My: Erotic Age Orientation," *Scientific American*, July 1, 2009, https://blogs.scientificamerican.com/bering-in-mind/pedophiles-hebephiles-and-ephebophiles-oh-my-erotic-age-orientation/.

7. For example, in Colorado the age of consent was sixteen until 1975, when it was changed to fifteen—such that regardless of consent, "sexual penetration or intrusion of a victim aged 14 or younger and an offender at least four years older" would be sexual assault in the second degree. H. Michael Steinberg, "Teen Age Sexual Contact," https://www.hmichaelsteinberg.com/teen-age-sexual-contact.html.

8. Allen Ginsberg, interview by Weine.

9. Allen Ginsberg, "Literary History of the Beat Generation," preliminary syllabus, Brooklyn College, 1987, 3.

10. Carl Solomon, *Emergency Messages: An Autobiographical Miscellany* (New York: Paragon House, 1989), 77.

11. John Clellon Holmes, "This Is the Beat Generation," *New York Times Magazine*, November 16, 1952.

12. Bob Rosenthal, *Straight around Allen: On the Business of Being Allen Ginsberg* (St. Andrews: Beatdom, 2018), 73.

13. Michael Pollan, *How to Change Your Mind: What the New Science of Psychedelics Teaches Us about Consciousness, Dying, Addiction, Depression, and Transcendence* (New York: Penguin, 2018).

14. Keith J. Holyoak, *The Spider's Thread: Metaphor in Mind, Brain, and Poetry* (Cambridge, MA: MIT Press, 2019).

15. Allen Ginsberg, journal, 1987, Allen Ginsberg Papers, Stanford.

16. Jason Shinder, *The Poem That Changed America: "Howl" Fifty Years Later* (New York: Farrar, Straus and Giroux, 2006), 12.

17. Ginsberg, *Collected Poems*, 142.

INDEX

Page numbers in *italics* reference images.

perception of, 217, 224; preparation for, 63, 75–78; "Psalm IV" inspiration from, 200–202; psychedelics and, 66; psychiatrists' recommendations on, 72–73, 121–122, 125, 129, 147, 155, 244; psychiatry medical records and notes on, 96–97, 107, 108, 111–112, 115, 119; renouncement of, 119, 121, 122, 125, 219; spiritual enlightenment and, 68–69, 76–79, 167–168, 170–171, 180–183, 212; unpublished poem recounting of, 221; visionary poetry inspiration from, 69, 71–72, 74–75, 78, 123, 181
Bloomingdale Hospital (New York), 34–35, 37–38
The Blue Hand (Baker), 213
blues: "Howl" and, 7, 156–157; "Kaddish" and, 5, 11, 191, 192
Bono, 13
Bow, Clara, 173
Bowering, George, 219
Bowles, Jane, 176
Bowles, Paul, 176
breath lines, 7, 242
Breton, Andre, 183–184, 191; "Free Union," 183–184
"The Bridge" (Crane), 191
bridges, 103, *104*
Bridget (friend), 51–52
Brill, Henry, 34, 56, 57–59
Brill, Norman, 33
Brilliant Corners (Monk), 189–190
Brook, Lyle (brother's son), 162
Brooklyn College, 16, 230, 244
Brooks, Connie (sister-in-law), 2, 162
Brooks, Eugene (brother), x; Allen's correspondence with, 3, 4, 10, 11, 155, 177–178, *177*, 180, 182; on Allen's homosexuality, 113; Allen's hospitalization consent signed by, 94; Allen's telegram announcing Naomi's death, 3, 3, 4; birth of, 37; on Blake visions, 97; early family life, 37, 38–39, 42; education and employment of, 42, 44, 194; marriage and family life, 154, 162, 219; military service of, 104; at Naomi's funeral, 2–3, 8; Naomi's letters

referencing, 54, 60, 73, 147, 161; Naomi's letters to, 10, *148*, 161, 165; Naomi's medical records requested by, 34; poetry published by, 173; visits to Naomi in hospital, x, 10, 38–39, 88, 149, 162
Bruce, Lenny (nephew), 220
Buber, Martin, 212, 219
Buddhism: Allen as practicing Buddhist, 1; Dalai Lama visit, 213; death and grief rituals of, 1, 192; independent study of, 150, 154, 172; poetic inspiration from, 150; spiritual discipline through, 219, 223, 235
"Burial" (L. Ginsberg), 173
Burroughs, William, 46; Allen's collaboration with, 175, 176, 205, 244; Allen's correspondence with, 5, 52, 72–73; Allen's relationship with, viii, 45, 47, 56–57, 105, 112; author's reaction to, 244; Beat Generation course visiting poet, 244; on Blake visions, 72–73; as late bloomer, 190; madness stories from, 157; marriage of, 144 (*see also* Vollmer, Joan); *Naked Lunch*, 176, 220; obscenity trial of, 220; as an outsider, 68; in Paris (1957–1958), 183, 188; as "Paterson" inspiration, viii; psychedelics and, 2, 205, 210; psychoanalysis by, 50–51, 52, 76, 112; *The Yage Letters* (with Ginsberg), 205, 244
Burton, Robert, 58
Butler, Nicholas Murray, 47

Café Select, 12
California trip (1953). *See* San Francisco (1955–1956); San Francisco (1963); San Francisco (1967)
Cannastra, William, 93, 144, 152
caregivers. *See* family caregivers of persons with mental illness
Carmichael, Stokely, 131
Carr, Lucien: Allen's physical attraction to, 52; Allen's relationship with, viii, 44–47, 189; on Huncke, 85; murder of Kammerer by, 47; "New Vision" and, 49; as "Paterson" inspiration, viii

Stevan M. Weine, MD, is Professor of Psychiatry at the University of Illinois College of Medicine, where he is also Director of Global Medicine and Director of the Center for Global Health. He is the author of two prior books: *When History Is a Nightmare: Lives and Memories of Ethnic Cleansing in Bosnia-Herzegovina* (Rutgers University Press, 1999) and *Testimony and Catastrophe: Narrating the Traumas of Political Violence* (Northwestern University Press, 2006).